Communications in Computer and Information Science 2810

Rationale

The CCIS series is devoted to the publication of proceedings of computer science conferences. Its aim is to efficiently disseminate original research results in informatics in printed and electronic form. While the focus is on publication of peer-reviewed full papers presenting mature work, inclusion of reviewed short papers reporting on work in progress is welcome, too. Besides globally relevant meetings with internationally representative program committees guaranteeing a strict peer-reviewing and paper selection process, conferences run by societies or of high regional or national relevance are also considered for publication.

Topics

The topical scope of CCIS spans the entire spectrum of informatics ranging from foundational topics in the theory of computing to information and communications science and technology and a broad variety of interdisciplinary application fields.

Information for Volume Editors and Authors

Publication in CCIS is free of charge. No royalties are paid, however, we offer registered conference participants temporary free access to the online version of the conference proceedings on SpringerLink (http://link.springer.com) by means of an http referrer from the conference website and/or a number of complimentary printed copies, as specified in the official acceptance email of the event.

CCIS proceedings can be published in time for distribution at conferences or as post-proceedings, and delivered in the form of printed books and/or electronically as USBs and/or e-content licenses for accessing proceedings at SpringerLink. Furthermore, CCIS proceedings are included in the CCIS electronic book series hosted in the SpringerLink digital library at http://link.springer.com/bookseries/7899. Conferences publishing in CCIS are allowed to use our online conference service (Meteor) for managing the whole proceedings lifecycle (from submission and reviewing to preparing for publication) free of charge.

Publication process

The language of publication is exclusively English. Authors publishing in CCIS have to sign the Springer CCIS copyright transfer form, however, they are free to use their material published in CCIS for substantially changed, more elaborate subsequent publications elsewhere. For the preparation of the camera-ready papers/files, authors have to strictly adhere to the Springer CCIS Authors' Instructions and are strongly encouraged to use the CCIS LaTeX style files or templates.

Abstracting/Indexing

CCIS is abstracted/indexed in DBLP, Google Scholar, EI-Compendex, Mathematical Reviews, SCImago, Scopus. CCIS volumes are also submitted for the inclusion in ISI Proceedings.

How to start

To start the evaluation of your proposal for inclusion in the CCIS series, please send an e-mail to ccis@springer.com

Tie Qiu · Guang Cheng · Wei Li · Qiao Xiang
Editors

Frontiers of Networking Technologies

The Third China Conference on Networking, CCF ChinaNet 2025
Shenyang, China, September 12–14, 2025
Proceedings

Editors
Tie Qiu
Northeastern University
Shenyang, China

Wei Li
Southeast University
Nanjing, China

Guang Cheng
Southeast University
Nanjing, China

Qiao Xiang
Xiamen University
Xiamen, China

ISSN 1865-0929 ISSN 1865-0937 (electronic)
Communications in Computer and Information Science
ISBN 978-981-95-8449-9 ISBN 978-981-95-8450-5 (eBook)
https://doi.org/10.1007/978-981-95-8450-5

This Springer imprint is published by the registered company Springer Nature Singapore Pte Ltd.
The registered company address is: 152 Beach Road, #21-01/04 Gateway East, Singapore 189721, Singapore

Preface

The CCF ChinaNet Conference is a premier annual academic event sponsored by CCF TCI and CCF TCCOMM. It provides a vibrant forum for researchers, practitioners, and industry experts to present and discuss high-quality research results and real-world applications in the field of Internet and computer networks. CCF ChinaNet 2025, the third edition of the conference series, was held from September 12 to 14, 2025, in Shenyang, Liaoning, hosted by Northeastern University, China.

This volume contains 13 high-quality papers from CCF ChinaNet 2025, as selected from 102 submissions after a single-blind peer review process. Each paper was reviewed by at least 3 Program Committee members. We hope this volume will be beneficial for readers from both academia and industry, who may understand and tackle the challenges in an efficient manner and adopt appropriate solutions in the related fields. We hope that you enjoy reading and benefit from the proceedings of ChinaNet 2025.

September 2025

Tie Qiu
Guang Cheng
Wei Li
Qiao Xiang

Organization

General Chairs

Xingwei Wang	Northeastern University, China
Keqiu Li	Tianjin University, China

Program Committee Chairs

Tie Qiu	Northeastern University, China
Guang Cheng	Southeastern University, China
Wei Li	Southeastern University, China
Qiao Xiang	Xiamen University, China

Program Committee Co-chairs

Jie Jia	Northeastern University, China
Yueqiu Jiang	Shenyang Ligong University, China
Tingwei Chen	Liaoning University, China
Qiang He	Northeastern University, China

Program Committee

Geng Sun	Jilin University, China
Jianxiong Guo	Beijing Normal University, China
Gongming Zhao	University of Science and Technology of China, China
Guyue Liu	Peking University, China
Fusang Zhang	Beihang University, China
Xiaoxi Zhang	Sun Yat-sen University, China
Peirui Cao	Nanjing University, China
Wenxin Li	Tianjin University, China
Menghao Zhang	Beihang University, China
Xiaocan Li	Hunan University, China

Zhiyuan Wang	Beihang University, China
Zehua Guo	Beijing Institute of Technology, China
Long Luo	University of Electronic Science and Technology of China, China
Wei Wang	Wuhan University, China
Rongfei Zeng	Northeastern University, China
Bo Wang	Tsinghua University, China
Shenglin Zhang	Nankai University, China
Zichuan Xu	Dalian University of Technology, China
Yifei Zhu	Shanghai Jiao Tong University, China
Danfeng Shan	Xi'an Jiaotong University, China
Ruiting Zhou	Northeastern University, China
Yifei Zou	Shandong University, China
Tong Li	Renmin University of China, China
Qiang Su	Xiamen University, China
Lu Tang	Xiamen University, China
Huan Zhou	National University of Defense Technology, China
Guiyan Liu	Chongqing University, China
Xudong Wu	East China Normal University, China
Deyu Zhang	Central South University, China
Huan Zhou	Northwestern Polytechnical University, China
Yu Zhang	Harbin Institute of Technology, China
Wanxin Shi	Fudan University, China
Yi Gao	Zhejiang University, China
Jingzhou Wang	Suzhou University, China
Zhaoxin Chang	Institut Polytechnique de Paris, France
Yuchao Zhang	Beijing University of Posts and Telecommunications, China
Weiting Zhang	Beijing Jiaotong University, China
Junqi Ma	Chinese Academy of Sciences, China
Kaihui Gao	Zhongguancun Lab, China
Ertong Shang	Xidian University, China
Le Tian	Information Engineering University, China
Bo Hu	Chinese Academy of Sciences, China
Xinyi Zhang	Chinese Academy of Sciences, China
Guoming Tang	Hong Kong University of Science and Technology (Guangzhou), China
Fangxin Wang	Chinese University of Hong Kong (Shenzhen), China
Wufan Wang	Beijing University of Posts and Telecommunications, China

Guiyun Fan — Tongji University, China
Shijia Liu — Southwest Jiaotong University, China
Yanru Chen — Sichuan University, China

Contents

4D Semantic Segmentation Method for Point Cloud Video Based on Cross-Modal Fusion

Jinhua Wang, Jie Li(✉), Di Xu, Zihan Liu, and Shuang Cao

Northeastern University, Shenyang 110819, China
lijie@mail.neu.edu.cn

Abstract. 4D point cloud video semantic segmentation is essential for dynamic 3D scene understanding but remains challenging due to data sparsity and lack of texture in point clouds. Existing methods, primarily based on geometric structures, are often limited in spatiotemporal modeling. To overcome these limitations, we propose a novel dual-branch cross-modal fusion network that leverages complementary information from RGB videos. Our framework features a dedicated RGB branch which separately extracts texture features and temporal gradient features. These are then fused by an internal cross-attention module to enhance the representation of appearance and motion. Subsequently, a cross-modal Transformer aligns and integrates these enriched RGB features with the spatiotemporal features from the point cloud branch—the latter modeled via self-attention mechanisms. Experiments on the Synthia 4D and HOI4D datasets demonstrate the superior performance of our approach in 4D semantic segmentation, which is supported by comprehensive ablation studies validating the contribution of each module.

Keywords: dynamic scene perception · point cloud video · 4D semantic segmentation · cross-modal feature fusion

1 Introduction

Point cloud videos, as dynamic sequences of 3D point clouds, integrate spatial structures with temporal evolution, providing accurate geometric and motion-aware representations of the physical world. They are crucial in robotics [1, 2], autonomous driving [3], human-computer interaction [4], and augmented reality [5], motivating growing research in 4D perception such as semantic segmentation [6–8].

However, processing point cloud videos remains challenging due to their sparsity, lack of texture, and unstructured nature, which hinder effective spatiotemporal modeling by conventional grid-based video models or static point cloud methods [9–11]. Although recent 4D approaches [6, 12–14] extend 3D architectures with temporal modules, they still face difficulties in fine-grained semantic understanding.

A promising direction is incorporating RGB sequences for complementary texture and appearance cues. We observe that: (1) point clouds provide precise 3D spatial and motion information; (2) RGB data offers rich semantic texture. These modalities are synergistic. We thus propose joint input of both, using RGB to enhance point cloud

T. Qiu et al. (Eds.): CCF ChinaNet 2025, CCIS 2810, pp. 1–10, 2026.
https://doi.org/10.1007/978-981-95-8450-5_1

representation. While early cross-modal methods like CrossVideo show potential, many underutilize modality synergy, treating RGB monolithically without capturing critical temporal dynamics.

To address this, we propose a dual-branch fusion framework for 4D semantic segmentation. A point cloud branch uses self-attention for spatiotemporal features, while an RGB branch employs CNNs to extract spatial and temporal-gradient features separately, fused via cross-attention. A cross-modal Transformer then aligns and transfers enhanced features from RGB to point clouds, enabling comprehensive segmentation. Introduction.

2 Related Work

4D semantic segmentation enables spatiotemporally continuous object recognition and tracking by dynamically analyzing semantic information and motion trajectories within 3D scenes over time.

SpSequenceNet [15] introduces cross-frame global attention and local interpolation modules to capture spatiotemporal information in 4D point clouds. Mamba4D [16], based on state space modeling, shows strong performance in tasks such as human action recognition and 4D semantic segmentation, particularly for long sequences. PointSDA [17] proposes a point deformation attention mechanism that adaptively focuses on informative regions and integrates multi-level features in a spatiotemporally decoupled manner, facilitating dynamic segmentation. PST-Transformer [12] employs self-attention to identify relevant points across video sequences. CrossVideo [18] leverages cross-modal relationships between point cloud videos and image sequences to derive meaningful representations. SemanticFlow [19] presents a method for LiDAR point cloud sequence segmentation using sparse frame annotations. SegNet4D [20] decomposes 4D segmentation into semantic and motion subtasks, combining results via a fusion module.

4D-CS [21] utilizes explicit clustering information to solve the prediction inconsistency problem of point categories within the same foreground object and develops a strategy for obtaining clustering labels, aiming to improve segmentation performance by leveraging instance information and integrating temporal features. Introduction.

3 Method

3.1 Overall Framework

The overall architecture of our proposed cross-modal fusion network for 4D point cloud video semantic segmentation is illustrated in Fig. 1. Designed to address challenges such as sparsity, lack of texture, and complex temporal dynamics in irregular point sets, our model employs a dual-branch structure that synergistically processes point cloud sequences and corresponding RGB videos. The input consists of three consecutive point cloud frames and their synchronized RGB images. Through novel fusion mechanisms, the model outputs semantically segmented point clouds, effectively enriching sparse geometric data with texture and motion cues from RGB.

In the point cloud branch, consecutive frames are processed by 4D convolutional layers to construct hierarchical geometric representations. A self-attention mechanism

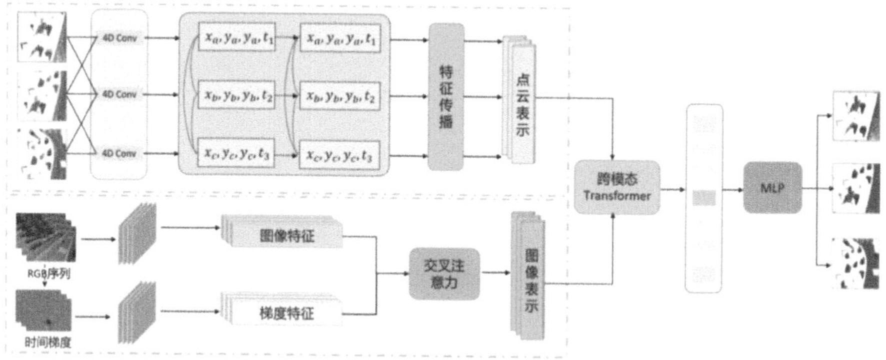

Fig. 1. Architecture of our 4D semantic segmentation model.

captures long-range spatiotemporal dependencies between points, enhancing robustness to density variations and occlusion through contextual feature aggregation. Simultaneously, the RGB branch processes image sequences in two paths: a CNN extracts texture features, while a parallel stream computes temporal gradient features. These are fused via cross-attention to dynamically integrate appearance and motion cues.

Subsequently, a cross-modal Transformer aligns RGB and point cloud features via contrastive learning. Finally, an MLP decoder merges the multimodal representations and produces a semantically labeled 4D point cloud sequence.

3.2 Point Cloud Self-attention Mechanism

To effectively preserve spatiotemporal structures in point cloud video modeling, we introduce a self-attention mechanism that adaptively associates relevant points across sequences without explicit motion tracking. Query $Q \in \mathbb{R}^{C' \times T \times N}$ and key $K \in \mathbb{R}^{C' \times T \times N}$ are generated through separate encodings. A scaled dot product $A \in \mathbb{R}^{T \times N \times T \times N}$ computes similarity across all points. Video-level self-attention with softmax normalization locates relevant points and produces attention weights.

This approach aggregates information from correlated points, enhancing spatiotemporal representations. The model employs multi-head attention, ReLU, LayerNorm, and residual connections to improve capacity and feature richness. As shown in Fig. 2, input features $F \in \mathbb{R}^{C \times T \times N}$ are first normalized via LayerNorm, then processed through attention. A stackable unit—comprising Linear layers, ReLU, and LayerNorm—enables deep refinement, outputting enhanced features $F \in \mathbb{R}^{C'' \times T \times N}$. Residual connections preserve original features and promote gradient flow.

To enhance the encoding of spatiotemporal structures in point cloud videos, we incorporate a dedicated spatiotemporal structure encoding module into the model. Given the irregular and unordered spatial nature of point clouds alongside their temporal order, we separately encode spatial and temporal structures to mitigate the impact of spatial irregularity on temporal modeling. Let $V_{pp'}$ be the value encoding the spatiotemporal structure of point p and point p′. The calculation method of $V_{pp'}$ is shown in Eq. (1).

$$V_{pp'} = \mathcal{T}_{\Delta t}\big(S_{\delta s}(F_{p'})\big) \tag{1}$$

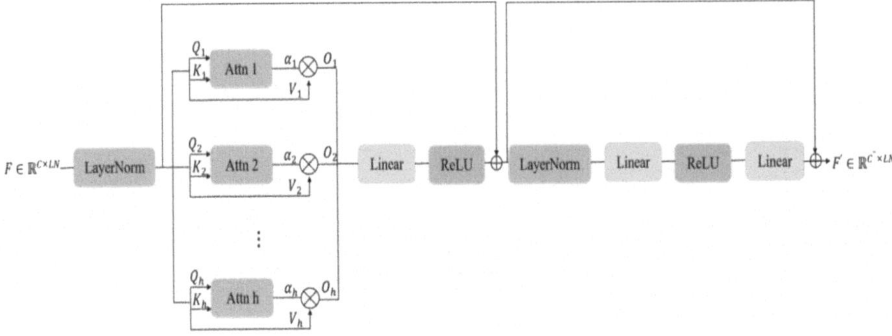

Fig. 2. Structure of our 4D self-attention mechanism.

where $\mathcal{T}_{\Delta t}(\cdot)$ is the encoding function of the temporal structure, and $S_{\delta s}(\cdot)$ is the function encoding the spatial structure.

3.3 RGB Image Cross-Attention Fusion Mechanism

To better capture the temporal correlations in video sequences, this paper extracts temporal gradient information from RGB sequences as additional input features. Considering the weak signal characteristics of gradient features, we design a specialized cross-attention fusion mechanism. This mechanism generates fused relevant features by mining the temporal relationships between RGB features F^I and temporal gradient features F^G. The cross-attention fusion mechanism framework is shown in Fig. 3, which contains three core feature streams: raw image features, temporal gradient features, and fused image representations.

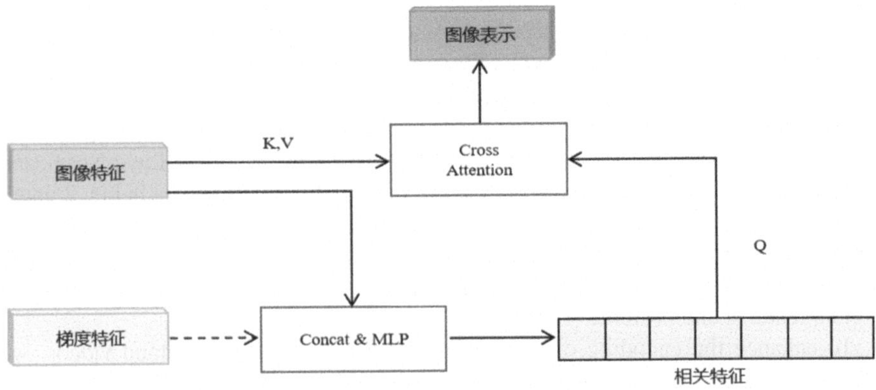

Fig. 3. Framework Diagram of the Cross-Attention Mechanism.

Specifically, we represent RGB features and temporal gradient features in the form of time series and perform feature fusion through a sliding window at each time step. By introducing learnable parameters and window sizes, we flexibly adjust the weights and ranges of feature fusion, obtaining RGB features $\widehat{F}^{I}$ and temporal gradient features $\widehat{F}^{G}$ after sliding window processing within frames. While retaining the texture information of the original images, the representation ability of temporal changes is enhanced. Finally, the two feature streams are deeply integrated through a multilayer perceptron (MLP) to generate fused feature representations F^{cor} with gradient perception capabilities. The calculation process is shown in Eq. (2).

$$F^{cor} = MLP\left(\left[\widehat{F}^{I}; \widehat{F}^{G}\right]\right) \tag{2}$$

where $[\cdot;\cdot]$ represents the concatenation operation.

3.4 Cross-Modal Transformer

To effectively transfer the texture information and gradient perception information in the image branch to the 4D point cloud model, this paper designs a cross-modal Transformer to fuse knowledge from the two modalities. First, to ensure temporal consistency between the two modalities, further enhance the generated features, and facilitate the prediction of motion trajectories by leveraging the geometric consistency of adjacent frames. This paper uses Eqs. (3) and (4) to align the temporal information between the two modalities.

$$L^{adv} = -\sum_{i=2}^{N} log\frac{exp\left(f_{i-1}^{I}\cdot f_{i}^{P}/\tau\right)}{\sum_{i=2}^{N} exp\left(f_{i-1}^{I}\cdot f_{i}^{P}/\tau\right)} \tag{3}$$

$$L^{lag} = -\sum_{i=1}^{N-1} log\frac{exp\left(f_{i-1}^{I}\cdot f_{i}^{P}/\tau\right)}{\sum_{i=1}^{N-1} exp\left(f_{i-1}^{I}\cdot f_{i}^{P}/\tau\right)} \tag{4}$$

where N represents the frame number, f_{i-1}^{I} represents the feature of the i-1-th frame in the RGB image sequence, f_{i}^{P} represents the feature of the i-th frame in the point cloud sequence, and τ is the temperature coefficient.

The temporal consistency between the two modalities is a linear combination of the above two loss functions, and its formula expression is shown in Eq. (5).

$$L_{PI}^{tac} = \left(L^{adv} + L^{lag}\right)/2 \tag{5}$$

After that, a cross-modal Transformer mechanism is adopted to merge the feature representations of the two modality data. Specifically, a stack of Transformer layers is used to jointly encode the two input modalities F_{H}^{P} and F_{H}^{I}. To avoid performance degradation when the RGB sequence is unavailable, this paper designs an attention mask. The introduced attention mask allows the model to refer to F_{H}^{P} and F_{H}^{I} when generating the final output of the image branch. Finally, the output features are used for 4D semantic segmentation.

4 Experiments

4.1 Experimental Setup

In the point cloud branch of the model, four 4D point convolution layers are used to extract features from video frames, with spatial subsampling rates set to 4, 4, 4, and 2 sequentially. Meanwhile, the self-attention mechanism model for spatiotemporal feature extraction contains 4 heads and 2 layers. Additionally, for the RGB branch, ResNet18 is used as the image encoder. This paper uses the SGD optimizer to train the model, setting the number of epochs to 75. The batch size is set to 8. The learning rate is set to 0.01 and decays at a rate of 0.1 at the 30th, 40th, and 50th epochs.

4.2 Experimental Dataset

Experiments are conducted on the Synthia 4D and HOI4D datasets to validate the effectiveness and general applicability of the proposed method.

The Synthia 4D dataset contains six driving scenarios under nine weather conditions, with 12 semantic annotations. Each sequence includes four stereo RGB-D images captured from a moving vehicle's roof. 3D point cloud sequences are reconstructed from both RGB and depth images, while the RGB images are used for training.

The HOI4D dataset consists of egocentric RGB-D video sequences, with 2,971 training and 892 testing videos. Each sequence comprises 300 point cloud frames, every frame containing 8,192 points and covering 43 indoor semantic categories. For each RGB-D sequence, depth maps are projected into point clouds, and the corresponding RGB images are also utilized during training.

4.3 Evaluation Metrics

This study employs mean Intersection over Union (mIoU), a core metric in semantic segmentation, to comprehensively evaluate the accuracy of the proposed 4D semantic segmentation model. mIoU quantifies the overlap between predicted and ground-truth segmentation regions, providing a robust measure of segmentation performance. Its calculation method is shown in Eq. (6).

$$\mathrm{mIoU} = \frac{1}{N}\sum_{i=1}^{N} \mathrm{IoU}_i \tag{6}$$

where N is the total number of categories, IoUi is the IoU value of the i-th category, representing the ratio of the intersection to the union of the predicted region and the real region for a single category. Its calculation method is shown in Eq. (7).

$$\mathrm{IoU} = \frac{\mathrm{TP}}{\mathrm{TP} + \mathrm{FP} + \mathrm{FN}} \tag{7}$$

where TP represents true positives, i.e., the number of correctly predicted pixels, FP represents false positives, i.e., the number of misreported pixels, and FN represents false negatives, i.e., the number of missed pixels.

4.4 Results

Under the aforementioned experimental settings, we comprehensively evaluated the performance of our proposed 4D semantic segmentation algorithm on both the Synthia 4D and HOI4D datasets. Table 1 shows the segmentation results on Synthia 4D.

Table 1. The Results of 4D Semantic Segmentation (mIoU %) on Synthia 4D.

Method	Bldn	Road	Scbulk	Fence	Vegitin	Pole	Car	T.Sign	Pedstm	Lane	T.Light
PSTNet	96.91	98.33	90.83	95.00	96.96	97.61	95.15	77.45	85.68	75.71	77.28
P4Transformer	96.73	98.35	94.03	95.23	98.28	98.01	95.61	81.54	85.18	75.95	79.07
PST-Transformer	96.11	98.44	94.94	96.58	98.98	98.11	96.06	82.67	87.86	76.01	81.67
Cross_video	96.27	98.17	95.13	95.26	98.07	98.35	96.35	84.25	90.39	78.69	81.97
CMF-Seg	97.48	98.85	95.65	97.15	98.54	98.61	96.95	87.49	89.75	80.35	83.27

Experimental results demonstrate our method demonstrates superior performance, achieving the highest mIoU in 9 out of 11 categories. This advantage can be attributed to two core designs: (1) Our explicit dual-path RGB feature extraction strategy, which separates texture and temporal gradient features, allows for more precise modeling of superior temporal correlation compared to methods like Cross_video that rely on implicit temporal learning through 3D CNNs. (2) The cross-modal Transformer effectively fuses these complementary features from the point cloud and RGB modalities, mitigating the inherent sparsity and lack of texture in point clouds. In summary, compared with existing methods, the model designed in this paper has good performance in the 4D semantic segmentation task and can greatly improve segmentation accuracy.

To validate the robustness and generalizability of our model, we extended evaluations to the HOI4D dataset. The experimental results are shown in Table 2.

Table 2. The Results of 4D Semantic Segmentation (mIoU %) on HOI4D.

Method	Table	Groud	Metope	Locker	Pliers	Laptop	Safe Deposit	Pillow	Hand and Arm
PSTNet	57.45	63.38	83.80	44.69	13.71	35.03	51.55	76.30	40.39
P4Transformer	63.58	66.60	87.17	58.39	32.29	72.03	65.87	57.41	54.36
PST-Transformer	67.49	74.92	87.92	62.12	41.22	71.86	71.39	77.02	62.50
Cross_video	66.78	73.76	88.21	59.43	38.74	71.25	72.04	78.64	61.27
CMF-Seg	67.76	75.68	90.67	60.83	40.95	72.82	73.41	83.13	63.26

Due to some characteristics of the dataset itself, the segmentation performance of all methods on the HOI4D dataset is significantly reduced compared with that on the Synthia 4D dataset. However, from the horizontal comparison of method performance, the 4D semantic segmentation method designed in this paper achieves the optimal performance in seven categories, and the mIoU index also reaches the highest. Compared with the method that only takes a single mode as input, the method proposed in this paper has a performance improvement of up to 18.20 and a minimum of 1.43 respectively. In addition, compared with the multimodal input method, the method proposed in this paper has an improvement of 2.04. This demonstrates that our method's ability to leverage texture and, crucially, explicit temporal gradients is not dataset-specific but translates effectively to more challenging and realistic environments. The performance boost in classes involving human-object interaction (a key feature of HOI4D) further confirms the importance of our temporal modeling.

To verify the effectiveness of the RGB branch in the 4D semantic segmentation model designed in this paper, ablation experiments are conducted. Experiments are carried out on the Synthia 4D dataset under four conditions: using only point cloud sequences, using point cloud sequences + RGB sequences, using point cloud sequences + temporal gradients, and the method designed in this paper. The experimental results are shown in Table 3.

Table 3. The Effect of RGB Branches on Segmentation Performance.

Point Cloud	RGB	Gradient	Frame	mIoU (%)
√	×	×	3	80.73
√	√	×	3	83.29
√	×	√	3	82.22
√	√	√	3	85.34

To more intuitively see the segmentation results on different objects, this paper also intercepts the specific performance data of five category objects in the Synthia 4D dataset under the four methods. The comparison results are shown in Fig. 4.

The data shows that when only point cloud sequences are used as input, the segmentation accuracy is the lowest due to the lack of feature information such as color and texture. After adding RGB sequences, the color and texture information or corresponding temporal gradient information provided by the RGB sequences can be utilized to better understand the semantics and dynamics of point cloud videos, thus improving performance. The method in this paper takes point cloud sequences, RGB sequences, and temporal gradients as the model input together. It not only uses the texture and semantic information provided by RGB sequences to enhance the understanding of videos but also obtains more temporal correlation information by taking temporal gradients as additional input. Therefore, it achieves the best performance, with performance improvements of 4.61, 2.05, and 3.12 compared with the other three methods, respectively. This effectively verifies the effectiveness of each module.

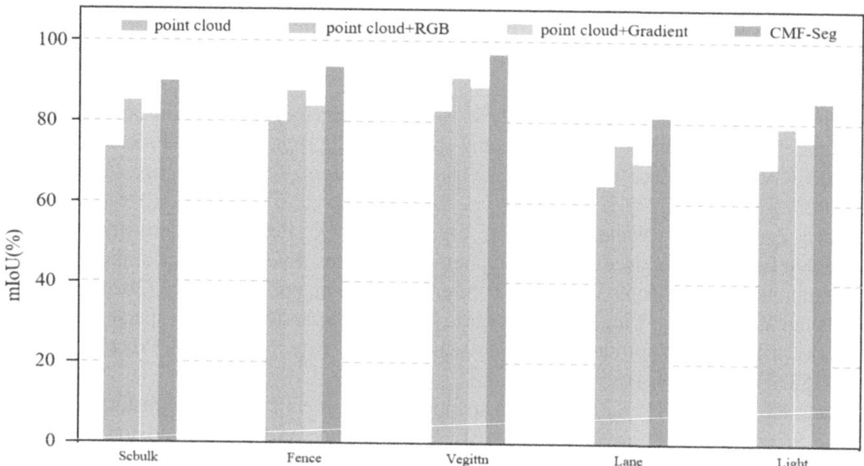

Fig. 4. Results of mIoU Comparison.

5 Conclusion

This paper proposes a cross-modal fusion-based method for 4D semantic segmentation of point cloud videos, addressing the challenges of spatiotemporal modeling caused by sparsity and lack of texture in dynamic point clouds. A dual-branch architecture integrates geometric information from point cloud sequences and texture cues from RGB sequences, significantly enhancing semantic understanding of dynamic scenes. Evaluations on the Synthia 4D and HOI4D datasets show the method achieves strong mIoU results and outperforms single-modal baselines in segmentation accuracy. Ablation studies confirm the contribution of both the RGB branch and the temporal gradient module.

References

1. Lin, J., Zhong, K., Gong, T., Zhang, X., Wang, N.: Prior information-assisted neural network for point cloud segmentation in human-robot interaction scenarios. IEEE Robot. Autom. Lett. **9**(5), 4186–4193 (2024)
2. Zhu, S., Wang, G., Blum, H., Liu, J., Song, L., Pollefeys, M., Wang, H.: Sni-slam: Semantic neural implicit slam. In: Proceedings of the IEEE/CVF Conference on Computer Vision and Pattern Recognition, pp. 21167--21177 (2024)
3. Nunes, L., Marcuzzi, R., Chen, X., Behley, J., Stachniss, C.: Segcontrast: 3d point cloud feature representation learning through self-supervised segment discrimination. IEEE Robot. Autom. Lett. **7**(2), 2116–2123 (2022)
4. Liu, Z., Lu, X., Liu, W., Qi, W., Su, H.: Human-robot collaboration through a multi-scale graph convolution neural network with temporal attention. IEEE Robot. Autom. Lett. **9**(3), 2248–2255 (2024)
5. Jiang, C., Wang, G., Miao, Y., Wang, H.: 3-d scene flow estimation on pseudo-lidar: Bridging the gap on estimating point motion. IEEE Trans. Industr. Inf. **19**(6), 7346–7354 (2022)

6. Wen, H., Liu, Y., Huang, J., Duan, B., Yi, L.: Point primitive transformer for long-term 4D point cloud video understanding. In: European Conference on Computer Vision, pp. 19--35. Springer (2022)
7. Shi, H., Wei, J., Li, R., Liu, F., Lin, G.: Weakly supervised segmentation on outdoor 4D point clouds with temporal matching and spatial graph propagation. In: Proceedings of the IEEE/CVF Conference on Computer Vision and Pattern Recognition, pp. 11840--11849 (2022)
8. Shen, Z., Sheng, X., Wang, L., Guo, Y., Liu, Q., Zhou, X.: Pointcmp: contrastive mask prediction for self-supervised learning on point cloud videos. In: Proceedings of the IEEE/CVF Conference on Computer Vision and Pattern Recognition, pp. 1212--1222 (2023)
9. Zheng, Y., Wang, G., Liu, J., Pollefeys, M., Wang, H.: Spherical frustum sparse convolution network for lidar point cloud semantic segmentation. Adv. Neural. Inf. Process. Syst. **37**, 121827–121858 (2024)
10. Hara, K., Kataoka, H., Satoh, Y.: Can spatiotemporal 3d cnns retrace the history of 2d cnns and imagenet? In: Proceedings of the IEEE Conference on Computer Vision and Pattern Recognition, pp. 6546--6555 (2018)
11. Liu, L., Hu, X., Zhu, L., Fu, C.-W., Qin, J., Heng, P.-A.: ψ-net: stacking densely convolutional lstms for sub-cortical brain structure segmentation. IEEE Trans. Med. Imaging **39**(9), 2806–2817 (2020)
12. Fan, H., Yang, Y., Kankanhalli, M.: Point spatio-temporal transformer networks for point cloud video modeling. IEEE Trans. Pattern Anal. Mach. Intell. **45**(2), 2181–2192 (2022)
13. Fan, H., Yu, X., Yang, Y., Kankanhalli, M.: Deep hierarchical representation of point cloud videos via spatio-temporal decomposition. IEEE Trans. Pattern Anal. Mach. Intell. **44**(12), 9918–9930 (2021)
14. Fan, H., Yu, X., Ding, Y., Yang, Y., Kankanhalli, M.: PSTNet: point spatio-temporal convolution on point cloud sequences. arXiv preprint arXiv:2205.13713 (2022)
15. Shi, H., Lin, G., Wang, H., Hung, T.-Y., Wang, Z.: SpSequenceNet: semantic segmentation network on 4D point clouds. In: Proceedings of the IEEE/CVF Conference on Computer Vision and Pattern Recognition, pp. 4574--4583 (2020)
16. Liu, J., Han, J., Liu, L., Aviles-Rivero, A.I., Jiang, C., Liu, Z., Wang, H.: Mamba4d: efficient long-sequence point cloud video understanding with disentangled spatial-temporal state space models. arXiv preprint arXiv:2405.14338 (2024)
17. Sheng, X., Shen, Z., Xiao, G.: PointSDA: spatio-temporal deformable attention network for point cloud video modeling. IEEE Robot. Autom. Lett. (2024)
18. Liu, Y., Chen, C., Wang, Z., Yi, L.: CrossVideo: self-supervised cross-modal contrastive learning for point cloud video understanding. In: 2024 IEEE International Conference on Robotics and Automation (ICRA), pp. 12436--12442. IEEE (2024)
19. Zhao, J., et al.: SemanticFlow: Semantic segmentation of sequential LiDAR point clouds from sparse frame annotations. IEEE Trans. Geosci. Remote Sens. **61**, 1–11 (2023)
20. Wang, N., Guo, R., Shi, C., Zhang, H., Lu, H., Zheng, Z., Chen, X.: SegNet4D: effective and efficient 4D LiDAR semantic segmentation in autonomous driving environments. arXiv preprint arXiv:2406.16279 (2024)
21. Zhong, J., Li, Z., Cui, Y., Fang, Z.: 4D-CS: exploiting cluster prior for 4D Spatio-Temporal LiDAR semantic segmentation. IEEE Robot. Autom. Lett. (2024)

When BBR Meets Live Streaming

Xu Yan[1], Tong Li[1,4](✉), Bo Wu[2], Cheng Luo[2], Jiuxiang Zhu[1], and Laizhong Cui[3]

[1] Renmin University of China, Beijing, China
{yanxu2,tong.li,2024103876}@ruc.edu.cn
[2] Tencent Technologies, Beijing, China
{brynwu,lancelotluo}@tencent.com
[3] Shenzhen University, Guangdong, China
cuilz@szu.edu.cn
[4] State Key Laboratory of Internet Architecture, Tsinghua University, Beijing, China

Abstract. Recently, industrial pioneers like Amazon, Tencent, ByteDance, and Huawei have been adopting BBR as their congestion control algorithm for live-streaming applications, including TikTok Live. However, BBR, originally crafted for bulk data transmission, faces multiple challenges in live-streaming scenarios. In this paper, we first explore two key issues associated with BBR due to inaccurate bandwidth estimation in live-streaming scenarios: (i) BBR cannot easily exit its startup phase, resulting in a fierce self-inflicted loss. (ii) BBR sends data at a lower rate than the available bandwidth during its stable phase. We then propose BBR-Copilot, an auxiliary congestion control component that cooperates with BBR, making BBR better adapt to live-streaming scenarios. BBR-Copilot allows for proactively generating accurate bandwidth measurement samples by smartly creating and sending extra data. We implement the BBR-Copilot prototype upon QUIC and evaluate it via testbed. Experimental evaluation results show that BBR-Copilot effectively enhances BBR's performance in live-streaming scenarios.

Keywords: BBR · Live Streaming · QUIC

1 Introduction

With the rapid development of the Internet, live-streaming services such as TikTok Live [26], YouTube Live [12], and Twitch [27] have become essential elements of our daily entertainment. Users tend to prefer live-streaming platforms that offer a better viewing experience for watching live streams for longer periods. For live-streaming service providers and Content Delivery Network (CDN) service

This work is partially supported by the National Natural Science Foundation of China (62572473, 62441230, U23B2026, and 62372305), the Scientific Research Innovation Capability Support Project for Young Faculty (SRICSPYF-ZY2025001), the funding from State Key Laboratory of Internet Architecture (HLW2025ZD17), the Guangdong Basic and Applied Basic Research Foundation (2024B1515040012), and the funding from Tencent Basic Platform Technology Rhino-Bird Focused Research Program.

T. Qiu et al. (Eds.): CCF ChinaNet 2025, CCIS 2810, pp. 11–27, 2026.
https://doi.org/10.1007/978-981-95-8450-5_2

providers, having more users and longer viewing times often translates to higher profits. Therefore, improving user's viewing experience has become a significant challenge for both live-streaming service providers and CDN service providers.

As a state-of-the-art congestion control algorithm, BBR (Bottleneck Bandwidth and Round-trip propagation time) [5] has been demonstrated to perform excellently and has been widely adopted (in Sect. 2.1). During its *Startup phase*, BBR rapidly increases its data-sending rate to quickly fill available bandwidth. In the *ProbeBW phase* (a.k.a, stable phase), BBR continuously monitors bottleneck bandwidth and Round-Trip Time (RTT) to reduce queuing delay in the intermediate buffer while maintaining high link utilization. Due to BBR's potential benefits in terms of Quality of Service (QoS) for data transmission and the user viewing experience, industrial pioneers such as Amazon [2], Tencent [25], ByteDance [4] and Huawei [14] have chosen BBR as their congestion control algorithm in cloud services or applications.

However, BBR encounters several issues due to lacking accurate bandwidth measurement samples in live-streaming scenarios. In live-streaming scenarios, the upper-layer application generates a frame of video periodically to be delivered to the transport layer. If the streaming bitrate is lower than the actual available bandwidth, it frequently causes the transport layer to enter a phase where it can send data but has no data to send, which is called the application-limited phase [8] (in Sect. 2.2). This frequent entry into the application-limited phase results in many inaccurate bandwidth measurement samples (in Sect. 2.3), which in turn causes BBR to encounter two key issues. **Firstly**, BBR fails to exit the Startup phase. During the Startup phase, the sender tends to send excessive data, leading to fierce losses. **Secondly**, even when BBR exits the Startup phase and turns into the ProbeBW phase, BBR cannot accurately estimate the available bandwidth, leading to long frame completion time. A high RTT prominently highlights these issues (in Sect. 2.4).

To tackle the issues BBR encounters in live-streaming scenarios, it is natural to consider transforming live streaming into bulk data transmission by sending extra data. This approach prevents the transport layer from entering the application-limited phase and ensures that bandwidth measurement samples are accurate. However, sending extra data at all times would incur excessive transmission costs, which is unacceptable. Therefore, we must exercise meticulous control over the sending of extra data (in Sect. 3.1).

In this paper, we propose BBR-Copilot (in Sect. 3.2), which can enhance the performance of BBR in live-streaming scenarios with transmission costs as low as possible. Specifically, when the *padding controller* (in Sect. 3.3) of BBR-Copilot detects that BBR is currently in the bandwidth probing phase (i.e., pacing_gain is greater than 1) and the current transport layer is in the application-limited phase, it will control the *data generator* (in Sect. 3.4) to generate and send extra data, enabling the bandwidth measurement mechanism to generate accurate bandwidth measurement samples when BBR requires them. Therefore, in the Startup phase, BBR can choose to exit the Startup phase based on the latest bandwidth measurement samples and the transition conditions of its state machine, avoiding the potentially large number of packet losses in a shallow buffer scenario. In the ProbeBW phase, BBR-Copilot can increase the accuracy of bandwidth measurement samples, helping BBR to adjust the sending rate more accurately based on the latest bandwidth measurement samples.

We implement BBR-Copilot prototype upon QUIC protocol [15,20,21] with just 200 lines of code and conduct experiments on our testbed (in Sect. 4.1). The evaluation results are as follows. (i) BBR-Copilot can increase the ratio of BBR exits from Startup to 100%, effectively reducing the retransmission ratio by 43.3% in live-streaming scenarios (in Sect. 4.2). (ii) BBR-Copilot helps BBR to reduce the Root Mean Square Error (RMSE) of the true bandwidth and the bandwidth measurement samples by 86.1% and adjust the sending rate to match the available bandwidth in live-streaming scenarios (in Sect. 4.3).

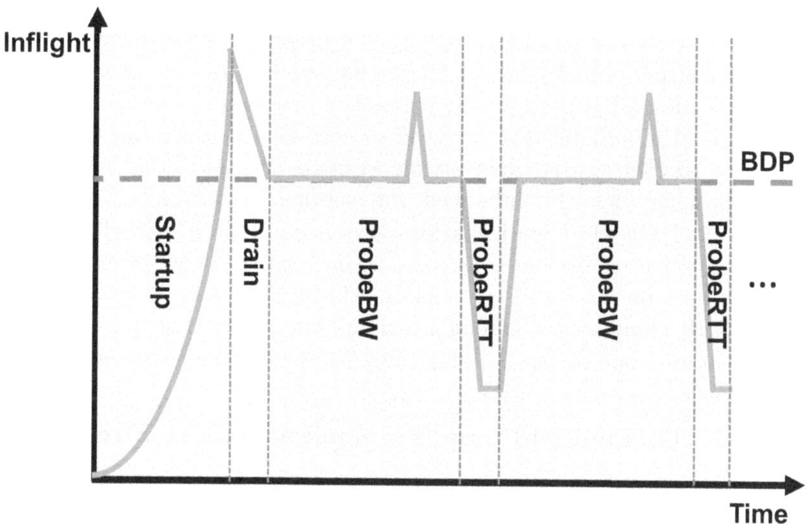

Fig. 1. BBR congestion control curve

2 Background and Motivation

In this section, we first introduce the BBR congestion control algorithm (in Sect. 2.1). Then, we highlight the recurrent occurrence of application-limited phases in live-streaming scenarios, contrasting sharply with bulk data transmission (in Sect. 2.2). Furthermore, we dissect BBR's bandwidth estimation process and diagnose estimation inaccuracy stemming from application-limited phase (in Sect. 2.3). Finally, we present two challenges faced by BBR in live-streaming scenarios (in Sect. 2.4).

2.1 BBR Overview

BBR is a new-type congestion control algorithm proposed by Google in 2016 [5]. BBR was originally designed for file transfer to optimize transfer performance. Traditional congestion control algorithms are mostly based on the signal of packet loss or RTT. However, BBR is based on active detection. The kernel method of BBR is an estimation of RTprop (round-trip propagation time) and BtlBw (bottleneck bandwidth) to maximize transport throughput and minimize delivery delay. Bandwidth-Delay Product (BDP) is the product of the BtlBw and RTprop. It quantifies the amount of data that can be in transit in the network at any given time. BBR uses this value to adjust its sending rate and congestion window to maximize throughput while avoiding potential congestion.

As Fig. 1 shows, BBR operates in four main phases: Startup, Drain, ProbeBW, and ProbeRTT. Startup is the initial phase, where BBR enables data to be sent at a rate that ramps up until available bandwidth is fully utilized. The Drain phase is carried out after the Startup phase, the sender stops sending follow-up packets until the in-flight data size (inflight) meets some condition (e.g., inflight $\leq$ BDP). When BBR exits the Drain phase, it enters the ProbeBW phase. BBR will periodically adjust the actual sending rate to probe BtlBw in this phase. Besides, BBR periodically enters the ProbeRTT phase, during which BBR maintains the inflight at a low level to precisely measure the RTprop.

BBR has revolutionized congestion control. Google, the developer of the BBR, has significantly enhanced the service performance of YouTube, Google.com, and Google Cloud Platform by using BBR. Cardwell et al. documented impressive results, such as a 2–25x decrease in video rebuffering rates on YouTube and up to a 14% increase in throughput for Google.com search queries [5]. BBR along with its Google variants are deployed at 22% of classified websites, becoming one of the popular congestion control algorithms [22].

2.2 Application-Limited Phase Is Ubiquitous in Live Streaming

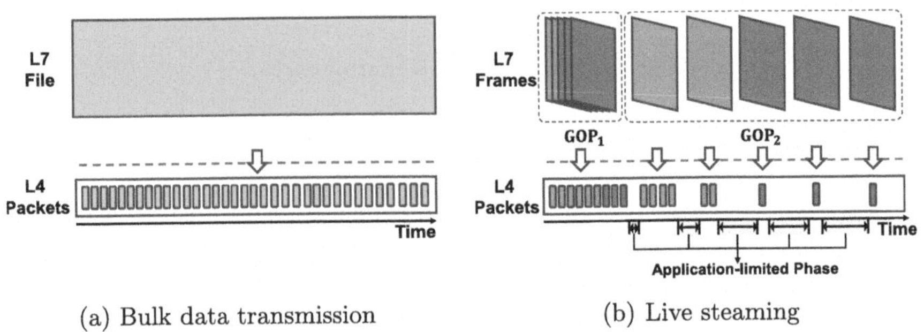

(a) Bulk data transmission (b) Live steaming

Fig. 2. Transmission characteristics.

In traditional bulk data transmission, once the client's request is processed, the server's application layer submits the entire requested file to the transport layer, as shown in Fig. 2a. Until the entire file is fully transmitted, there will be no instances where there is no data available to send in the send buffer. Therefore, when transmitting bulk data, the transport layer will hardly ever enter a phase where it can send data but has no data to send, which is called the application-limited phase. However, the situation is significantly different in live-streaming scenarios. As shown in Fig. 2b, after the client's request is processed, to allow the client to buffer some frames and reduce the impact of network fluctuations, the server will first send the latest Group of Pictures (GOP) to the client, and then successively send the real-time generated video and audio frames. Therefore, when the connection is just established, the server has a lot of data to send, and the transmission characteristics at this time are similar to those of transmitting bulk data. However, after the data of this GOP is transmitted, the upper-layer application will generate a new video or audio frame to be sent by the transport layer at intervals according to the frame rate. If the current frame is sent before the next frame is generated, and the current congestion control algorithm allows us to continue sending data, the transport layer will fall into a situation where it can send data but has no data to send (i.e., it enters the application-limited phase). Since the bitrate of the live stream must be less than or equal to the true bandwidth, otherwise the client will not be able to receive the corresponding frames in time and will frequently experience freezing, the transport layer of the sender will frequently enter the application-limited phase in live-streaming scenarios [32] (Fig. 3).

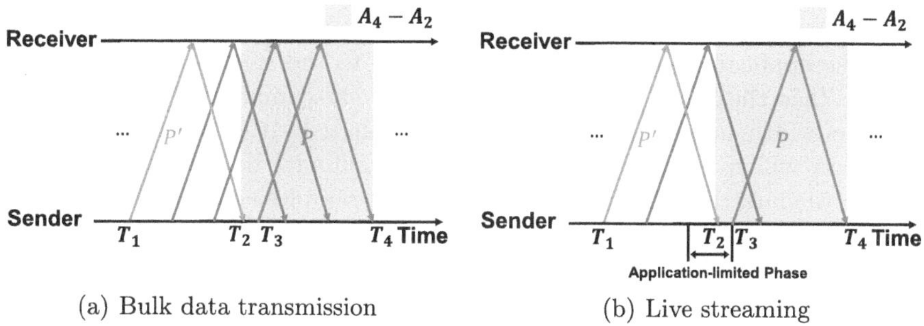

(a) Bulk data transmission

(b) Live streaming

Fig. 3. Bandwidth measurement sample calculation.

2.3 BBR Bandwidth Estimation Suffers From Application-Limited Phase

Bandwidth Estimation in BBR is Based on Bandwidth Measurement Samples. BBR estimates bandwidth by taking the maximum value of all bandwidth measurement samples computed from packets within a specific time window. The sample calculation procedure is as follows: As shown in Figure 2.3a, when packet P is sent, we record the time T_3. When P is acknowledged, we record the time T_4 when P is acknowledged and the total amount of data A_4 acknowledged from the start of the connection to the time T_4. In addition, we also record some information about the *most recently acknowledged packet* P'

when P is sent. This includes the time T_1 when P' is sent, the time T_2 when P' is acknowledged, and the total amount of data A_2 acknowledged from the start of the connection to the time T_2. When P is acknowledged, we can calculate the average sending rate (*send_rate*) and the average acknowledging rate (*ack_rate*) of the packets sent from the time T_1 to T_3 according to Equation (1) and Equation (2).

$$send\_rate = \frac{A_4 - A_2}{T_3 - T_1} \tag{1}$$

$$ack\_rate = \frac{A_4 - A_2}{T_4 - T_2} \tag{2}$$

Ultimately, upon acknowledging P, the bandwidth measurement sample is derived from the lower of *send_rate* and *ack_rate*.

The Application-Limited Phase Causes the Bandwidth Measurement Samples to Fail to Reflect the Underlying True Bandwidth. After the transport layer exits the application-limited phase, all bandwidth measurement samples generated by the packets sent from the time when the next packet is sent to the time when this packet is acknowledged are inaccurate. This is because the most recent acknowledged packet when these data packets were sent was sent before the transport layer entered the application-limited phase. According to Eqs. 1 and 2, since no data was sent when the transport layer was in the application-limited phase, this leads to the *send_rate* and *ack_rate* being less than the actual sending rate. Therefore, we cannot distinguish whether these bandwidth measurement samples are limited by the true bandwidth or the rate at which the upper-layer application submits data to the transport layer. So we mark these bandwidth measurement samples as inaccurate. In other words, when the transport layer enters the application-limited phase within the time of one RTT before a packet is sent, the bandwidth measurement sample generated by that packet becomes inaccurate. Therefore, the larger the RTT, the more inaccurate bandwidth measurement samples are caused by entering the application-limited phase. This is consistent with our experimental results in §4.

Figure 4 provides an example illustrating how RTT affects the accuracy of bandwidth measurement samples in live-streaming scenarios. The RTT in Fig. 4a is higher compared to Fig. 4b, while all other conditions remain the same. At the time T_1, the transport layer enters the application-limited phase. In Fig. 4a, this leads to all bandwidth samples measured between T_2 and T_4 being inaccurate. However, in Fig. 4b, an accurate bandwidth sample can be calculated when the packet sent at time T_4 has been acknowledged.

2.4 Challenges When BBR Meets Live-Streaming

Challenge in Startup Phase. In live-streaming scenarios, BBR does not easily exit the Startup phase. We conducted large-scale measurements on over 570,000 live-streaming flows in real-world networks and found that 88.4% of them end

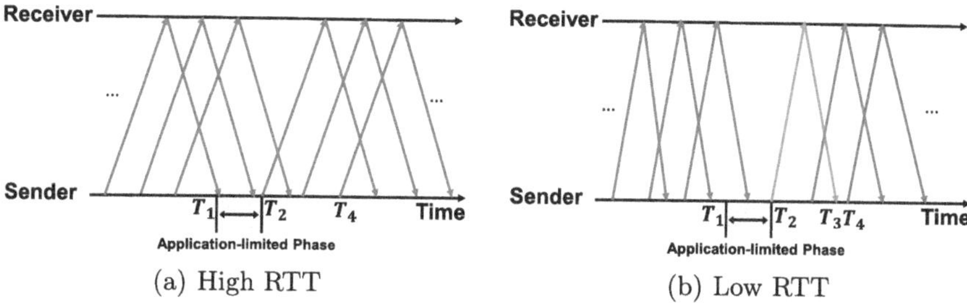

(a) High RTT (b) Low RTT

Fig. 4. Bandwidth measurement sample calculation in live streaming.

with BBR remaining in the Startup phase. The specific reasons impeding BBR's smooth exit from Startup phase are examined in the following analysis. When the current round ends, BBR checks if the last bandwidth measurement sample is accurate. If it is inaccurate, BBR will not exit the Startup phase at this point. Otherwise, if the BtlBw estimated in the current round is 25% higher than the BtlBw estimated in the previous round, a counter is reset to 0. Otherwise, the counter is incremented by 1. BBR exits the Startup phase when the counter reaches 3. In live-streaming scenarios, frequent transitions to the application-limited phase at the transport layer result in a large number of inaccurate bandwidth measurement samples. If the last bandwidth measurement sample within each round remains inaccurate, BBR can not exit the Startup phase. Based on the transmission characteristics mentioned in §2.2, in live-streaming scenarios, the server first sends a GOP to the client. If this data allows BBR to estimate a BtlBw close to the true bandwidth but not enough to exit the Startup phase, considering that BBR's sending rate is 2.885 times the BtlBw in the Startup phase, the sending rate will exceed the true bandwidth, leading to a high packet loss rate in shallow buffer scenarios. This phenomenon is exemplified in Fig. 7 (in §4.2).

Challenge in ProbeBW Phase. During the ProbeBW phase, BBR periodically sets the pacing_gain to 1.25, which means it will send data at a rate of 1.25 times the BtlBw to probe for more available bandwidth. When the true bandwidth increases, if a bandwidth measurement sample is generated during a period where the transport layer does not enter the application-limited phase and the pacing_gain is set to 1.25, then the value of that bandwidth measurement sample will be greater than BBR's current estimated BtlBw, and BBR will update its BtlBw to the value of that bandwidth measurement sample, which allows the sending rate to continuously increase and eventually approach the true bandwidth. However, if all bandwidth measurement samples are taken during periods where the transport layer frequently enters the application-limited phase, resulting in an average sending rate within the measurement period that is lower than BBR's BtlBw, BBR will not use these bandwidth measurement samples to update its BtlBw. This leads to a problem where the sending rate does not increase even when the true bandwidth increases. Figure 8 (in Sect. 4.3) demonstrates a representative scenario of this phenomenon.

3 Design

In this section, we first discuss the design rationale of how to allow for the generation of accurate bandwidth measurement samples (in Sect. 3.1). We then dive into the detailed design of BBR-Copilot by introducing the framework (in Sect. 3.2) and its two key components (in Sect. 3.3 and Sect. 3.4).

3.1 Design Rationale

To address the issues encountered by BBR mentioned above, one simple solution is to transform the live-streaming scenarios into bulk data transmission scenarios. This means generating extra data for transmission when the transport layer is about to enter the application-limited phase. By doing so, the transport layer will never enter the application-limited phase, ensuring that all bandwidth measurement samples are accurate. This naturally resolves the problems faced by BBR in live-streaming scenarios. However, this approach has a significant consequence: it results in the transmission of a large amount of extra data, wasting network resources and significantly increasing transmission costs.

Based on our understanding of BBR, we have identified that the two issues encountered by BBR in live-streaming scenarios are caused by a lack of accurate bandwidth measurement samples when the pacing_gain is greater than 1. Therefore, we believe that only when the pacing_gain of BBR is greater than 1 and the transport layer is about to enter the application-limited phase, extra data needs to be generated to avoid the transport layer being in an application-limited phase and ensure accurate bandwidth sampling, solving BBR's issue in live streaming.

3.2 Framework of BBR-Copilot

As illustrated in Fig. 5, BBR-Copilot primarily consists of two modules: The *padding controller* and the *data generator*. The padding controller is responsible for detecting whether the current conditions for generating extra data are met, thereby controlling the data generator. The data generator is responsible for receiving control signals from the padding controller and generating extra data to send when the conditions are met. When the sending module completes sending the packets that can be sent, BBR-Copilot checks if there is a need to generate extra data. It generates extra data when the transport layer is in an application-limited phase and BBR's pacing_gain is greater than 1. Through this mechanism, we have achieved the function of the transport layer not entering an application-limited phase when BBR needs to probe bandwidth, enabling BBR to obtain accurate bandwidth measurement samples.

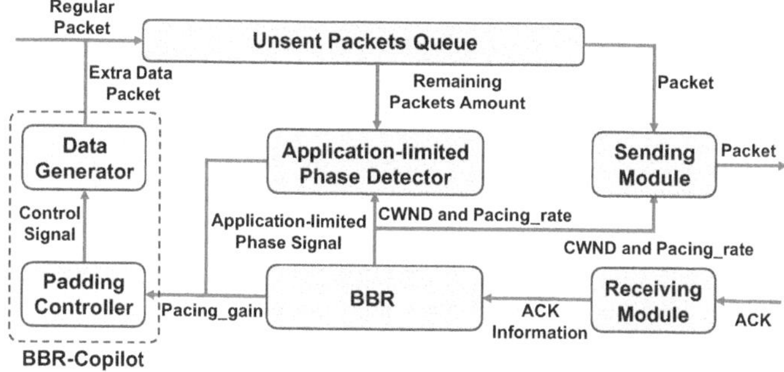

Fig. 5. The framework of BBR-Copilot mechanism.

3.3 Padding Controller

After sending a packet, the padding controller starts checking if there is a need to generate extra data. Firstly, the padding controller queries the existing application-limited phase detector to determine if the transport layer is currently in an application-limited phase. If the application-limited phase detector determines that packets can be sent and detects that the unsent packet queue is empty, it returns an application-limited signal to the padding controller. Simultaneously, the padding controller obtains BBR's pacing_gain. If the padding controller receives an application-limited signal and detects that the BBR's pacing_gain is greater than 1, it sends the signal to the data generator to generate extra data.

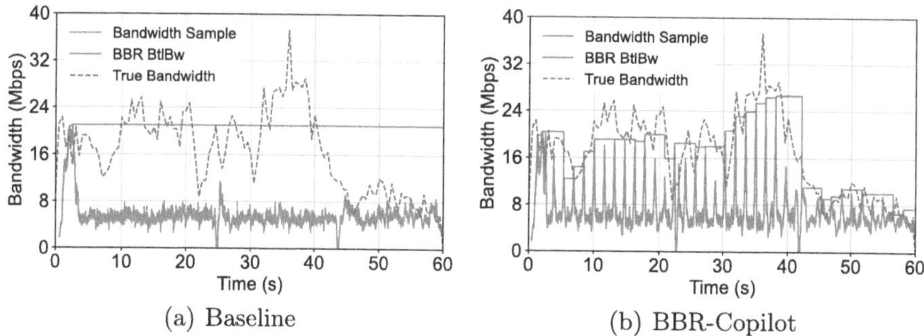

Fig. 6. Bandwidth measurement in a network environment where BBR cannot exit the Startup phase. Bandwidth measurement in a network environment where BBR cannot exit the Startup phase.

3.4 Data Generator

When the data generator receives the signal sent by the padding controller, it will generate a packet containing extra data, and then put this packet into the unsent packets queue, allowing it to be sent by the sending module. The extra data generated here is meaningless and is only used for assisting bandwidth estimation. After receiving this packet, the receiver will only return acknowledgment (ACK) and the data will not be submitted to the upper layer. This packet does not need to be resent after being lost, avoiding the problem of affecting subsequent normal data transmission.

4 Evaluation

In this section, we will introduce the experimental evaluation results of BBR-Copilot. We first introduce the specific architecture of the testbed (in §4.1). Then, we evaluate the optimization effects of BBR-Copilot on the issue BBR encounters during the Startup phase (in §4.2). Finally, we evaluate the optimization effects of BBR-Copilot on the issue BBR faces during the ProbeBW phase (in §4.3).

4.1 Architecture of the Testbed

We set up a test platform to evaluate BBR-Copilot. The test platform consists of a physical machine and two containers deployed on the physical machine. One of the containers simulates the source station, providing live streams. The physical machine simulates a CDN server, used to proxy the live streams, and BBR-Copilot is deployed on it. The other container simulates a client, which can send requests to the CDN server and obtain live-streaming data, and Mahimahi [23] is deployed on it to simulate the network environment between the CDN server and the client.

4.2 Optimization of BBR-Copilot in the Startup Phase

To evaluate the optimization effect of BBR-Copilot on addressing issue in the Startup phase of BBR, we need to select a network environment where BBR hardly exits the Startup phase and the buffer size is small. In this case, we evaluate the performance of the BBR-Copilot in an environment with a streaming bitrate of 5.4 Mbps, RTT of 200 ms, network buffer of 40 KB, and using the Verizon-LTE-driving.up and Verizon-LTE-driving.down traces provided by Mahimahi to set the uplink and downlink bandwidth.

As shown in Fig. 6a, in this environment, for BBR without BBR-Copilot deployed, there is sufficient data to be sent within the first 3 s. BBR updates its BtlBw to a larger value based on accurate bandwidth measurement samples. After 3 s, due to the transport layer's frequent entry into the application-limited phase, BBR without BBR-Copilot cannot exit the Startup phase due to a lack of accurate bandwidth measurement samples. Since BBR does not reduce the sending rate during the Startup phase, the sender continues to send data at a rate of pacing_gain times the BtlBw, resulting in a sending rate of 60.5 Mbps, even exceeding the maximum available bandwidth of 37.2 Mbps within 60 s. With only a 40 KB buffer size, a large number of packet losses occur, with a retransmission ratio of 27.5%. When BBR-Copilot is deployed, as shown in Fig. 6b, BBR smoothly exits the Startup phase, and the sending rate adjusts according to the true bandwidth, closely matching the true bandwidth. Packet losses are significantly reduced, with a retransmission ratio of 12.6%.

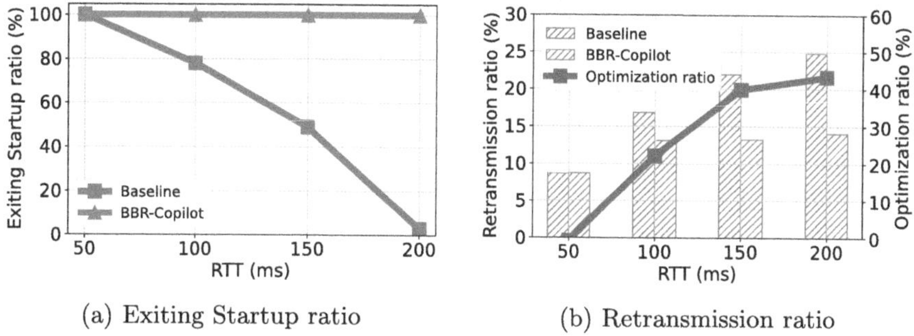

(a) Exiting Startup ratio

(b) Retransmission ratio

Fig. 7. The optimization effect of BBR-Copilot varies with RTT.

Then, with all other network environment parameters unchanged, we tested the optimization effect of the BBR-Copilot on the issue BBR encounters in the Startup phase under environments with RTTs of 50 ms, 100 ms, 150 ms, and 200 ms, respectively, to examine how the optimization effect changes with RTT.

As shown in Fig. 7a, for BBR without BBR-Copilot deployed, as the RTT increases from 50 ms to 200 ms, the proportion of live streams in which BBR exits the Startup phase within 60 s decreases from 100% to 3%. For BBR with BBR-Copilot deployed, regardless of the RTT variation, the proportion of live streams in which BBR exits the Startup phase remains at 100%. This demonstrates that BBR-Copilot effectively helps BBR exit the Startup phase.

As shown in Fig. 7b, as the RTT increases from 50 ms to 200 ms, for BBR without BBR-Copilot deployed, the retransmission ratio gradually increases from 8.6% to 24.8%. However, for BBR with BBR-Copilot deployed, the retransmission ratio increases from 8.7% to 14.1%. The optimization ratio relative to BBR without BBR-Copilot gradually increases from nearly 0% to 43.3%. It is evident that as the RTT increases, the proportion of live streams in which BBR exits the Startup phase decreases, leading to a higher retransmission ratio. BBR Copilot effectively addresses the issue of a high retransmission ratio caused by BBR's failure to exit the Startup phase.

4.3 Optimization of BBR-Copilot in The ProbeBW Phase

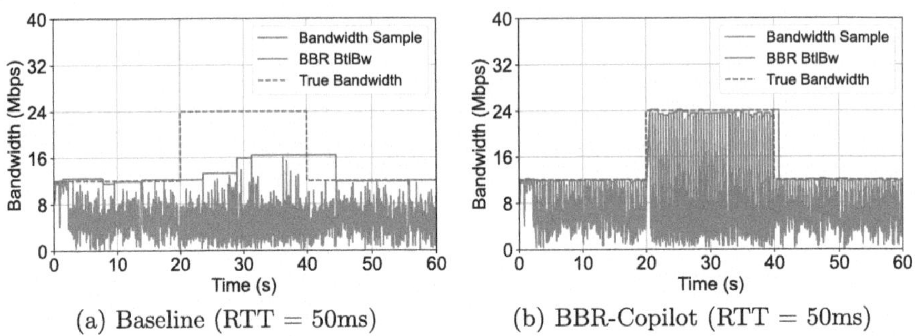

(a) Baseline (RTT = 50ms)

(b) BBR-Copilot (RTT = 50ms)

Fig. 8. Bandwidth measurement in a low-RTT network environment where BBR can exit the Startup phase.

To evaluate the optimization effect of BBR-Copilot on addressing the issue in the ProbeBW phase of BBR, we need to select a network environment where BBR easily exits the Startup phase and the available network bandwidth increases. Here we evaluate the performance of the BBR-Copilot in an environment with a streaming bitrate of 5.4 Mbps and RTT values of 50 ms and 200 ms. The uplink bandwidth is set at 12 Mbps, while the downlink bandwidth varies as follows: 12 Mbps from 0 to 20 s, 24 Mbps from 20 to 40 s, and 12 Mbps from 40 to 60 s. In this environment, regardless of whether BBR-Copilot is deployed or not, BBR can exit the Startup phase and enter the ProbeBW phase after the Drain phase.

As shown in Fig. 8a, when the RTT is 50 ms, between the 20th and 40th seconds, BBR without BBR-Copilot deployed can only obtain a larger bandwidth measurement sample of 16.4 Mbps, which is much lower than the true bandwidth of 24.0 Mbps, and the RMSE of the true bandwidth and the bandwidth measurement samples is 9.41. As shown in Fig. 8b, BBR with BBR-Copilot deployed can quickly obtain accurate bandwidth measurement samples that are close to the true bandwidth. The RMSE of the true bandwidth and the bandwidth measurement samples is 1.31 between the 20th and 40th seconds, which is 86.1% lower than the RMSE of the true bandwidth and the bandwidth measurement samples without BBR-Copilot deployed.

As shown in Fig. 9a, when the RTT is 200 ms, BBR without BBR-Copilot deployed can not even obtain larger bandwidth measurement samples and continues using the bandwidth measurement sample of 11.8 Mbps obtained between the 0th and 20th seconds, which results in the RMSE of the true bandwidth and the bandwidth measurement samples being 12.18 between the 20th and 40th seconds. However, as shown in Fig. 9b, BBR with BBR-Copilot deployed performs better. It can obtain an accurate bandwidth measurement sample exceeding 23.0 Mbps. The RMSE of the true bandwidth and the bandwidth measurement samples is 2.72. This is 77.7% lower than the RMSE of the true bandwidth and

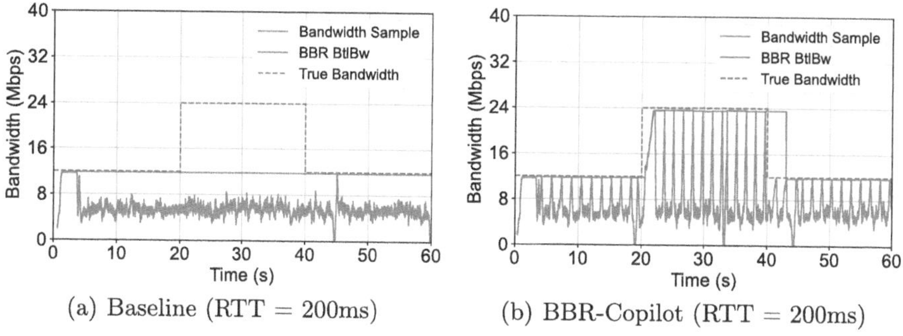

(a) Baseline (RTT = 200ms)

(b) BBR-Copilot (RTT = 200ms)

Fig. 9. Bandwidth measurement in a high-RTT network environment where BBR can exit the Startup phase.

the bandwidth measurement samples without BBR-Copilot deployed. Therefore, BBR's sending rate can be more precisely aligned with the available bandwidth. It is evident that BBR-Copilot can effectively improve the accuracy of bandwidth estimation of BBR during the ProbeBW phase, which helps BBR to adjust the sending rate accurately to match the available bandwidth.

5 Discussion and Future Work

Extra Transmission Costs: Generating extra data to prevent the transport layer from entering the application-limited phase will introduce extra transmission costs. The larger the gap between the true bandwidth and the live-streaming bitrate, the more extra data is needed, and the higher the cost. Therefore, accurately and timely generating accurate bandwidth measurement samples requires the introduction of significant extra transmission costs. The current solution of BBR-Copilot is to generate accurate bandwidth measurement samples only at certain key moments. In future work, we plan to reduce extra transmission costs further, that is, to balance the bandwidth required for live streaming and the extra transmission costs, and choose an appropriate bandwidth as the upper limit for our bandwidth probing, rather than precisely detecting the maximum available bandwidth of the entire link.

Content of Extra Data: The extra data currently generated by BBR-Copilot consists of some meaningless filler data. However, we believe that if we can make full use of this extra data, it can also optimize the transmission of normal data. We plan to utilize copies of in-flight packets as extra data. When we send these extra data to prevent the transport layer from entering an application-limited phase, even if the in-flight data packets are lost, the receiving end can recover the content of these lost packets when it receives these extra data, reducing the time for packet loss recovery.

Higher Versions of BBR: In this paper, we conducted evaluation tests based on version 1 of BBR and did not involve higher versions of BBR. Compared to BBRv1, which only chooses to exit the Startup phase based on estimated BtlBw increase, BBRv2 [7] and BBRv3 [6] also choose to exit the Startup phase based on packet loss rate. This may solve the problem of BBRv1 not being able to exit the Startup phase easily in live-streaming scenarios. However, it still cannot solve the problem that BBR cannot adjust the sending rate in time as the actual bandwidth increases in the ProbeBW phase. We plan to continue testing the effects of BBR-Copilot on BBRv2 and BBRv3 in future work.

6 Related Work

Congestion Control Algorithm. Currently, widely-deployed congestion control algorithms (CCAs) are mostly rule-based [5,13,30,34]. Designed by domain experts, they adjust packet sending rate and congestion window according to network feedback (e.g., loss, throughput, delay). These algorithms are optimized for specific network environments, yet no single rule-based CCA works universally. This has led to the rise of learning-based CCAs, which use modern machine-learning tools like supervised learning (e.g., Indigo [31], Muses [37]) or reinforcement learning (e.g., Aurora [16], DeepCC [1]). They perform well in diverse network scenarios. However, their black-box design causes performance degradation in new environments [17,35], and high computation overhead restricts large-scale deployment. Recently, the poly-algorithmic congestion control paradigm has been proposed [11,33,38], aiming to combine multiple CCAs to leverage strengths and mitigate limitations. Combining rule-based and learning-based CCAs has balanced stability and generality, but the built-in learning-based CCAs still result in high deployment overhead. In summary, compared to other CCAs, BBR performs excellently in common network scenarios, with low overhead and stable performance, making it widely used.

Optimization of BBR. Since the introduction of BBR, many efforts have been made to optimize the issues inherent in BBR. BBR-S [9], when measuring bandwidth, uses an Adaptive Tobit Kalman Filter (ATKF) to replace the maximum filter that may lead to overestimation of bandwidth, thereby reducing queuing delay. oBBR [3] avoids substantial packet loss in shallow buffer links by detecting the size of the bottleneck buffer and adjusting the upper limit of data in transmission. It can also accurately and promptly detect bandwidth drops and adjust its sending rate, significantly reducing the retransmission ratio. BBR-E [18] enhances the fairness of flows that share the same bottleneck link but have different RTTs by reducing cwnd when a larger RTT is detected. Unlike previous works, BBR-Copilot does not directly modify BBR. Instead, it adds a mechanism to help BBR more accurately estimate bandwidth in live-streaming scenarios.

On-off Traffic Pattern. Many previous works [10,19,24,28,32,36] have demonstrated the on-off traffic pattern is not conducive to transmission control. The work most closely related to BBR-Copilot in recent years is Amphis [24]. Amphis is a congestion control algorithm framework that enhances the accuracy of bandwidth estimation and the speed of data transmission at the message granularity level under the on-off traffic pattern by dividing the sent data into messages and using FEC coding [29] to generate extra data to assist in bandwidth estimation. The main differences between BBR-Copilot and Amphis are as follows: (i) We have conducted a detailed analysis of the problems with BBR in the on-off traffic pattern and their causes. (ii) We have provided conditions for generating extra data and the implementation method coupled with BBR in detail.

7 Conclusion

BBR-Copilot assists BBR in obtaining accurate bandwidth measurement samples, enabling it to quickly exit the Startup phase and adjust the sending rate accurately and promptly in the ProbeBW phase. Evaluation results have demonstrated that BBR-Copilot significantly enhances the performance of BBR in livestreaming scenarios. In the future, we plan to further reduce the transmission cost associated with BBR-Copilot and improve the timeliness of generating accurate bandwidth measurement samples. Subsequently, we will deploy it on our CDN servers, serving millions of users worldwide.

References

1. Abbasloo, S., Yen, C.Y., Chao, H.J.: Wanna make your tcp scheme great for cellular networks? let machines do it for you! IEEE J. Sel. Areas Commun. **39**(1), 265–279 (2020)
2. Amazon: Amazon (2025). https://aws.amazon.com/cn/cloudfront
3. Bi, P., Xiao, M., Yu, D., Zhang, G.: oBBR: optimize retransmissions of BBR flows on the internet. In: USENIX ATC 23, pp. 537–551 (2023)
4. ByteDance: Bytedance (2025). https://www.bytedance.com
5. Cardwell, N., Cheng, Y., Gunn, C.S., Yeganeh, S.H., Jacobson, V.: BBR: congestion-based congestion control: measuring bottleneck bandwidth and round-trip propagation time. ACM Queue **14**(5), 20–53 (2016)
6. Cardwell, N., et al.: BBRv3: algorithm bug fixes and public internet deployment. In: IETF 117th Meeting, pp. 1–13 (2023)
7. Cardwell, N., et al.: BBRv2: a model-based congestion control performance optimization. In: IETF 106th Meeting, pp. 1–32 (2019)
8. Cheng, Y., Cardwell, N., Hassas Yeganeh, S., Jacobson, V.: Delivery rate estimation. IETF. Internet-Draft draft-cheng-iccrg-delivery-rate-estimation-02 (2022)
9. Chiariotti, F., Zanella, A., Kucera, S., Claussen, H.: BBR-S: a low-latency bbr modification for fast-varying connections. IEEE Access **9**, 76364–76378 (2021)

10. De Cicco, L., Caldaralo, V., Palmisano, V., Mascolo, S.: Elastic: a client-side controller for dynamic adaptive streaming over http (dash). In: PV, pp. 1–8 (2013)
11. Emara, S., Li, B., Chen, Y.: Eagle: refining congestion control by learning from the experts. In: IEEE INFOCOM, pp. 676–685 (2020)
12. Google: Youtube live (2025). https://www.youtube.com/live
13. Ha, S., Rhee, I., Xu, L.: Cubic: a new tcp-friendly high-speed tcp variant. ACM SIGOPS **42**(5), 64–74 (2008)
14. Huawei: Huawei. https://www.huawei.com (2025)
15. Iyengar, J., Thomson, M.: QUIC: A UDP-Based Multiplexed and Secure Transport. RFC 9000 (2021). https://www.rfc-editor.org/info/rfc9000
16. Jay, N., Rotman, N., Godfrey, B., Schapira, M., Tamar, A.: A deep reinforcement learning perspective on internet congestion control. In: ICML, pp. 3050–3059 (2019)
17. Jiang, H., et al.: When machine learning meets congestion control: a survey and comparison. Comput. Netw. **192**, 108033 (2021)
18. Kim, G.H., Song, Y.J., Mahmud, I., Cho, Y.Z.: Enhanced bbr congestion control algorithm for improving rtt fairness. In: ICUFN, pp. 358–360 (2019)
19. Kupka, T., Halvorsen, P., Griwodz, C.: Performance of on-off traffic stemming from live adaptive segmented http video streaming. In: LCN, pp. 401–409 (2012)
20. Langley, A., et al.: The quic transport protocol: design and internet-scale deployment. In: ACM SIGCOMM, pp. 183–196 (2017)
21. LiteSpeed: LiteSpeed QUIC and HTTP/3 Library (2025). https://github.com/litespeedtech/lsquic
22. Mishra, A., Sun, X., Jain, A., Pande, S., Joshi, R., Leong, B.: The great internet TCP congestion control census. Proc. ACM Meas. Anal. Comput. Syst. **3**(3), 1–24 (2019)
23. Netravali, R., et al.: Mahimahi: accurate record-and-Replay for HTTP. In: USENIX ATC 15, pp. 417–429 (2015)
24. Pan, T., et al.: Amphis: rearchitecturing congestion control for capturing internet application variety. In: APNet, pp. 95–101 (2023)
25. Tencent: Tencent (2025). https://www.tencent.com
26. TikTok: Tiktok (2025). https://www.tiktok.com
27. Twitch: Twitch (2025). https://www.twitch.tv
28. Wierman, A., Osogami, T., Olsén, J.: Modeling tcp-vegas under on/off traffic. SIGMETRICS Perform. Eval. Rev. **31**(2), 6–8 (2003)
29. Wikipedia: Forward error correction (fec) (2025). https://en.wikipedia.org/wiki/Error_correction_code
30. Winstein, K., Sivaraman, A., Balakrishnan, H., et al.: Stochastic forecasts achieve high throughput and low delay over cellular networks. In: NSDI, vol. 1, pp. 2–3 (2013)
31. Yan, F.Y., et al.: Pantheon: the training ground for internet congestion-control research. In: USENIX ATC 2018, pp. 731–743 (2018)
32. Yan, X., et al.: Poster: too: accelerating loss recovery by taming on-off traffic patterns. In: ACM SIGCOMM, pp. 1147–1149 (2023)
33. Yang, W., Liu, Y., Tian, C., Jiang, J., Guo, L.: Gemini: divide-and-conquer for practical learning-based internet congestion control. In: INFOCOM, pp. 1–10 (2023)
34. Zaki, Y., Pötsch, T., Chen, J., Subramanian, L., Görg, C.: Adaptive congestion control for unpredictable cellular networks. In: SIGCOMM, pp. 509–522 (2015)
35. Zhang, T., Mao, S.: Machine learning for end-to-end congestion control. IEEE Commun. Mag. **58**(6), 52–57 (2020)

36. Zhao, Y., Zhang, B., Li, C., Chen, C.: On/off traffic shaping in the internet: motivation, challenges, and solutions. IEEE Netw. **31**(2), 48–57 (2017)
37. Zhong, Z., et al.: Muses: enabling lightweight learning-based congestion control for mobile devices. In: IEEE INFOCOM, pp. 2208–2217 (2022)
38. Zhou, J., et al.: Antelope: a framework for dynamic selection of congestion control algorithms. In: ICNP, pp. 1–11 (2021)

An Adaptive Particle Swarm Optimization-Based Algorithm for Industrial Control Network Situation Prediction

Li Shen, Qiuyu Huang, Liangyin Chen, and Yanru Chen(✉)

College of Computer Science, Sichuan University, Chengdu 610065, China
shen_li@stu.scu.edu.cn, {chenliangyin,chenyanru}@scu.edu.cn

Abstract. Situation element acquisition, assessment, and prediction are critical components of situation awareness. Enhancing the accuracy of risk trend extraction in security frameworks is essential. To address the issues of low prediction accuracy and slow convergence in industrial control network situation prediction, this paper proposes SAIPSO-BiLSTM, an adaptive particle swarm optimization-based prediction algorithm. Opposition-based learning is used to initialize the particle swarm to improve population diversity, while Gaussian and Cauchy mutation mechanisms dynamically adjust inertia weights to accelerate convergence. In addition, a Levy flight-based perturbation strategy, integrating similarity and aggregation degree, helps particles escape local optima. Taking into account the temporal dependencies in the situation data, a BiLSTM network is employed, with model optimization performed via the adaptive PSO. The experimental results show that the proposed SAIPSO-BiLSTM improves prediction accuracy and convergence speed, achieving a lowest MAPE of 1.40 and up to 0.16 increase in R^2 compared to baseline models, demonstrating its clear advantage.

Keywords: Industrial Control Systems · Network Security · Situation Awareness · Situation Prediction · Particle Swarm Optimization

1 Introduction

Network Security Situation Prediction (NSSP) is a critical research topic in industrial control networks (ICS). It aims to predict future network states and trends by identifying correlations within historical data. As the final stage of network situation awareness, accurate prediction of attack trends enables proactive

This work was supported in part by the National Natural Science Foundation of China (Grant 62302324); in part by the Sichuan Province Science and Technology Support Program (Grant 2024NSFSC0500 and 2024YFHZ0023); in part by the Fundamental Research Funds for the Central Universities (Grant YJ202420); in part by Sichuan University young teachers science and technology innovation ability improvement project (Grant 2024SCUQJTX028).

T. Qiu et al. (Eds.): CCF ChinaNet 2025, CCIS 2810, pp. 28–42, 2026.
https://doi.org/10.1007/978-981-95-8450-5_3

defenses, ensuring timely and targeted security measures. However, achieving high prediction accuracy and real-time performance remains a major challenge. Therefore, the development of effective NSSP methods is essential to ensure the safe and stable operation of ICS.

Research on NSSP can be broadly categorized into two main directions: improving prediction accuracy through traditional machine learning and deep learning models, and enhancing model performance and convergence speed via hyperparameter optimization algorithms. In the realm of deep learning, long short-term memory (LSTM) networks have been widely applied due to their capability to handle large datasets and capture long-range dependencies. However, standard LSTM architectures are unidirectional, which limits their ability to model the bidirectional dependencies inherent in situation data [2,3,7,15]. To address this limitation, Bidirectional LSTM (BiLSTM) networks have been adopted, as they can extract information from both past and future contexts, making them better suited for NSSP tasks. Regarding hyperparameter tuning, various optimization algorithms such as Cuckoo Search, Ant Colony Optimization, Genetic Algorithms, and Particle Swarm Optimization (PSO) have been proposed to enhance BiLSTM performance. Previous studies have demonstrated that PSO can effectively optimize LSTM parameters and improve model accuracy. Nevertheless, the standard PSO algorithm often suffers from premature convergence and tends to get trapped in local optima, which constrains its ability to further enhance model performance.

To address the challenges of low prediction accuracy, insufficient temporal modeling, and slow convergence, we proposes SAIPSO-BiLSTM (Situation Prediction Algorithm for Industrial Control Systems based on Improved Particle Swarm Optimization), which leverages an improved PSO algorithm to optimize BiLSTM networks. In SAIPSO-BiLSTM, the proposed enhancements include: (1) opposition-based learning to improve initial population diversity and accelerate convergence; (2) dynamic position adjustment using Cauchy and Gaussian distributions to balance exploration and exploitation; (3) Levy flight perturbations, guided by particle similarity and aggregation, to prevent premature convergence and enhance global search capability. Once optimal hyperparameters are found, the BiLSTM network is optimized and trained on historical data to predict future situations. Experiments on the UNSW-NB15 dataset validate the effectiveness of the proposed method. Evaluations based on Mean Absolute Error (MAE), Coefficient of Determination (R^2), and Mean Absolute Percentage Error (MAPE) demonstrate that SAIPSO-BiLSTM outperforms baseline PSO-based methods in terms of accuracy and convergence speed.

Our contributions are summarized as follows:

1. We propose an improved Particle Swarm Optimization (PSO) algorithm for BiLSTM hyperparameter optimization. In SAIPSO-BiLSTM, opposition-based initialization increases swarm diversity, dynamic position adjustment using Cauchy and Gaussian distributions improves convergence speed and solution quality, and aggregation-driven Levy flights help particles escape local optima.

2. We propose the SAIPSO-BiLSTM model, which effectively captures complex temporal dependencies for NSSP tasks. By automatically tuning BiLSTM hyperparameters, SAIPSO-BiLSTM enhances the modeling of bidirectional dependencies and improves prediction accuracy on large-scale situation data.
3. We validate the proposed method on the UNSW-NB15 dataset. Results show that SAIPSO-BiLSTM outperforms baseline PSO-based models in prediction accuracy and convergence speed, achieving improvements in MAE, a lowest MAPE of 1.40, and up to 0.16 increase in R^2

The remainder of this paper is organized as follows. Section 2 reviews related work. Section 3 introduces the SAIPSO-BiLSTM algorithm. Section 4 presents experimental validation. Section 5 concludes the paper and discusses future directions.

2 Related Work

Network security situation prediction has become an important approach for protecting network systems, with applications in sensor networks and mobile environments [2,3,7]. Various techniques have been explored, including artificial neural networks, mathematical modeling, clustering algorithms, and machine learning methods [5,12]. Neural networks extract features through hidden layers but suffer from high computational complexity and long training times. Clustering algorithms, although useful, face challenges such as selecting initial nodes and similarly incur high costs. Consequently, research has increasingly shifted toward machine learning and deep learning-based approaches for industrial control network security prediction.

Zhang et al. [11] used a backpropagation (BP) neural network optimized via simulated annealing; however, BP networks are unsuitable for time-series data. Hu et al. [16] proposed a MapReduce-based framework to accelerate SVM training, but their model was limited by the use of only two nodes. Holsopple et al. [17] developed the FuSIA framework to predict threats using uncertain observability. Panigrahi et al. [19] combined ARIMA models with ANNs and fuzzy filters to improve time series forecasting.

Liu et al. [8] integrated PSO with LSTM, improving accuracy compared to traditional LSTM but failing to fully model temporal logic. Zhang et al. [13] improved CNN-based situation prediction through lightweight factorization, although stability and precision still require refinement.

Although substantial progress has been achieved, a significant proportion of existing studies fail to adequately capture temporal dependencies, which are pivotal for precise situation prediction. Furthermore, persistent challenges such as suboptimal accuracy and slow convergence underscore the necessity of developing advanced methodologies capable of more effectively modeling temporal correlations to enhance predictive performance, particularly in the context of industrial control systems.

3 Proposed Method

The proposed SAIPSO-BiLSTM framework combines an improved Particle Swarm Optimization (PSO) algorithm with a Bidirectional Long Short-Term Memory (BiLSTM) network for network security situation prediction. The method first enhances PSO with opposition-based learning to improve population diversity and convergence speed, and introduces Cauchy/Gaussian perturbations with Levy flight to balance exploration and exploitation while avoiding premature convergence. The optimized hyperparameters are then used to train the BiLSTM network, which captures bidirectional temporal dependencies to generate accurate predictions.

3.1 Adaptive Particle Swarm Optimization-Based Network Security Situation Prediction Algorithm

Fitness Function Selection. The fitness function often viewed as an objective function [18], evaluates candidate solutions by assigning fitness values, guiding the search process toward the global optimum. In PSO, fitness functions determine which particles are retained during iterations. A computationally simple function is preferred for efficiency, especially when optimizing BiLSTM-based prediction models. Therefore, the fitness function adopted in our work is as follows:

$$\text{Fitness} = \frac{1}{k}\sum_{k=1}^{k}\left|y_k' - y_k\right|, \tag{1}$$

where y_k' is the actual value and y_k is the predicted output from the network.

3.2 Particle Swarm Initialization Based on Opposition-Based Learning Strategy

Particle Swarm Initialization Based on Random Strategy. In conventional PSO, initialization typically follows a random strategy. The process consists of:

- Randomly initializing swarm parameters: maximum iterations, learning factors, population size, and inertia weight.
- Selecting the fitness function (Eq. (1)).
- Evaluating particle fitness to guide updates.
- Updating personal best (pbest_{id}) and global best (gbest_{id}) positions.
- Terminating when convergence criteria are met or continuing iterations otherwise.

The particle position is initialized as an S-dimensional vector:

$$x_{id} = [x_{id1},\ x_{id2},\ \ldots,\ x_{ids}] \tag{2}$$

The velocity update rule is given by:

$$v_{id}^{t+1} = \beta * v_{id}^{t} + c_1 * \text{rand}_1 \left(\text{pbest}_{id} - x_{id}^{t}\right) + c_2 * \text{rand}_2 \left(\text{gbest}_{id} - x_{id}^{t}\right) \tag{3}$$

where c_1 and c_2 are learning factors, rand_1 and rand_2 are random numbers in $[0, 1]$, and β is the inertia weight controlling exploration versus exploitation.

The inertia weight is dynamically updated as:

$$\beta(k) = \beta_{\max} - \frac{\beta_{\max} - \beta_{\min}}{K_{\max}} * k, \tag{4}$$

where k is the current iteration, and $\beta_{\max}$ and $\beta_{\min}$ are the upper and lower bounds, respectively.

Discussion on Random Initialization Strategy. Purely random initialization leads to highly stochastic distributions and may compromise optimization efficiency. If the initial population is near the global optimum, convergence is rapid but risks local optima entrapment; otherwise, convergence slows significantly.

Research shows that a diverse initial population with high-quality solutions improves PSO performance. Therefore, our work adopts a hybrid initialization strategy combining random solutions with opposition-based learning, aiming to enhance diversity and accelerate convergence.

Particle Swarm Initialization Based on Opposition-Based Learning Strategy. Opposition-Based Learning (OBL), first proposed by Tizhoosh in 2005 [20], initially introduced the concept of "opposite numbers", later extended to "quasi-opposite" and "quasi-reflected opposite" numbers. OBL has been widely applied in PSO to improve population initialization and dynamic jumping mechanisms.

The quality and diversity of the initial population significantly affect PSO convergence. Populations containing multiple high-quality solutions converge faster. To enhance diversity and acceleration, our work integrates random solutions with opposition-based solutions during initialization.

The fundamental definitions of OBL are as follows:

Definition 1. *Opposite number: Given $x \in [k, e]$, its opposite number x^{op} is:*

$$x^{op} = k + e - x \tag{5}$$

Definition 2. *Opposite point: In an m-dimensional space, for $X_i = (x_i^1, x_i^2, \ldots, x_i^m)$ with $x_i^j \in [k_j, e_j]$, its opposite point X_i' is:*

$$X_i' = (x_i^{1'}, x_i^{2'}, \ldots, x_i^{m'}) \quad \textit{where} \quad x_i^{j'} = k_j + e_j - x_i^j \tag{6}$$

The improved initialization process based on OBL is summarized as:

- **Parameter Initialization:** Set the population size N.
- **Random Generation:** Generate the initial swarm $\{X\}$.
- **Opposite Generation:** For each particle dimension, compute $x'_i = k_i + e_i - x_i$.
- **Merging:** Combine original and opposite populations: $X_{\text{merge}} = X \cup X'$.
- **Fitness Evaluation:** Calculate fitness for all particles in X_{merge} and sort them.
- **Selection:** Choose the top N particles as the final initialized population X_{end}.

Gaussian and Cauchy Distribution Mutations. The inertia weight β affects particle velocity and convergence in PSO: larger values promote exploration, while smaller values risk premature convergence.

In standard PSO, β is fixed, limiting both convergence speed and search capability. To address this, a nonlinear and randomly perturbed inertia weight adjustment [10] is adopted. The inertia weight at iteration t is defined as:

$$\beta(t) = \beta_{\text{fix}} * e^{-\left(\frac{t}{t_{\max}}\right)^{\varepsilon}}, \tag{7}$$

where β_{fix} is the maximum inertia coefficient, $t_{\max}$ is the maximum number of iterations, and $\varepsilon \in (0, 1)$ is a random variable.

Equation (7) shows that $\beta(t)$ decreases nonlinearly, encouraging exploration early and refining local search later, thus improving convergence speed and solution quality.

To further balance exploration and exploitation, Gaussian and Cauchy distribution-based mutation strategies [6] are introduced. The Cauchy distribution, with a broader spread along the x-axis, promotes large jumps for global search; the Gaussian distribution, broader along the y-axis, supports fine-grained local refinement.

During iteration k, if a particle i satisfies $\text{Fitness}_i^k > \text{Fitness}_{pi}^k$ and a random number $r_3 > 0.9$, a mutation is triggered as:

$$x_{id}^{k*} = \begin{cases} |x_{id}^k + \text{Cauchy} * (\text{pbest}_{id}^k - x_{id}^k)|, \\ \quad \text{if } \frac{k}{k_{\max}} \leq 0.5, \quad r_3 > 0.9 \\ \\ x_{id}^k * \left(1 + \frac{2}{5} - \frac{1}{5} * \tan\left(\frac{\pi}{4} * \frac{k}{k_{\max}} * \text{Normal}\right)\right), \\ \quad \text{if } \frac{k}{k_{\max}} > 0.5, \quad r_3 > 0.9 \end{cases} . \tag{8}$$

As seen in Eq. (8), Cauchy-based mutations dominate early iterations, promoting particle diversity, while Gaussian-based mutations refine local searches in later stages. This two-phase strategy, combined with dynamic inertia adjustment, enhances both global exploration and local convergence.

3.3 Particle Perturbation Based on Levy Flight and Aggregation Degree

Levy Flight. Levy flight proposed by French mathematician Paul Lévy, is a stochastic search model widely used to describe random processes in fields such as earthquake modeling, bird foraging, astronomy, and biology. Due to its distinctive step-length characteristics, Levy flight has been incorporated into various optimization algorithms [14].

In a typical Levy flight, most movements are small steps interspersed with occasional large jumps, combining local exploration with global search. This randomness broadens the search space, allowing particles to escape local optima and discover diverse solutions. Therefore, Levy flight is introduced here to enhance particle global search capability.

The step-length probability distribution is defined by:

$$\text{LevyDistribution}(\mu) = \frac{r}{|v|^{-\mu}} \tag{9}$$

where $\mu \in (0, 2)$, $r \sim N(0, \delta^2)$, and $v \sim N(0, 1)$. The scaling factor δ is computed as:

$$\delta = \frac{\Gamma(1+\mu)\sin\left(\frac{\pi\mu}{2}\right)}{\mu\Gamma\left(\frac{1+\mu}{2}\right)2^{\frac{\mu-1}{2}}}. \tag{10}$$

Based on the Levy distribution, the particle position is updated as:

$$x(t+1) = x(t) + \text{random}(\text{size}(d)) \oplus \text{Levy}(\mu), \tag{11}$$

where random(size(d)) generates a random step vector matching dimensionality d, and $\oplus$ denotes element-wise multiplication.

By employing Levy flights via Equations (9)–(11), particles can explore a wider search space, effectively avoiding premature convergence and enhancing the overall global search ability.

Particle Position Update Based on Aggregation Degree and Similarity. During optimization, the global best guides particles toward better solutions. However, excessive clustering can trap the swarm in local optima. Thus, perturbations based on aggregation degree and similarity are introduced.

The similarity $p(x, y)$ between two particles is defined as:

$$p(x, y) = 1 - \frac{\text{distance}(x, y)}{\text{distance}_{\max}}, \tag{12}$$

where distance(x, y) is the Euclidean distance between x and y, and $\text{distance}_{\max}$ is the maximum inter-particle distance.

The aggregation degree measures average similarity relative to the global best:

$$\text{gather}(k) = \frac{1}{N}\sum_{j=1}^{N} p(j, g) \tag{13}$$

Higher gather(k) implies tighter clustering and increased risk of local trapping.

When the following condition holds:

$$\text{rand} < b_1 \times p(i, g) \times \text{gather}(k) \tag{14}$$

The particle position is updated by:

$$x_i^{k+1} = x_i^k + b_2 \oplus k^{-\lambda} \tag{15}$$

where b_2 is the step-size (set to 0.01 here) and $1 < \lambda < 3$.

The threshold parameter b_1 dynamically decays with iterations:

$$b_1 = \frac{1}{k} \tag{16}$$

By triggering perturbations when particles cluster excessively, swarm diversity is preserved, allowing effective escape from local optima.

The overall Levy flight-enhanced PSO process is summarized in Algorithm 1.

Algorithm 1. Levy Flight Enhanced PSO

Input: Standard Gaussian noise v, particles N, max iterations max_iterations
Output: global best *g_best*

```
while (it < max_iterations) do
  for each particle i do
    Update position and velocity
    Update personal best p_best and global best g_best
  end for
  if (Levy flight triggered) {Equation 14}
    then Apply Levy perturbation {Update position and v}
  else Continue normal update
  end if
  Increment it
end while
return g_best
```

Overall Optimization Strategy. Early iterations use Cauchy mutations with large inertia to expand the search space and enhance diversity, while later iterations adopt Gaussian mutations for finer local search. When stagnation occurs, aggregation-degree-based perturbations are applied to help the swarm escape and approach the global optimum.

3.4 Bidirectional Long Short-Term Memory (BiLSTM) Model for Prediction Optimization

Standard LSTM networks use gating mechanisms to control information flow [2], effectively addressing long-term dependencies. However, traditional LSTM is unidirectional, which limits its ability to capture bidirectional dependencies essential for industrial control network situation prediction. To overcome this, a Bidirectional LSTM (BiLSTM) model is adopted, leveraging both past and future context to improve prediction accuracy.

BiLSTM performance heavily depends on hyperparameter settings, such as learning rate, hidden layer size, and training iterations. Manual tuning is inefficient and subjective; thus, metaheuristic algorithms like Ant Colony Optimization, Cuckoo Search, and PSO have been widely applied [9]. Although PSO effectively optimizes hyperparameters, it suffers from premature convergence and limited search speed.

To address these issues, an improved adaptive PSO method (SAIPSO) is employed to optimize the hyperparameters of the BiLSTM model, including the number of training iterations (Iterator), the learning rate, the number of hidden units in the first hidden layer (n_1), and the number of hidden units in the second hidden layer (n_2).

The SAIPSO optimization procedure includes:

1. Data preprocessing and normalization
2. Setting SAIPSO parameters (swarm size, iterations, learning factors, inertia weights)
3. Defining the fitness function (Eq. (1))
4. Randomly initializing particles
5. Updating particle positions and velocities (Eqs. (2) and (3))
6. Building BiLSTM models based on particle-represented hyperparameters
7. Applying Cauchy/Gaussian mutations or Levy perturbations as needed
8. Updating personal best and global best solutions
9. Checking termination conditions

In summary, SAIPSO integrates opposition-based initialization, dynamic mutation strategies, and aggregation-driven Levy perturbations, significantly improving the search efficiency, convergence speed, and prediction performance of BiLSTM models.

4 Experimental Evaluation

4.1 Experimental Data

This study uses the UNSW-NB15 dataset [1], a widely recognized benchmark for network security research. Collected in 2015 by the University of New South Wales, it contains 49 features across 9 attack types, split into a training set (175,341 instances) and a testing set (82,232 instances).

To avoid short-term bias, situation values are quantified following the threat assessment method from [4]. Attack records are transformed into security situation values for time-series analysis, resulting in 58 training samples and 27 testing samples. The situation value at time t is computed as:

$$S\_Value(t) = \sum_{i=1}^{N} Z_i, \tag{17}$$

where Z_i denotes the threat value and N the number of attacks within the time window.

4.2 Evaluation Metrics and Benchmark Models

The performance of the model is evaluated using Coefficient of Determination (R^2), Mean Absolute Error (MAE), and Mean Absolute Percentage Error (MAPE).

MAE measures the average absolute difference between predicted and actual values:

$$\text{MAE} = \frac{1}{N} \sum_{i=1}^{N} |y_i - y_i'| \tag{18}$$

R^2 evaluates the goodness of fit, ranging from 0 to 1:

$$R^2 = 1 - \frac{\sum_{i=1}^{N} (y_i - y_i')^2}{\sum_{i=1}^{N} (y_i - \overline{y})^2} \tag{19}$$

MAPE assesses the average relative error:

$$\text{MAPE} = \frac{1}{N} \sum_{i=1}^{N} \left| \frac{y_i - y_i'}{y_i} \right| \tag{20}$$

where y_i and y_i' represent the actual and predicted values, $\overline{y}$ is the mean actual value, and N is the number of samples.

4.3 Experimental Results and Analysis

The SAIPSO algorithm optimizes three BiLSTM hyperparameters: number of hidden layer neurons, training iterations, and learning rate. Specifically, neuron counts are set within $[1, 100]$, training iterations within $[100, 500]$, and learning rates between $[0.001, 0.01]$.

To ensure fair comparison, all other parameters remain constant across configurations. The main difference is the treatment of the inertia weight $\beta(k)$: SAIPSO dynamically adjusts $\beta(k)$ adaptively, while standard PSO uses a fixed value.

The parameter settings are summarized in Table 1.

Table 1. Parameter Settings for PSO and SAIPSO Algorithms

Parameter	PSO	SAIPSO
Inertia Weight β	0.8 (Fixed)	[0.3, 0.8] (Adaptive)
Swarm Size N	20	20
Maximum Iterations	50	50
Learning Factor c_1, c_2	2, 2	2, 2
Learning Rate Range	[0.001, 0.1]	[0.001, 0.1]

Fitness Function Evaluation. The fitness function measures individual quality and directly affects convergence speed and algorithm complexity. Comparing fitness evolution across algorithms provides insight into optimization performance.

As shown in Fig. 1, the fitness value changes of standard PSO and the proposed SAIPSO algorithm are compared. SAIPSO exhibits fewer inflection points and less frequent convergence to local optima, indicating a more stable optimization trajectory. Moreover, SAIPSO reaches the global optimum with fewer iterations, demonstrating significantly faster convergence.

These improvements stem from the dynamic adjustment of the inertia weight $\beta(k)$, which enhances swarm diversity and prevents premature convergence. In addition, Cauchy-distributed mutations promote global exploration in early iterations, while Gaussian-distributed refinements improve local precision in later stages. Aggregation-guided perturbations further assist particles in escaping local optima and accelerating convergence.

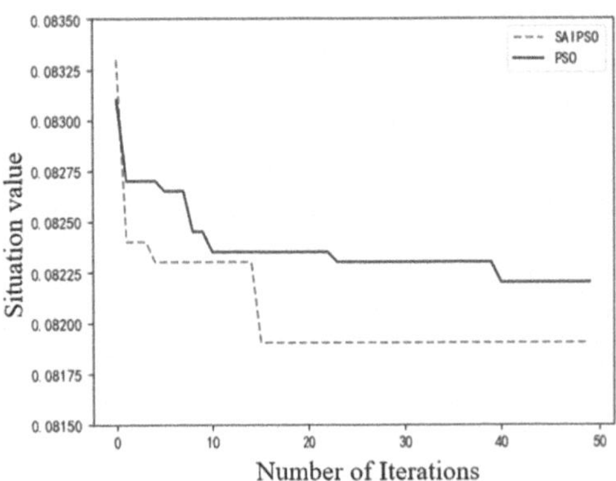

Fig. 1. Fitness evolution comparison between PSO and SAIPSO algorithms.

Prediction Performance Evaluation. This section evaluates the SAIPSO algorithm by comparing predicted and actual situation values across 20 random samples.

Experiments were conducted with two window sizes (2 and 3), and the performance of BiLSTM, PSO-LSTM, PSO-BiLSTM, and SAIPSO-BiLSTM was visually compared, as shown in Fig. 2 and Fig. 3.

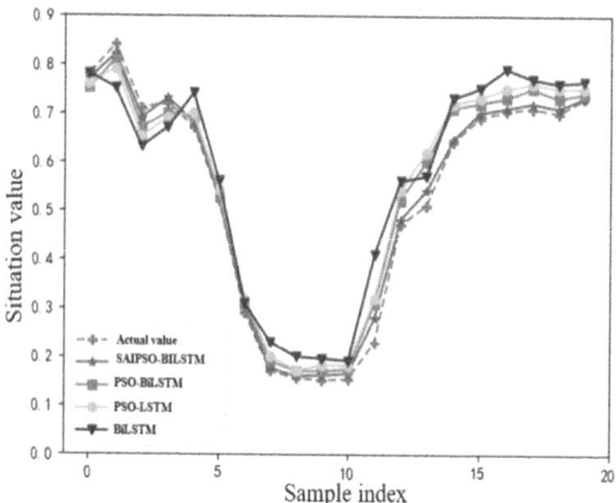

Fig. 2. Prediction Results (Window Size = 2)

As seen in Fig. 2, SAIPSO achieves a closer fit to the true values with window size 2, while other methods show larger deviations. In Fig. 3, SAIPSO maintains good alignment even with minor fluctuations.

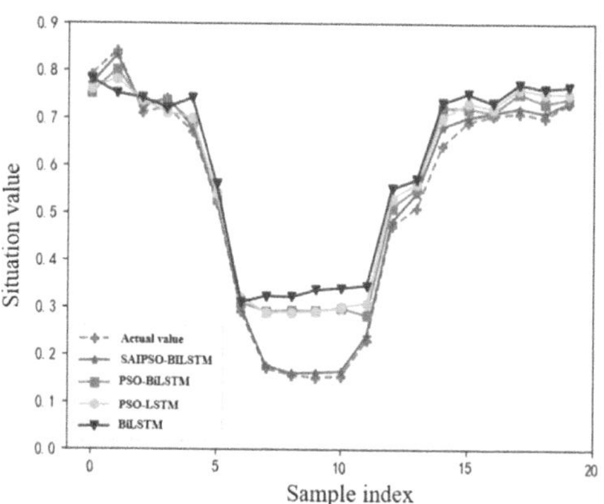

Fig. 3. Prediction Results (Window Size = 3)

Among baseline models, PSO-BiLSTM outperforms BiLSTM and PSO-LSTM due to PSO-driven hyperparameter optimization and BiLSTM's ability to capture bidirectional dependencies. SAIPSO-BiLSTM further improves over PSO-BiLSTM, benefiting from adaptive weight adjustment and dynamic position perturbations.

Overall, SAIPSO demonstrates clear advantages in prediction accuracy compared to conventional approaches.

Mean Absolute Percentage Error (MAPE) Evaluation. The Mean Absolute Percentage Error (MAPE) is used to assess prediction accuracy, where lower values indicate better performance. The MAPE results of BiLSTM, PSO-LSTM, PSO-BiLSTM, and SAIPSO-BiLSTM under different window sizes are shown in Fig. 4a.

As seen in Fig. 4a, with window size 2, SAIPSO achieves an average MAPE of 1.44, reducing errors by 0.07, 0.10, and 0.08 compared to BiLSTM, PSO-LSTM, and PSO-BiLSTM, respectively. With window size 3, SAIPSO achieves 1.40, still outperforming the others.

These results demonstrate that SAIPSO better captures nonlinear patterns and improves parameter optimization across learning rate, iteration count, and hidden layer size, thus enhancing convergence and prediction accuracy.

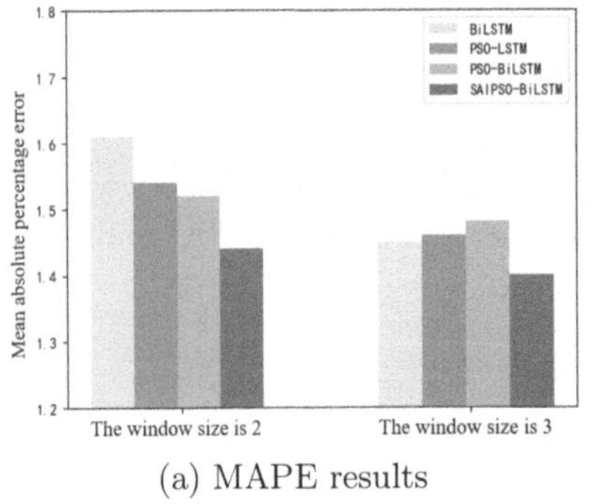

(a) MAPE results

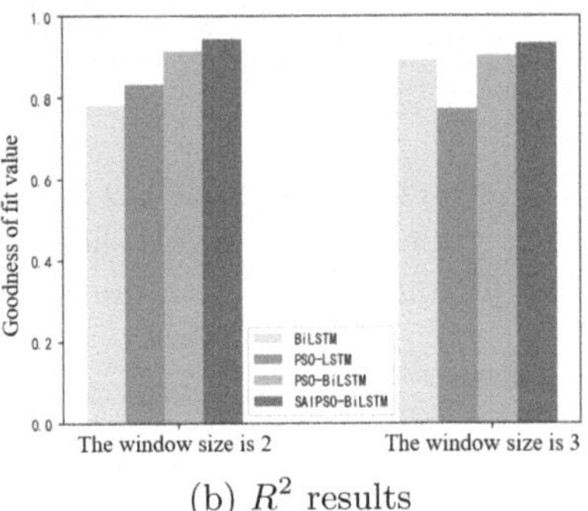

(b) R^2 results

Fig. 4. Evaluation Metrics for Different Algorithms

Goodness of Fit ($\mathbf{R^2}$) Evaluation. The Coefficient of Determination (R^2) measures the goodness of fit, with higher values indicating better agreement between predictions and ground truth. Figure 4b shows the R^2 comparison among BiLSTM, PSO-LSTM, PSO-BiLSTM, and SAIPSO-BiLSTM models.

With a window size of 2, SAIPSO achieves R^2 improvements of 0.16, 0.11, and 0.03 over BiLSTM, PSO-LSTM, and PSO-BiLSTM, respectively. When the window size is increased to 3, the corresponding gains are 0.04, 0.16, and 0.03.

These results show that PSO improves fitting performance, and SAIPSO's dynamic inertia adjustment and hybrid mutation strategies further enhance accuracy. To visualize the distribution, Fig. 5 presents box plots for R^2 under window size 2.

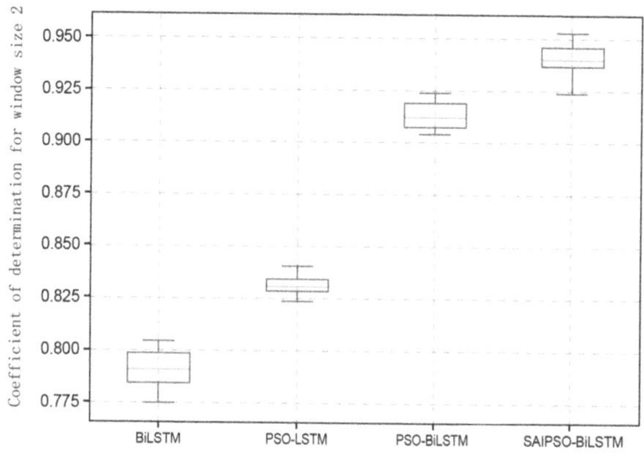

Fig. 5. Box Plot of R^2 for Window Size 2

Although SAIPSO achieves higher mean R^2, variability increases due to a broader optimization space and diverse optimal solutions.

Summary of Prediction Performance. Experimental results show that SAIPSO-BiLSTM outperforms BiLSTM, PSO-LSTM, and PSO-BiLSTM in prediction accuracy, convergence speed, and robustness.

5 Conclusion

Our work presents SAIPSO-BiLSTM, an industrial control system (ICS) situation prediction algorithm combining adaptive PSO and BiLSTM. The method incorporates opposition-based initialization, dynamic inertia adjustment, and Levy flight perturbations to improve particle diversity and convergence. Experiments on the UNSW-NB15 dataset demonstrate that SAIPSO-BiLSTM achieves superior accuracy, faster convergence, and greater robustness compared to baseline models. Future work will explore extending the approach to more dynamic and complex ICS environments.

References

1. Althubiti, S.A., Jones, E.M., Roy, K.: LSTM for anomaly-based network intrusion detection. In: 2018 28th International Telecommunication Networks and Applications Conference (ITNAC), pp. 1–3. IEEE (2018)
2. Bento, M.E.: A hybrid particle swarm optimization algorithm for the wide-area damping control design. IEEE Trans. Industr. Inf. **18**(1), 592–599 (2021)
3. Chen, J., Cui, M.: Multi-class intrusion detection system in SDN based on hybrid LSTM model. In: China Conference on Networking, pp. 99–111. Springer (2023)
4. Ding, N., Li, H., Yin, Z., Jiang, F.: A novel method for journal bearing degradation evaluation and remaining useful life prediction under different working conditions. Measurement **177**, 109273 (2021)

5. Djaidja, T.E.T., Brik, B., Senouci, S.M., Boualouache, A., Ghamri-Doudane, Y.: Early network intrusion detection enabled by attention mechanisms and RNNs. IEEE Trans. Inf. Forensics Secur. (2024)
6. Graves, A., Graves, A.: Long short-term memory. In: Supervised Sequence Labelling with Recurrent Neural Networks, pp. 37–45 (2012)
7. Hochreiter, S., Schmidhuber, J.: LSTM can solve hard long time lag problems. Adv. Neural Inf. Process. Syst. **9** (1996)
8. Holsopple, J., Yang, S.J.: FuSIA: future situation and impact awareness. In: 2008 11th International Conference on Information Fusion, pp. 1–8. IEEE (2008)
9. Hu, J., Ma, D., Liu, C., Shi, Z., Yan, H., Hu, C.: Network security situation prediction based on MR-SVM. IEEE Access **7**, 130937–130945 (2019)
10. Kennedy, J., Eberhart, R.: Proceedings of ICNN'95-international conference on neural networks. Particle Swarm Optim. **4**, 1942–1948 (1995)
11. Li, D., Liu, Z.: Situation element extraction of network security based on logistic regression and improved particle swarm optimization. In: 2013 Ninth International Conference on Natural Computation (ICNC), pp. 569–573. IEEE (2013)
12. Nakıp, M., Gelenbe, E.: Online self-supervised deep learning for intrusion detection systems. IEEE Trans. Inf. Forensics Secur. **19**, 5668–5683 (2024)
13. Panigrahi, S., Behera, H.S., Abraham, A.: A fuzzy filter based hybrid ARIMA-ANN model for time series forecasting. In: International Conference on Soft Computing and Pattern Recognition, pp. 592–601. Springer (2016)
14. Tizhoosh, H.R.: Opposition-based learning: a new scheme for machine intelligence. In: International Conference on Computational Intelligence for Modelling, Control and Automation and International Conference on Intelligent Agents, Web Technologies and Internet Commerce (CIMCA-IAWTIC 2006), vol. 1, pp. 695–701. IEEE (2005)
15. Wang, Y.: Advanced network traffic prediction using deep learning techniques: a comparative study of SVR, LSTM, GRU, and bidirectional LSTM models. In: ITM Web of Conferences, vol. 70, p. 03021. EDP Sciences (2025)
16. Wen, B., Guo, W., Chen, G.: Network security situation element extraction based on projection pursuit regression. In: 2012 Sixth International Conference on Innovative Mobile and Internet Services in Ubiquitous Computing, pp. 405–408. IEEE (2012)
17. Zhang, H., Kang, C., Xiao, Y.: Research on network security situation awareness based on the LSTM-DT model. Sensors **21**(14), 4788 (2021)
18. Zhang, K., Liang, L., Huang, Y.: A network traffic prediction model based on quantum inspired PSO and neural network. In: 2013 Sixth International Symposium on Computational Intelligence and Design, vol. 2, pp. 219–222. IEEE (2013)
19. Zhang, R., Liu, M., Yin, Y., Zhang, Q., Cai, Z.: Prediction algorithm for network security situation based on bp neural network optimized by SA-SOA. Int. J. Perform. Eng. **16**(8), 1171 (2020)
20. Zhang, R., Zhang, Y., Liu, J., Fan, Y.: Network security situation prediction method using improved convolution neural network. Comput. Eng. Appl. **55**(06), 86–93 (2019)

SJ-GNN: A Graph Neural Network-Based Spatio-Temporal Joint Optimization Routing Algorithm

Changwei Liu, Jie Li(✉), Yuhe Zhang, Yinrui Yu, Jiaxin Lu, and Hongjun Ma

Northeastern University, Shenyang 110819, China
lijie@mail.neu.edu.cn

Abstract. The convergence of 5G, AI, and IoT technologies is enabling the transition of Unmanned Aerial Vehicle (UAV) systems from single-unit operations to intelligent swarm collaboration. Addressing the challenges of dynamic topologies and resource constraints in these networks, this paper proposes a spatiotemporal joint optimization framework. Our cross-layer design integrates an enhanced time synchronization algorithm with an intelligent routing mechanism to improve network performance. First, to mitigate cumulative clock errors, our synchronization protocol combines multi-path broadcasting with bidirectional exchange, using Maximum Likelihood Estimation (MLE) to transform the exponential accumulation of multi-hop errors into linear growth. Second, a Dueling Double Deep Q-Network (D3QN) routing algorithm uses a mobility-aware state representation and a multi-objective reward function to optimize for energy efficiency, link stability, and low latency. We fuse these components into a unified model using a Graph Neural Network (GNN) that enables closed-loop interaction via a bidirectional feedback mechanism. Experimental results demonstrate our architecture excels in suppressing cumulative errors, enhancing network throughput, and reducing packet loss, validating the effectiveness of the spatiotemporal joint optimization design.

Keywords: UAV networks · Time synchronization · Routing selection · Spatiotemporal joint optimization · D3QN · Graph Neural Network (GNN)

1 Introduction

With the deep integration of fifth-generation mobile communication, artificial intelligence, and Internet of Things (IoT) technologies, unmanned aerial vehicle (UAV) systems are evolving from single-unit operations to intelligent swarm collaboration. These swarms enhance service coverage and operational resilience through multi-agent cooperative architectures [1], demonstrating irreplaceable value in tactical surveillance [2] and smart city management [3]. The successful execution of these missions depends critically on two foundational yet interdependent network pillars: high-precision time synchronization and efficient data routing.

T. Qiu et al. (Eds.): CCF ChinaNet 2025, CCIS 2810, pp. 43–53, 2026.
https://doi.org/10.1007/978-981-95-8450-5_4

In the high-mobility, resource-constrained environment of UAV swarms, these pillars are deeply, often detrimentally, coupled. Time synchronization faces formidable challenges: low-cost oscillators exhibit frequency instability and accumulating clock drift [4], while high-speed mobility induces Doppler shifts and dynamic topologies create unpredictable propagation delays [5]. Traditional solutions prove inadequate; GPS fails in signal-denied environments, and network protocols struggle with non-deterministic latency in multi-hop wireless networks [6].

Simultaneously, routing protocols must address transient link stability, constrained energy resources, and multi-objective optimization needs [7]. This creates a vicious cycle—inaccurate synchronization produces unreliable delay metrics, leading to suboptimal routing decisions, while inefficient routing introduces excessive jitter that further degrades synchronization accuracy, preventing network-wide convergence.

Existing research has predominantly tackled these issues in isolation. This paper addresses this critical gap by proposing a novel cross-layer framework, SJ-GNN, that employs synergistic co-design of synchronization and routing. Our work establishes a new optimization paradigm with these contributions:

1. We propose a cross-layer optimization framework that reframes time synchronization and routing as a unified spatiotemporal problem, implementing a bidirectional feedback mechanism where routing quality impacts synchronization accuracy, while synchronization precision enhances routing decisions, breaking their cycle of mutual degradation.
2. We design two core technical components: (a) An enhanced time synchronization protocol using hybrid multi-path flooding with Maximum Likelihood Estimation, transforming exponential multi-hop error accumulation into linear growth; (b) A synchronization-aware DRL agent leveraging a Graph Neural Network to create topology-aware representations that integrate clock parameters directly into routing decisions.
3. Through extensive simulations, we demonstrate the quantitative synergistic gains of our joint approach. By optimizing routes for synchronization stability, SJ-GNN improves key routing metrics while reciprocally enhancing time synchronization precision, validating our design's effectiveness.

2 Related Work

2.1 Time Synchronization Algorithms

Time synchronization is fundamental for wireless network coordination. Hierarchical methods achieve microsecond-level accuracy in static environments [8] but prove unsuitable for dynamic UAV networks due to their reliance on stable topologies and vulnerability to reference node failure. Distributed consensus algorithms [9] offer more robust decentralized calibration, yet despite advances in fault tolerance and convergence, most still inadequately address random, time-varying network delays [10].

This fundamental trade-off—hierarchical methods vulnerable to topology changes versus consensus methods overlooking network QoS variability—highlights the need for more adaptive solutions. Our work addresses these limitations through an enhanced rapid-flooding protocol with multi-path redundancy and an MLE-based approach that effectively combats the error accumulation induced by routing jitter.

2.2 Routing Algorithms

Routing approaches have evolved from traditional protocols like AODV [11], which struggle with UAV mobility, to deep reinforcement learning (DRL) solutions. Initial DQN implementations faced limitations from discrete action spaces, leading to hybrid DDPG-DQN architectures. For complex network representations, Graph Neural Networks (GNNs) [12] have been integrated with DRL, creating topology-aware embeddings by aggregating features across nodes [13].

A critical flaw in current DRL-based routing is their assumption of perfect network synchronization. These approaches rely on link-state metrics potentially corrupted by synchronization errors, resulting in suboptimal policies. Our framework addresses this by developing a synchronization-aware GNN-D3QN agent that incorporates clock parameters directly into its state representation. By training in a closed loop with our synchronization module, it creates a routing policy that simultaneously optimizes network efficiency and maintains conditions conducive to precise time synchronization—solving both challenges synergistically.

3 System Model and Problem Formulation

3.1 Network and Clock Model

We model the UAV swarm as a time-evolving undirected graph $G_t = (V, E_t)$, where V represents UAV nodes and E_t represents communication links that exist when nodes are within range R_c Each node's local clock follows a linear model:

$$C_i(t) = (1 + d_i)t + \theta_i \tag{1}$$

where d_i is clock drift rate and θ_i is initial offset. Time synchronization aims to estimate and compensate for these parameters network-wide.

3.2 Problem Definition: The Spatiotemporal Challenge

Our challenge is designing a framework that simultaneously achieves microsecond-level synchronization and low-latency routing in dynamic environments-goals that traditional approaches fail to reconcile due to their interdependence.

This comprises two interlinked sub-problems; Firstly, The Synchronization Problem: Designing a distributed protocol that withstands topology changes and suppresses the exponential accumulation of clock errors—a problem worsened by routing-induced unpredictable delays.

And secondly, The Routing Problem: Creating an intelligent algorithm that adapts to rapid link changes when the primary quality metric delay is inherently compromised by synchronization errors.

We reformulate these as a joint optimization problem, seeking a policy π^* that co-designs both strategies to minimize a unified objective function.

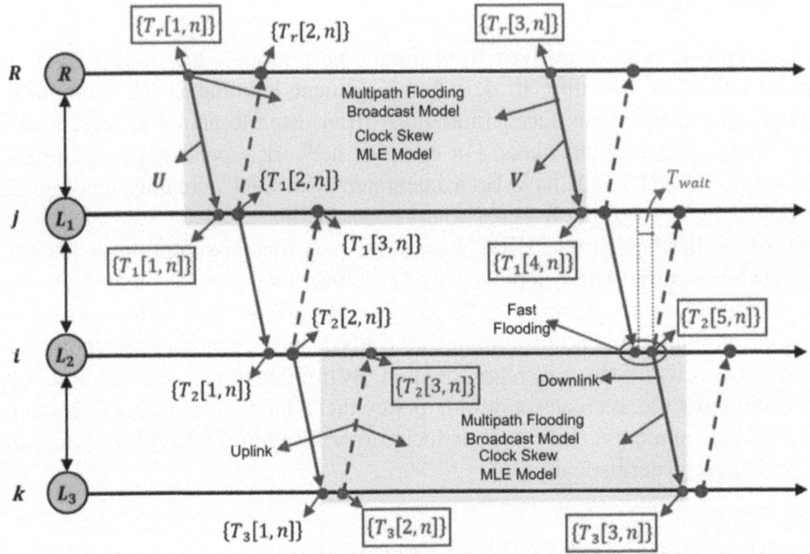

Fig. 1. Overall architecture of the enhanced time synchronization algorithm, showing the data flow from raw timestamp input to final clock calibration.

4 Proposed SJ-GNN Algorithm

4.1 Enhanced Rapid Flooding Time Synchronization

Hybrid Synchronization Model. Our approach combines two complementary techniques for robust data collection. First, we employ multi-path flooding where a reference node disseminates synchronization messages through multiple paths simultaneously. This redundancy provides inherent protection against link failures while allowing receiving nodes to prioritize first-arriving time information, effectively mitigating the impact of variable transmission delays [14]. Second, nodes engage in bidirectional exchange by performing two-way timestamp exchanges with their neighbors. This critical process facilitates the mathematical separation of symmetric propagation delay from asymmetric clock offset, enabling more precise synchronization in dynamic environments.

Parameter Estimation and Calibration. Collected timestamps undergo processing as shown in Fig. 1. After jitter buffering, we apply Maximum Likelihood Estimation (MLE) to estimate clock parameters. Assuming Gaussian-distributed link delays, we derive relative clock drift d_{ij} independently of clock offset, followed by calculating offset θ_{ij} using the drift estimate. This decoupled approach transforms multi-hop error accumulation from exponential to linear growth [15], with results feeding into clock calibration.

D3QN-based Intelligent Routing. We formulate routing as an MDP solved via a D3QN agent [16] that enhances standard DQN with Double Q-learning to reduce overestimation and Dueling architecture for better policy evaluation.

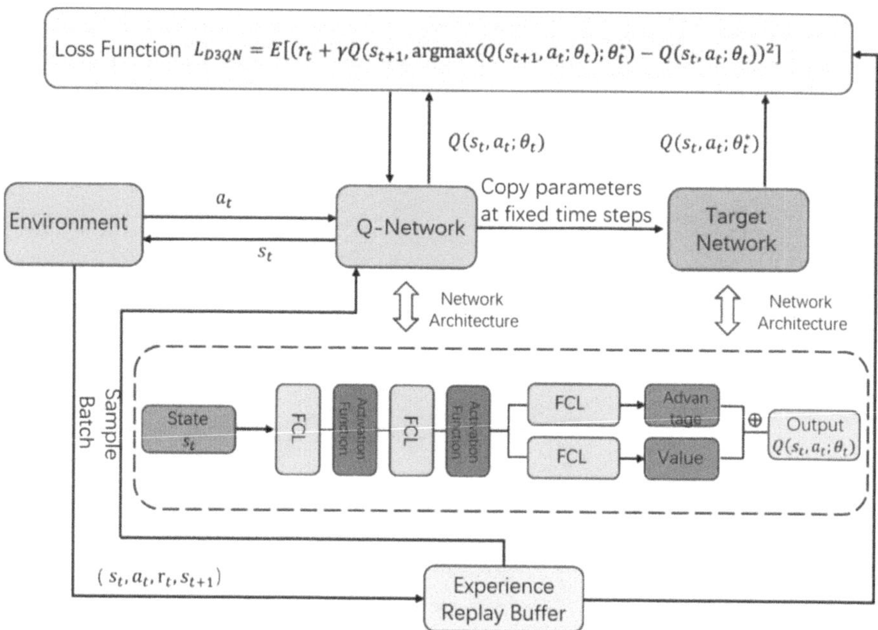

Fig. 2. D3QN-based Intelligent Routing

The Dueling architecture (Fig. 2) decomposes Q values into state-value e $V(s)$ and action-advantage A(s, a) functions:

$$Q(s, a; \psi, \alpha, \beta) = V(s; \psi, \beta) + \left(A(s, a; \psi, \alpha) - \frac{1}{|A|} \sum_{a\prime \in A} A(s, a\prime; \psi, \alpha) \right) \quad (2)$$

where ψ represents shared layers' parameters, while α and β represent advantage and state-value stream parameters.

The target Q-value uses Double DQN to decouple action selection and evaluation:

$$y_t = r_{t+1} + \gamma Q(s_{t+1}, arg\max_{a\prime} Q(s_{t+1}, a\prime; \theta_t); \theta_t^-) \quad (3)$$

State, Action, and Reward. The state representation for each UAV node comprises a comprehensive feature vector that includes spatial coordinates, destination information, remaining energy, and neighborhood connectivity data. Crucially, we augment this representation with estimated clock parameters $(\hat{d}_i, \hat{\theta}_i)$ obtained from the synchronization module, providing the agent with an integrated view of the network's spatiotemporal characteristics. The action space is defined as the discrete set of one-hop neighbors, offering a practical and efficient choice for routing decisions in dynamic environments. For reward design, we implement a composite function that balances multiple competing objectives:

$$R_t = w_1 R_{\text{energy}} + w_2 R_{\text{dist}} + w_3 R_{\text{delay}} + w_4 R_{\text{hops}} \quad (4)$$

This weighted formulation rewards energy conservation (promoting network lifetime and load balancing), geographical progress toward destinations, latency minimization using synchronization-corrected delay measurements, and hop count reduction to minimize transmission overhead across the network.

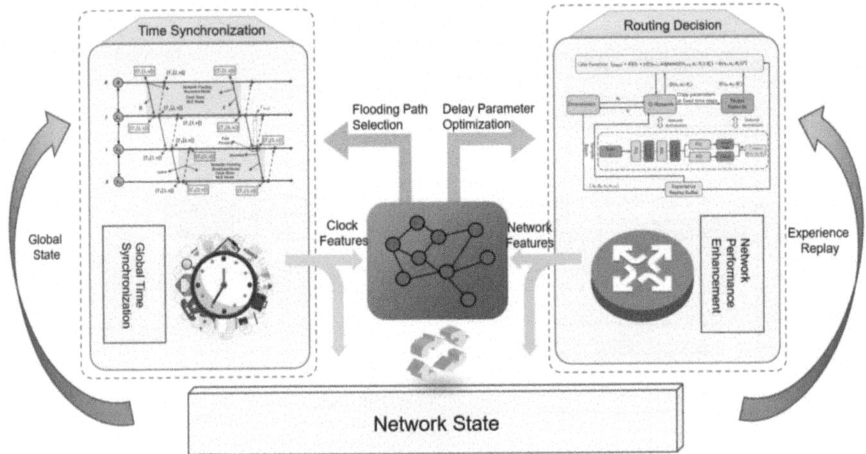

Fig. 3. The proposed SJ-GNN framework, illustrating the synergistic feedback loop between the synchronization and routing modules, mediated by the GNN.

4.2 GNN-Based Cross-Layer Integration

The synchronization-routing synergy is orchestrated by a GNN (Fig. 3).

Spatiotemporal Graph Modeling. We model the network as a dynamic graph $G_t = (V, E_t)$ where each node has a hidden state h_i^t incorporating both routing and synchronization features. The GNN updates states via message-passing with GRU-based temporal processing:

$$m_{ji}^t = \mathrm{MLP}([h_j^{t-1} || h_i^{t-1} || e_{ji}^t]) \tag{5}$$

Nodes aggregate messages and update states:

$$M_i^t = \sum_{j \in \mathcal{N}(i)} m_{ji}^t \tag{6}$$

$$h_i^t = \mathrm{GRU}(h_i^{t-1}, M_i^t) \tag{7}$$

This creates a comprehensive network embedding for the D3QN agent.

Bidirectional Feedback Mechanism. The core of our joint optimization framework is a closed-loop feedback mechanism that creates a virtuous cycle between synchronization and routing. In the forward direction (Sync $\rightarrow$ Route), precise clock parameters enable accurate delay calculations that prevent the selection of falsely attractive paths—paths that appear optimal due to clock errors but are suboptimal in reality. In the reverse direction (Route → Sync), the intelligent routing policy leverages its multi-objective optimization capabilities to prioritize stable, low-jitter physical paths, thereby providing clean timestamp data to the synchronization module. This high-quality input significantly improves the accuracy of clock parameter estimation, demonstrating how routing decisions can actively enhance synchronization performance.

Joint Loss Function. The system trains end-to-end by minimizing:

$$\mathcal{L}_{\text{total}} = w_{\text{route}}\mathcal{L}_{\text{D3QN}} + w_{\text{sync}}\mathcal{L}_{\text{sync\_error}} \tag{8}$$

These weights adapt the system to different operational contexts—increasing w_{route} for high-mobility scenarios or w_{sync} for large static networks.

Summary of Integration. The GNN integration forms the cornerstone of SJ-GNN, unifying network state representation and breaking traditional layered barriers. This enables learning policies that account for complex interdependencies between routing and synchronization, exploiting synergistic gains unattainable when treating these problems separately.

Algorithm 1 Spatiotemporal Joint Optimization Algorithm

Initialize: D3QN networks (θ, θ^{-}), GNN network(ϕ), replay buffer M.
for each episode do
  Reset environment and get initial spatiotemporal graph G_0.
  for each time step t do
    // Time Synchronization Stage
    Nodes perform multi-path flooding and bidirectional exchange.
    Each node computes clock parameters $(\hat{d}, \hat{\theta})$ using MLE.
    Update node features in graph G_t with new sync data.
    // Routing and Learning Stage
    Aggregate spatiotemporal state: $\mathcal{H}^t \leftarrow \mathrm{GNN}(G_t; \phi)$.
    For each packet, select action a_t using $\epsilon - greedy$ policy on D3QN output from $\mathcal{H}^t$.
    Execute a_t, observe reward R_t and new state G_{t+1}.
    Store transition (G_t, a_t, R_t, G_{t+1}) in M.
    Sample a mini-batch from M and update networks by minimizing the joint loss $\mathcal{L}_{\text{total}}$.
    Periodically update target network: $\theta^{-} \leftarrow \theta$.
  end for
end for

5 Performance Evaluation

5.1 Simulation Setup

Environment and Models. We validated our framework using a Python/PyTorch simulation platform modeling a UAV swarm in a 1500m × 1500m area. Network dynamics were simulated using the Random Waypoint mobility model with speeds of 0–10 m/s. The network stack implemented IEEE 802.11 MAC and FIFO queuing. Key parameters are in Table 1.

Table 1. Key Simulation Parameters.

Parameter	Value
Simulation Time	2000 s
Number of UAV Nodes	50 – 350
Network Area	1500 m × 1500 m
Communication Radius	200 m
Node Speed	0 – 10 m/s
Packet Size	4000 bits
Packet Generation Rate	1 packet/s
Initial Node Energy	100 J

Comparison Algorithms. We benchmarked SJ-GNN against two representative algorithms to provide a comprehensive evaluation. The first baseline, FCSA + AODV, represents a traditional decoupled approach that combines Fast Convergence Synchronization Algorithm with the reactive AODV routing protocol [11]. In this configuration, the synchronization and routing layers operate independently without information exchange, typifying conventional layered network designs. The second baseline, D3QN-Only, serves as an ablation study that utilizes our D3QN routing agent without the synchronization data integration or bidirectional feedback mechanisms. This comparison is particularly valuable as it isolates and quantifies the specific performance gains achieved through our proposed cross-layer design.

5.2 Results and Analysis

QoS Performance. Figure 4 demonstrates SJ-GNN's superior performance across all QoS metrics compared to both baselines. In throughput, SJ-GNN achieves up to 20% improvement over D3QN-Only in dense networks through two mechanisms: the GNN's holistic network view enabling proactive congestion avoidance and synchronization-corrected delay metrics providing accurate channel capacity assessment. The FCSA + AODV baseline suffers from reactive route discovery overhead, while D3QN-Only relies on noisy, unsynchronized delay data that compromises its effectiveness.

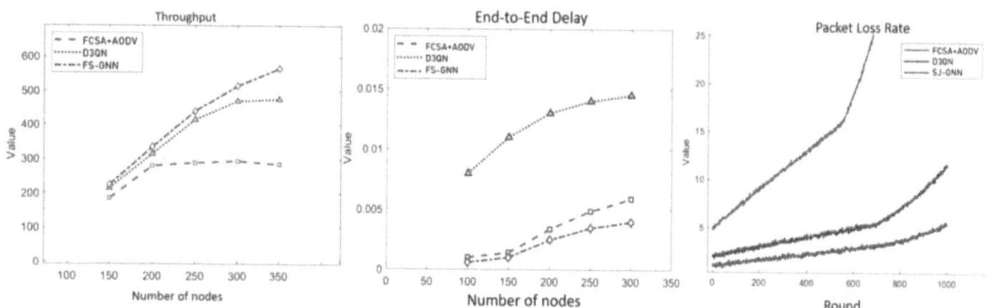

Fig. 4. Performance comparison of SJ-GNN with baseline algorithms across key QoS metrics. The joint optimization framework demonstrates superior throughput, lower packet loss, and reduced delay.

Our framework exhibits significant resilience in packet loss, reducing rates by approximately 40% compared to the AODV-based approach by avoiding transient links and preventing timeout-related drops through accurate timekeeping. This synchronization-routing coordination creates a more reliable communication infrastructure in dynamic scenarios.

End-to-end delay measurements highlight our framework's direct benefit: by continuously correcting for clock errors, the routing policy reflects true physical path latency rather than being misled by apparent shortcuts resulting from clock offset artifacts. This temporal awareness ensures data packets follow genuinely efficient paths across varying network conditions.

Synchronization Error Suppression. Figure 5 validates our core hypothesis on bidirectional optimization benefits. By selecting low-jitter, stable paths, the routing agent provides clean input data to the synchronization module's MLE process, enabling more accurate clock parameter estimation. In contrast, the D3QN-Only baseline lacks this feedback mechanism, resulting in greater error accumulation as synchronization messages traverse suboptimal paths. Our SJ-GNN successfully transforms traditional exponential error growth into linear accumulation, reducing terminal node clock errors by up to 80%. This improvement confirms that routing decisions directly impact network-wide time synchronization precision, underscoring our joint optimization approach's superiority.

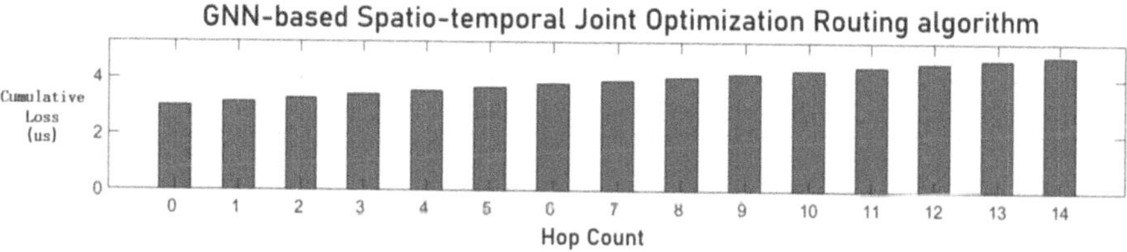

Fig. 5. Global synchronization error as a function of hop count, demonstrating SJ-GNN's ability to suppress error accumulation.

6 Conclusion

This paper introduced a spatiotemporal joint optimization framework for dynamic UAV swarm networks, demonstrating that tightly coupled, cross-layer design significantly outperforms conventional separated approaches. Our key contributions include an enhanced synchronization protocol achieving linear error accumulation and its integration with a GNN-D3QN routing agent through a novel bidirectional feedback mechanism. Simulations confirmed that SJ-GNN substantially improves throughput, delay, and packet loss while enhancing global synchronization accuracy. This establishes a new optimization paradigm for dynamic wireless networks by solving interdependent problems in unison rather than isolation.

References

1. Dai, M., Huang, N., Wu, Y., et al.: Unmanned-aerial-vehicle-assisted wireless networks: advancements, challenges, and solutions. IEEE Internet Things J. **10**(5), 4117–4147 (2022)
2. Hua, Z., Lu, Y., Pan, G., et al.: Computer vision-aided mmWave UAV communication systems. IEEE Internet Things J. **10**(14), 12548–12561 (2023)
3. Zheng, X., Zhang, J., Pan, G.: On secrecy analysis of underlay cognitive UAV-aided NOMA systems with TAS/MRC. IEEE Internet Things J. **9**(22), 22631–22642 (2022)
4. Wu, Y.C., Chaudhari, Q., Serpedin, E.: Clock synchronization of wireless sensor networks. IEEE Signal Process. Mag. **28**(1), 124–138 (2010)
5. Yan, J., Zhang, X., Luo, X., et al.: Asynchronous localization with mobility prediction for underwater acoustic sensor networks. IEEE Trans. Veh. Technol. **67**(3), 2543–2556 (2017)
6. Hasan, K.F., Feng, Y., Tian, Y.C.: GNSS time synchronization in vehicular ad-hoc networks: benefits and feasibility. IEEE Trans. Intell. Transp. Syst. **19**(12), 3915–3924 (2018)
7. Kumar, S.M.D.: Multi-objective stochastic gradient based ADR mechanism for throughput and latency optimization in LoRaWAN. Inter. J. Sensors Wireless Commun. Control **13**(6), 403–417 (2023)
8. Yildirim, K.S., Kantarci, A.: Time synchronization based on slow-flooding in wireless sensor networks. IEEE Trans. Parallel Distrib. Syst. **25**(1), 244–253 (2013)
9. Sutton, R.S., Barto, A.G.: Reinforcement learning: An introduction. MIT Press, Cambridge (1998)
10. Moerland, T.M., Broekens, J., Plaat, A., et al.: Model-based reinforcement learning: a survey. Foundat. Trends® Mach. Learn. **16**(1), 1–118 (2023)
11. Hosseinzadeh, M., Yousefpoor, M.S., Yousefpoor, E., et al.: A new version of the greedy perimeter stateless routing scheme in flying ad hoc networks. J. King Saud University-Comput. Inform. Sci. **36**(5), 102066 (2024)
12. Shi, X., Ren, P., Du, Q.: Reinforcement Learning Routing in Space-Air-Ground Integrated Networks. In: Proc. 13th Int. Conf. Wireless Commun. Signal Process. (WCSP), pp. 1–6 (2021)
13. Pareja, A., Domeniconi, G., Chen, J., et al.: EvolveGCN: evolving graph convolutional networks for dynamic graphs. In: Proc. AAAI Conference on Artificial Intelligence, vol. 34(04), pp. 5363–5370 (2020)
14. Shi, F., Tuo, X., Yang, S.X., et al.: Rapid-flooding time synchronization for large-scale wireless sensor networks. IEEE Trans. Industr. Inf. **16**(3), 1581–1590 (2019)

15. Chaudhari, Q.M., Serpedin, E., Qaraqe, K.: On maximum likelihood estimation of clock offset and skew in networks with exponential delays. IEEE Trans. Signal Process. **56**(4), 1685–1697 (2008)
16. Van Hasselt, H., Guez, A., Silver, D.: Deep reinforcement learning with double q-learning. In: Proc. AAAI Conference on Artificial Intelligence, vol. 30(1) (2016)

FedCog: Synergistic Task-Driven Client Collaboration and Contribution-Aware Aggregation for Federated Continual Learning at the Edge

Shilu Wang, Shuai Yu(✉), and Xu Chen

School of Computer Science and Engineering, Sun Yat-sen University, GuangZhou 51006, China
wangshlu@mail2.sysu.edu.cn, {yushuai,chenxu35}@mail.sysu.edu.cn

Abstract. Model updates in edge intelligence (EI) rely on server station centralized processing, suffering from limited uplink bandwidth, prolonged update cycles, underutilized edge computing resources, and catastrophic forgetting. To overcome these challenges, we propose FedCog, a communication-efficient federated continual learning (FCL) framework using task-driven client collaboration and contribution-aware aggregation. FedCog enables collaborative processing of new task data across edge nodes, effectively mitigating catastrophic forgetting through three innovations: Dynamic communication partnership where clients calculate data change rates to skip 70% of communication rounds and dynamically match partners via task relevance scoring; Selective parameter distribution that filters knowledge transfer using task correlation scores, maximizing relevant sharing while blocking interference; and Contribution-oriented gradient aggregation weighting updates by directional alignment with global objectives to accelerate convergence. Building on these strategies, we formulate an optimization problem to minimize communication cost while ignoring rate constraints and accuracy requirements. Extensive experimental results demonstrate that FedCog outperforms state-of-the-art approaches, achieving up to 10.0% absolute accuracy gain and 30.8% communication cost reduction.

Keywords: Edge computing · Edge intelligence · Federated learning · Continual learning

1 Introduction

The rapid proliferation of Internet of Things (IoT) devices and edge computing infrastructures has catalyzed the emergence of edge intelligence (EI) [1], enabling real-time data processing and decision-making near data sources. This paradigm leverages federated learning (FL) to collaboratively train machine learning models across distributed edge devices without centralizing raw data. Traditional

T. Qiu et al. (Eds.): CCF ChinaNet 2025, CCIS 2810, pp. 54–66, 2026.
https://doi.org/10.1007/978-981-95-8450-5_5

CL methods reduce forgetting but assume centralized data access [2]. Federated CL variants [3], either local forgetting on one edge device propagates through model aggregation or indiscriminate knowledge transfer across clients with non-overlapping task distributions wastes bandwidth and introduces harmful interference [4], leading to suboptimal convergence and accuracy erosion in large-scale heterogeneous settings [5].

To address these challenges, this paper proposes FedCog, a communication-efficient federated continuous learning framework for edge intelligence. This framework combines the advantages of federated learning and continuous learning. Figure 1 illustrates the superiority of multi-platform collaborative sensing: multiple platforms can significantly enhancing the overall environmental understanding capability.

Our main contributions include:

1. **Task-Driven Client Matching**: Edge nodes calculate data change rates and data correlations through task features. They decide whether to communicate in the current round based on data change rates and dynamically match suitable communication partners based on task relevance, thereby minimizing redundant transmission;
2. **Context-Aware Knowledge Transfer**: When transferring adaptive parameters from old tasks across edge nodes, filters and weights transferred parameters using task correlation scores, maximizing knowledge sharing only between task-related clients while minimizing interference between different tasks;
3. **Gradient Contribution-Aware Aggregation**: Weighting local updates based on the contribution of each edge's local gradient to the global gradient direction, ensuring consistency with the global update direction and accelerating convergence.

2 Related Work

2.1 Evolution of Edge Intelligence

Edge intelligence represents the convergence of edge computing and artificial intelligence, enabling real-time data processing and decision-making at the network periphery [5]. The integration of continuous learning (CL) with edge deployments emerged to handle non-stationary data streams, employing techniques like experience replay and parameter regularization to mitigate catastrophic forgetting [6]. Nevertheless, these approaches assumed centralized data access, violating privacy constraints inherent in distributed edges. Federated learning (FL) subsequently bridged this gap by enabling collaborative model training without raw data exchange, though standard FL frameworks struggled with sequential task learning and resource heterogeneity at the edge [7].

2.2 Federated and Continuous Learning at the Edge

The fusion of federated learning with continuous learning–termed Federated Continuous Learning (FCL)–has gained traction for edge intelligence applications requiring both privacy preservation and adaptability [2]. Current research tackles three primary challenges: i) Non-IID Data and Heterogeneity: Hierarchical FL architectures group edge nodes into clusters, reducing communication overhead with the central server. But leading to propagated forgetting when devices handle non-overlapping task sequences [8]. ii) Catastrophic Forgetting in Federated Settings: While CL techniques like Elastic Weight Consolidation (EWC) and generative replay mitigate forgetting on single devices, their federated extensions face scalability issues [9]. Federated generative replay trains GANs on devices, but incurs prohibitive computational costs [10]. iii) Communication Efficiency: Bandwidth constraints in edge networks demand communication-aware FCL [10]. Model sparsification and gradient filtering reduce payload sizes yet discard potentially critical information for incremental learning.

While significant progress has been made in lightweight architectures, communication efficiency, and environmental adaptability about Edge intelligence, few studies have addressed incremental learning, heterogeneous edge clients, and sparse connectivity issues collectively. Table 1 compares FedCog's refined strategies with those of mainstream methods, focusing on its unique solutions to propagating forgetting and negative transfer:

Table 1. Comparation of Different Strategies.

Strategy Dimensions	FedCog	FedWEIT	GEM	FedRep
Dynamic Participation Mechanism	Task-Driven Matching	Full participation	Full device synchronization	Static client grouping
Selective Transfer Design	Relevance Filtering	Indiscriminate Transfer	Local gradient constraints only	Layer-wise Transfer
Gradient Weighted Innovation	Contribution-aware Aggregation	Equal weighting	No global gradient alignment	Data volume weighting
Propagation forgetting mitigation	Selective Activation of Previous Knowledge	Unconstrained Reuse of Previous Parameters	Gradient Projection Constraints	No Dedicated Mechanism
Negative Transfer Suppression Effect	Task Correlation Matrix Irrelevant Transmission	Full History Transfer	lobal Aggregation Amplifies Local Differences	Partial Mitigation
Adaptability to heterogeneous environments	Dynamic adjustment of gradient contribution weights	Sensitivity decay	Convergence oscillation	Convergence delay

3 FedCog Overview

FedCog is characterized by a new concept of contribution-oriented selective transfer, which further enables lightweight computation and communication on resource-constrained edge devices. As shown in Fig. 1, the FedCog framework consists of four main stages, which are collaborative request matching, local training, global aggregation and selective transfer, respectively. The entire process proceeds as follows: i) client parameters are matched, and a relevance score matrix is calculated (i.e., step 1 in Fig. 1, details will be shown in Sect. 4.2). ii) the client with the highest data change rate in the current task is selected for communication (i.e., step 2 in Fig. 1, details will be shown in Sect. 4.1). During local training, sparse vector masks are used to selectively activate base parameters in convolutional filters to activate relevant parameters, while task-adaptive parameters selectively utilize knowledge from other clients based on relevance scores. iii) global aggregation is performed using the optimized weights (i.e., step 3 in Fig. 1, details will be shown in Sect. 4.2). This process is repeated iteratively until the model converges or reaches a threshold. iv) the server multiplies the adaptive parameters from the previous task by the correlation scores between the corresponding client and other clients to selectively transmit shared knowledge (i.e., step 4 in Fig. 1, details will be shown in Sect. 4.2).

Based on the above framework, we then define the system model as follows. All input training data are represented as the global dataset $\mathcal{D} = \{(\mathbf{x}, y) \mid \mathbf{x} \in \mathbb{X}, y \in \mathbb{Y}\}$, which consists of image set $\mathbb{X}$ together with their corresponding class labels from a predefined label space $\mathbb{Y}$. $\mathcal{D}$ is divided into T incremental tasks, where task $\mathcal{T}^t = \{(\mathbf{x}_i^t, y_i^t)\}_{i=1}^{N^t}$ and the label sets $\mathbb{Y}^t$ of different tasks are disjoint. In addition, we define C client nodes and an aggregation server node s. The task datasets $\mathcal{T}^t$ are distributed across the C clients, forming client-task

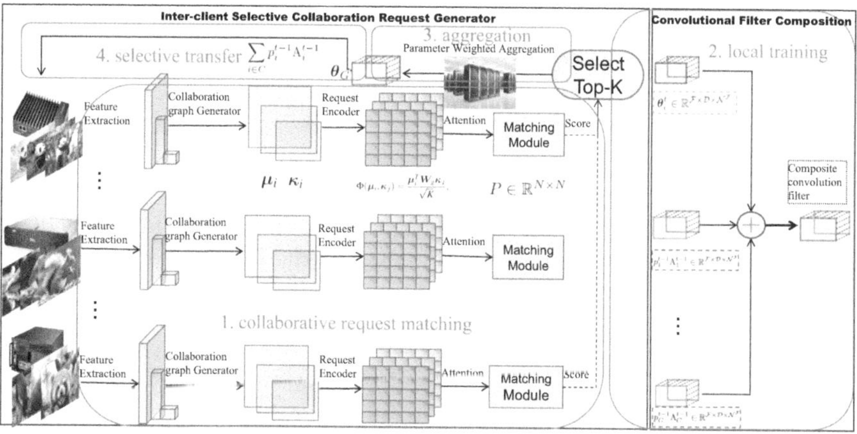

Fig. 1. (a) Schematic diagram of the proposed FedCog framework. (b) Combination of weighted additive filters performed in local model training.

Table 2. Description of Key Notations.

Notation	Description
c, s	Client c, server s
t, r	Current task index, current round
C, T, R	Total clients, tasks, rounds
$\mathcal{D}, \mathcal{T}^t$	Global dataset, dataset for task t
$\mathbb{X}, \mathbb{Y}^t$	Input space, label space for task t
$\mathcal{T}_c^t$	Training dataset for task t on client c
$\boldsymbol{\theta}_c^{t,r}$	Client c model (task t, round r)
$\boldsymbol{\theta}_{\mathcal{G}}^r$	Global server model (round r)
$\mathbf{x}_i^{c,t}, y_i^{c,t}$	Input vector, label for sample i in $\mathcal{T}_c^t$
$\mathbf{B}_c^t, \mathbf{A}_c^t$	Local base & task-adaptive parameters
p_c^t, m_c^t	Scalar attention and mask parameters
$\oplus$	Concatenation operation
K	Clients selected per round
D	Word embedding dimension
$\mathbb{L}_{\mathcal{D}}, \mathbb{L}_{\mathcal{T}^t}$	Unique label sets
λ_1, λ_2	Hyperparameters (sparsity, forgetting)
G_q, G_k	query generator parameterized by θ_q,key generator parameterized by θ_k
$\mathbf{W}_g$	learnable parameter to match the size of query and key
α_1, α_2	upper and lower bounds

datasets: $\mathcal{T}^t = \{\mathcal{T}_1^t, \mathcal{T}_2^t, \ldots, \mathcal{T}_C^t\}$. Therefore, each client $c_c \in \{c_1, ..., c_C\}$ learns its local model using its private sequence of task datasets $\{\mathcal{T}_c^t\}_{t=1}^T$. Here, $\mathcal{T}_c^t = \{(\mathbf{x}_i^{c,t}, y_i^{c,t})\}_{i=1}^{N_c^t}$ represents the dataset specific to client c for task t, consisting of N_c^t input-label pairs. Note that the datasets $\{\mathcal{T}_c^t\}_{c=1}^C$ for a given task t are disjoint across clients. The model parameters of the server s at round r are denoted $\boldsymbol{\theta}_{\mathcal{G}}^r$, while client c at task t and round r are denoted $\boldsymbol{\theta}_c^{t,r}$.

4 Problem Formulation and Algorithm Design

In this section, we will formulate the joint optimization problem for the FedCog framework, and an algorithm is designed to tackle the formulated optimization problem. For ease of reference, we list the key notations in Table 2.

4.1 Problem Formulation

At each training round r for task t, FedCog achieves three objectives:

- **Catastrophic forgetting prevention:** Each client c effectively optimizes $\boldsymbol{\theta}_c^{t,r}$ using $\mathcal{T}_c^t$ in a continual learning setting, mixing old adaptive parameters with new data to minimize forgetting while boosting current task learning.

Algorithm 1. Proposed Algorithm

Input: Task datasets $\{\mathcal{T}_c^{1:t}\}_{c=1}^{C}$, Global parameter $\boldsymbol{\theta}_{\mathcal{G}}$, hyperparameters λ_1, λ_2, $\{\mathbf{x}_i^{1:t}\}_{i=1}^{C} \in \mathcal{T}_c^{1:t}$

Output: $\{\mathbf{B}_c^t, \mathbf{m}_c^{1:t}, \boldsymbol{\alpha}_c^{1:t}, \mathbf{p}_c^{1:t}, \mathbf{A}_c^{1:t}\}_{c=1}^{C}$

Each client $c \in \mathcal{C} \equiv \{1, ..., C\}$ connects with server
Initialize $\mathbf{B}_c$ to $\boldsymbol{\theta}_{\mathcal{G}}$ for all clients $c \in \mathcal{C}$
for task $t = 1$ **to** T **do**
    Server transmits global parameter $\boldsymbol{\theta}_{\mathcal{G}}$ to all $c \in \mathcal{C}$
    Each client $c \in \tilde{\mathcal{C}}$ initializes $\mathbf{B}_c^t$ using $\boldsymbol{\theta}_{\mathcal{G}}$
    Each client $c \in \mathcal{C}$ initializes $\mathbf{A}_c^t, \mathbf{m}_c^t$
    if $t \neq 1$ **then**
        Server transmits $\{\mathbf{A}_c^{(t-1,R)}\}_{c=1}^{C}$ to all $c \in \mathcal{C}$
    end if
    for round $r = 1, \ldots, R$ **do**
        Each client $c \in \mathcal{C}$ Compute matching score: $p_{i,j}^t$ using Equations 3, 4, 5, 6
        Select top-K clients $\mathcal{K} \subset \mathcal{C}$ with smallest $p_{i,i}^t$
        Each client computes: $\boldsymbol{\theta}_c^{t,r} \leftarrow \mathbf{B}_c^t \odot \mathbf{m}_c^t + \mathbf{A}_c^t + \sum_{i \in \mathcal{C}} p_i^{t-1} \mathbf{A}_i^{t-1}$
        Minimize Equation 2 with regularization
        Each client $c \in \mathcal{K}$ transmits $\hat{\mathbf{B}}_c^{(t,r)}$ to server
        $\boldsymbol{\theta}_{\mathcal{G}} \leftarrow \mathrm{Agg}(\{\hat{\mathbf{B}}_c^{(t,r)}\}_{c \in \mathcal{C}}) = \sum_{c=1}^{C} w_c^{(t,r)} \hat{\mathbf{B}}_c^{(t,r)}$ using Equations 8
        Server distributes $\boldsymbol{\theta}_{\mathcal{G}}$ to all clients $c \in \mathcal{K}$
    end for
    Selected clients transmit $\{\mathbf{p}_c^{(t,R)}, \mathbf{A}_c^{(t,R)}\}$ to server
    Server distributes $\{\mathbf{p}_c^{(t,R)}, \mathbf{A}_c^{(t,R)}\}_{c=1}^{C}$ to all $c \in \mathcal{C}$
end for

- **Negative knowledge transfer prevention:** Through our attention mechanism, we maximize relevant knowledge transfer between clients while minimizing inter-client interference and communication costs.
- **Communication-efficiency:** At the server, $\boldsymbol{\theta}_{\mathcal{G}}$ aggregates parameters $\boldsymbol{\theta}_c^{t,r}$ from clients using optimized aggregation weights, accelerating convergence while reducing negative transfer.

To this end, we decompose each client's model parameters $\boldsymbol{\theta}_c^t$ into three components: i) Dense local base parameters $\mathbf{B}_c^t$ encoding task-agnostic knowledge; ii) Sparse task-adaptive parameters $\mathbf{A}_c^t$ capturing task-specific patterns; iii) Sparse mask parameters $\mathbf{m}_c^t$ that govern selective integration of global knowledge. The client parameterization follows:

$$\boldsymbol{\theta}_c^t = \mathbf{B}_c^t \odot \mathbf{m}_c^t + \mathbf{A}_c^t + \sum_{i \in \mathcal{C}} p_i^{t-1} \mathbf{A}_i^{t-1} \tag{1}$$

The optimization objective combines loss $\mathcal{L}(\boldsymbol{\theta}_c^{(t)}; \mathcal{T}_c^{(t)})$ with dual regularization:

$$\begin{aligned} \min_{\mathbf{B}_c^{(t)}, \mathbf{m}_c^{(t)}, \mathbf{A}_c^{(1:t)}, \mathbf{p}_c^{(t)}} \quad & \mathcal{L}\left(\boldsymbol{\theta}_c^{(t)}; \mathcal{T}_c^{(t)}\right) + \lambda_1 \|\mathbf{m}_c^{(t)}\|_1 + \lambda_1 \|\mathbf{A}_c^{(1:t)}\|_1 \\ & + \lambda_2 \sum_{i=1}^{t-1} \|\Delta \mathbf{B}_c^{(t)} \odot \mathbf{m}_c^{(i)} + \Delta \mathbf{A}_c^{(i)}\|_2^2 \end{aligned} \tag{2}$$

The ℓ_1-norm regularization enforces sparsity, while the quadratic term preserves historical task solutions through backward-compatible updates.

4.2 Algorithm Design

As illustrated in Algorithm 1, problem Eq. (2) can be tackled in two steps, which are task-driven client matching and gradient contribution-aware aggregation, respectively.

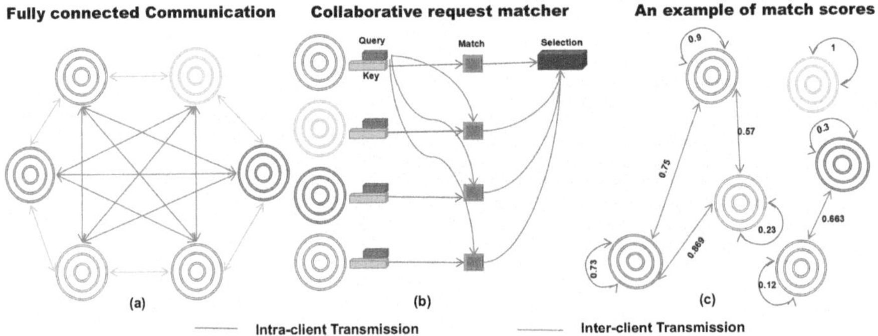

Fig. 2. (a) Fully connected, (b) Collaborative request matcher, (c) An example of matching matrix.

Task-Driven Client Matching. As shown in Fig. 2(a), previous work on federated learning communication applied fully connected communication to enable information exchange between clients, which leads to a large amount of bandwidth usage. As demonstrated in Fig. 2(b), based on established principles of communication network protocols, we present a Task-Driven Client Matching methodology. **Request phase:** Client i broadcasts compressed vectors:

$$\boldsymbol{\mu}_i = G_q(\mathbf{x}_i; \boldsymbol{\theta}_q) \in \mathbb{R}^Q \tag{3}$$

$$\boldsymbol{\kappa}_i = G_k(\mathbf{x}_i; \boldsymbol{\theta}_k) \in \mathbb{R}^K \tag{4}$$

Matching phase: Communication affinity between clients i and j:

$$p_{i,j} = \mathcal{F}(\boldsymbol{\mu}_i, \boldsymbol{\kappa}_j) = \frac{\boldsymbol{\mu}_i^\top \mathbf{W}_g \boldsymbol{\kappa}_j}{\sqrt{K}} \tag{5}$$

where $\mathbf{W}_g \in \mathbb{R}^{Q \times K}$ is a projection matrix.

Selection phase: Adjacency matrix derived via:

$$\mathbf{P} = \sigma\left([\mathcal{F}(\boldsymbol{\mu}_i, \boldsymbol{\kappa}_j)]_{i,j=1}^N\right) \tag{6}$$

where $\sigma(\cdot)$ applies row-wise softmax normalization and sparsification. As shown in Fig. 2(c), $p_{i,j}$ quantifies pairwise correlation and informational utility, while $p_{i,i}$ optimizes communication timing.

Cross-client knowledge transfer is mediated by attention-weighted combinations $p_c^{(t-1)}\mathbf{A}_{c'}^{(t-1)}$ of compressed foreign parameters, where $p_c^{(t)}$ modulates relevance to mitigate heterogeneity-induced misalignment.

Gradient Contribution-Aware Aggregation. The inherent statistical heterogeneity in federated learning induces a fundamental divergence between local empirical risk minimization and global optimization objectives, undermining convergence guarantees. We combine the theory about Lipschitz continuous gradient with the definitions of global aggregation and stochastic gradient descent (SGD) optimization:

Table 3. Key Experimental Parameters

Category	Parameter	Value/Range
Non-IID Setting	Classes/client/task	2–5 random classes
	Samples/class	5–10% stratified
DNN Models	CIFAR-100	6-layer CNN
	TinyImgNet	ResNet-18
Training	Local iter/round	25 (5 epochs)
	Tuning set	SVHN (2×5 classes)
	Comm rounds	**Per-dataset:** C100:15, Tiny:5
	Learning rate (η)	**Per-dataset:** C100:0.001, Tiny:0.0008
	Decay rate	**Per-dataset:** C100:1e-4, Tiny:1e-5
	Baseline HP bounds	Half to double original values

$$G(\boldsymbol{\theta}^{t+1}) \leq G(\boldsymbol{\theta}^t) + H - \eta\mathbb{E}_{k\sim\mathcal{K}}\left[\langle\nabla G(\boldsymbol{\theta}^t), \nabla T_k(\boldsymbol{\theta}^t)\rangle\right] \tag{7}$$

Here, η denotes the SGD learning rate and H bounds the stochastic gradient variance. Critical analysis of Eq. (7) reveals that client updates satisfying $\langle\nabla G(\boldsymbol{\theta}^t), \nabla T_k(\boldsymbol{\theta}^t)\rangle < 0$ impede convergence by counteracting global gradient directions.

To mitigate client drift induced by non-IID data distributions, we propose gradient alignment weighted aggregation that quantifies each client's contribution through directional consistency with the global objective. For client $S_k \in \mathcal{K}$, compute the gradient alignment metric:

$$w_k = \max\left[\min\left[\frac{\left\langle\nabla\widetilde{G}(\boldsymbol{\theta}^t), \nabla T_k(\boldsymbol{\theta}^t)\right\rangle}{\langle\nabla G(\boldsymbol{\theta}^t), \nabla T_k(\boldsymbol{\theta}^t)\rangle}, \alpha_1\right], \alpha_2\right] \tag{8}$$

where $\nabla \widetilde{G}(\boldsymbol{\theta}^t) = \frac{1}{|\mathcal{K}|-1} \sum_{i \in \mathcal{K}, i \neq k} \nabla \mathcal{T}_i(\boldsymbol{\theta}^t)$ represents the leave-one-out global gradient. The numerator evaluates S_k's alignment with the residual global manifold, while the denominator measures baseline alignment.

When $\left\langle \nabla \widetilde{G}(\boldsymbol{\theta}^t), \nabla \mathcal{T}_k(\boldsymbol{\theta}^t) \right\rangle > \langle \nabla G(\boldsymbol{\theta}^t), \nabla \mathcal{T}_k(\boldsymbol{\theta}^t) \rangle$, client S_k exhibits supra-linear convergence contribution, justifying higher aggregation weights. The hyperparameters $\alpha_1 = 0.2$ and $\alpha_2 = 5.0$ constrain the explosion/disappearance of the weight.

Complexity Analysis of the Proposed Solutions FedCog significantly reduces communication overhead through sparse parameter transmission, achieving client-to-server complexity $\mathcal{O}(|\mathcal{C}| \cdot (R \cdot |\hat{\mathbf{B}}| + |\mathbf{A}|))$ versus $\mathcal{O}(|\mathcal{C}| \cdot R \cdot |\boldsymbol{\theta}|)$ for baseline FCL, where $|\cdot|$ denotes number of parameters and R is rounds per task. Similarly, server-to-client costs scale as $\mathcal{O}(|\mathcal{C}| \cdot (R \cdot |\boldsymbol{\theta}_{\mathcal{G}}| + (|\mathcal{C}| - 1) \cdot |\mathbf{A}|_0))$ under FedCog compared to $\mathcal{O}(|\mathcal{C}| \cdot R \cdot |\boldsymbol{\theta}|)$.

5 Evaluation

In this section, we evaluate the FedCog framework on exhaustive experimental scenarios against various datasets, and present qualitative and quantitative analysis in setup.

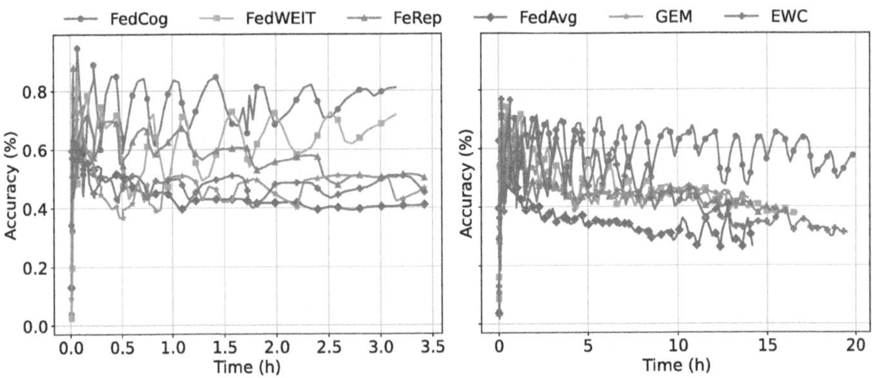

Fig. 3. Comparison of model accuracy and training time between FedCog and 5 baseline methods.

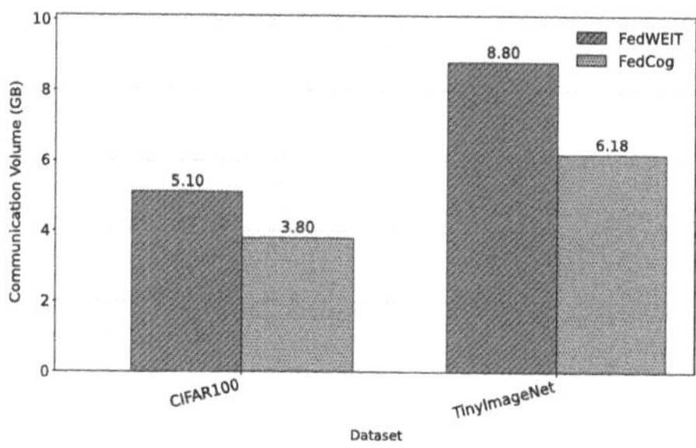

Fig. 4. Comparison of communication time under different datasets.

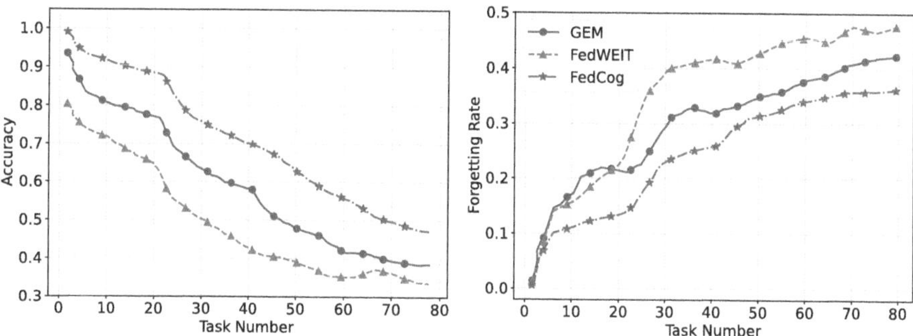

Fig. 5. Discussion of model accuracies and forgetting under different numbers of tasks.

5.1 Experimental Setup

Tested: Experiments are conducted on a Linux-based cloud instance (ali Cloud) using Python 3.12 and the PyTorch framework. Computation is accelerated by an NVIDIA A100 GPU with CUDA support. A federated incremental learning scenario involving 20 clients is simulated, with all clients executed concurrently on a single machine via parallel processes.

Datasets and DNN Models: Two benchmark datasets are adopted in the non-IID federated continuous learning (FCL) scenario: CIFAR-100 [11] and Tiny-ImageNet [12]. In evaluation, the first dataset are trained with a 6layer CNN model and the last datasets are trained with the ResNet-18 model.

Baseline Methods: The evaluation compares with five baseline methods in three categories:

- *Continual Learning:*
  - Gradient Episodic Memory (GEM) [13]: mitigates catastrophic forgetting by incorporating historical gradient constraints;

  - Elastic Weight Consolidation (EWC) [14]: pioneers parameter regularization using Fisher information matrices.
- *Federated Learning:*
  - FedAvg [15]: establishes client-specific aggregation weights proportional to local dataset cardinality;
  - FedRep [16]: enabling federated synchronization of common features while preserving local task adaptation.
- *Federated Continual Learning:*
  - FedWEIT [17]: segregating parameters into persistent base weights and task-adaptive components.

Evaluation Metric: i) Top-1 Accuracy: averaged over test sets, ii) Training Efficiency: Wall-clock time per communication round, iii) Forgetting Rate and iv) Communication cost. Table 3 shows the specific parameter settings.

5.2 Comparative Evaluations Under Different FCL Scenarios

We evaluate FedCog against five baseline methods by comparing model accuracy and training efficiency under standardized conditions. Figure 3 presents the comparative performance. FedCog achieved an accuracy rate of 72.3% on TinyImageNet, outperforming FedRep (68.5%) and FedWEIT (65.2%) by 3.8% points. Its convergence speed is 15% slower than FedAvg (which converges quickly but has low accuracy), but 40% faster than FedWEIT, and the standard deviation of the training curve is reduced by 62%.

Impact of Catastrophic Forgetting. The two federated learning baselines converge faster but achieve lower final accuracy, because disregard for prior task information. FedCog exhibits the smallest accuracy degradation, because this integrates knowledge similar to the current task. In contrast, FedWEIT utilizes knowledge aggregated from all previously learned tasks, which risks diluting the influence of critical tasks.

Impact of Negative Knowledge Transfer. While the two continual learning baselines effectively mitigate catastrophic forgetting, they suffer from negative knowledge transfer originating from other clients. Consequently, Large fluctuations in global model weights hinder the convergence of continual learning.

5.3 Evaluation of Communication Cost

As shown in Fig. 4, the FedCog model that includes the proposed match selection shows a significant improvement in the communication cost compared to the model that does not include when performing the same model training task. FedCog only needs to upload the adaptive weights of the clients that need to communicate and distribute historical parameters of matched tasks (reducing single-client payload by 60%). Overall, FedCog reduces communication costs by

34.7% on TinyImageNet (6.4 GB vs. 9.8 GB) and 26.9% on CIFAR100 (3.8 GB vs. 5.2 GB). This finding proves scheduling based on task similarity and client communication probability reduces redundancy (e.g. 70% clients skipped per round).

5.4 Fogetting Rate

We examine how numbers of task influences metrics i) average accuracy, ii) average forgetting rate, FedWEIT and GEM were selected as baselines due to their strong performance. To investigate the effect of task quantity, tasks from CIFAR-100 and TinyImageNet were combined into a single dataset comprising 80 tasks, and ensuring data heterogeneity. Figure 5 depicts the evolution of accuracy and forgetting rate as the number of tasks increases from 1 to 80. When the number of tasks reaches 80, compared to the baseline, FedCog improves the average accuracy from 52% in FedWEIT to 62% (a relative increase of 19.2%), while reducing the forgetting rate from 48% to 35% (a relative decrease of 27.1%). Notably, FedCog's forgetting rate growth rate (0.375% per task) is significantly lower than FedWEIT's (0.5% per task), which demonstrating that its knowledge selection mechanism can sustainably resist the catastrophic forgetting.

6 Conclusion

Our proposed framework incorporates a selective message-sharing matching module to dynamically determine the timing and methodology for selective transferring, coupled with a refined gradient aggregation mechanism that prioritizes updates with high utility. This approach facilitates efficient collaboration among edge devices, enabling continuous learning while minimizing resource overhead.

Acknowledgments. This work was supported in part by Guangdong S&T Programme (No. 2024B0101040007 and 2022B1515120002), in part by Guangdong Basic and Applied Basic Research Foundation (No. 2023B1515120058).

References

1. Cui, Y., Cao, K., Zhou, J., Wei, T.: Optimizing training efficiency and cost of hierarchical federated learning in heterogeneous mobile-edge cloud computing. IEEE Trans. Comput. Aided Des. Integr. Circuits Syst. **42**(5), 1518–1531 (2022)
2. Yang, X., Yu, H., Gao, X., Wang, H., Zhang, J., Li, T.: Federated continual learning via knowledge fusion: a survey. IEEE Trans. Knowl. Data Eng. **36**(8), 3832–3850 (2024)
3. Li, Y., Wang, H., Qi, Y., Liu, W., Li, R.: Re-fed+: a better replay strategy for federated incremental learning. IEEE Trans. Pattern Anal. Mach. Intell. (2025)
4. Xu, Z., et al.: Age-aware data selection and aggregator placement for timely federated continual learning in mobile edge computing. IEEE Trans. Comput. **73**(2), 466–480 (2023)

5. Luo, L., Zhang, C., Yu, H., Sun, G., Luo, S., Dustdar, S.: Communication-efficient federated learning with adaptive aggregation for heterogeneous client-edge-cloud network. IEEE Trans. Serv. Comput. (2024)
6. Wang, L., Zhang, X., Su, H., Zhu, J.: A comprehensive survey of continual learning: theory, method and application. IEEE Trans. Pattern Anal. Mach. Intell. (2024)
7. Jiang, Z., Xu, Y., Xu, H., Wang, Z., Qian, C.: Heterogeneity-aware federated learning with adaptive client selection and gradient compression. In: IEEE INFOCOM 2023-IEEE Conference on Computer Communications, pp. 1–10. IEEE (2023)
8. Liang, J., et al.: Diffusion-driven data replay: A novel approach to combat forgetting in federated class continual learning. In: European Conference on Computer Vision, pp. 303–319. Springer, Cham (2024)
9. Chen, J., He, J., Tang, J., Li, W., Yin, Z.: Knowledge efficient federated continual learning for industrial edge systems. IEEE Trans. Netw. Sci. Eng. (2025)
10. Li, Y., Li, Q., Wang, H., Li, R., Zhong, W., Zhang, G.: Towards efficient replay in federated incremental learning. In: Proceedings of the IEEE/CVF Conference on Computer Vision and Pattern Recognition, pp. 12820–12829 (2024)
11. Krizhevsky, A., Hinton, G., et al.: Learning multiple layers of features from tiny images (2009)
12. Le, Y., Yang, X.: Tiny imagenet visual recognition challenge. CS 231N **7**(7), 3 (2015)
13. Huang, Z., et al.: Gradient episodic memory for continual learning. In: Proceedings of the 31st Conference on Neural Information Processing Systems (NeurIPS) (2017)
14. Kirkpatrick, J., et al.: Overcoming catastrophic forgetting in neural networks. Proc. Natl. Acad. Sci. **114**(13), 3521–3526 (2017)
15. McMahan, B., Moore, E., Ramage, D., Hampson, S., y Arcas, B.A.: Communication-efficient learning of deep networks from decentralized data. In: AIR 2017, pp. 1273–1282. PMLR (2017)
16. Collins, L., Hassani, H., Mokhtari, A., Shakkottai, S.: Exploiting shared representations for personalized federated learning. In: ICML 2021, pp. 2089–2099. PMLR (2021)
17. Yoon, J., Jeong, W., Lee, G., Yang, E., Hwang, S.J.: Federated continual learning with weighted inter-client transfer. In: ICML 2021, pp. 12073–12086. PMLR (2021)

A Multi-agent Security Testing Framework on Software-Defined Space-Based Network

Liqiang He(✉), Jinjing Zhao, Ruonan Wang, Hongzheng Zhang, and Ling Pang

Institute of System Engineering, Academy of Military Sciences, Beijing, China
904826002@qq.com

Abstract. With the continuous development of space-based networks, Software Defined Networking (SDN), relying on its decoupled architecture of control plane and data plane, has become an important method for space networking. However, while the centralized scheduling characteristic of satellite-borne controllers strengthens space-ground collaboration capabilities, traditional ground-based security testing methods face the risk of failure when confronted with the high latency and dynamic topology characteristics of space-based networks. Therefore, this study designed a multi-agent security testing framework. It proposed three algorithms: a topology construction algorithm, a routing prediction algorithm, and an attack propagation analysis algorithm. It designed a triplet model for four types of flow risks, covering 14 types of space-based network risks, achieving risk quantification. This study provides a security testing framework for space-based networks, facilitating the evolution of software-defined space-based networks towards high resilience.

Keywords: Space-based Network · Software-define Network · Security Testing

1 Introduction

Today, various countries attach great importance to space-based networks, as a new type of information infrastructure, which constitute a necessary extension and critical supplement to the terrestrial internet, representing the primary trend in the future development of global communication network structures [1]. Regarding the challenges of heterogeneous network collaboration and global resource optimization in space-based networks, as shown in Fig. 1, the Software Defined Networking (SDN) architecture is introduced in the design, addressing these issues through the network design philosophy of decoupling the data plane from the control plane [2]. In this regard, foreign development started relatively early, with SpaceX proposing the “Starlink” [3] low-Earth-orbit satellite internet plan in 2015, and Europe’s SES-17 [4] satellite carrying a fifth-generation digital transparent processor with reprogrammable beam-forming capability in 2021. China is also actively promoting the construction of the Hongyan Constellation [5] and the Xingyun Project [6].

However, when the high latency and dynamic topology characteristics of space-based networks are combined with SDN, new security risks emerge: firstly, existing security

T. Qiu et al. (Eds.): CCF ChinaNet 2025, CCIS 2810, pp. 67–88, 2026.
https://doi.org/10.1007/978-981-95-8450-5_6

testing research mostly focuses on terrestrial networks, with less consideration for high latency and dynamically changing topology, making it difficult to directly apply to the model-based analysis of software-defined space-based networks; secondly, there is a lack of systematic risk assessment specifically for software-defined space-based networks, with research predominantly focusing on one specific attack or one category of attacks. Therefore, there is an urgent need to establish a set of scientific, systematic security risk assessment indicators.

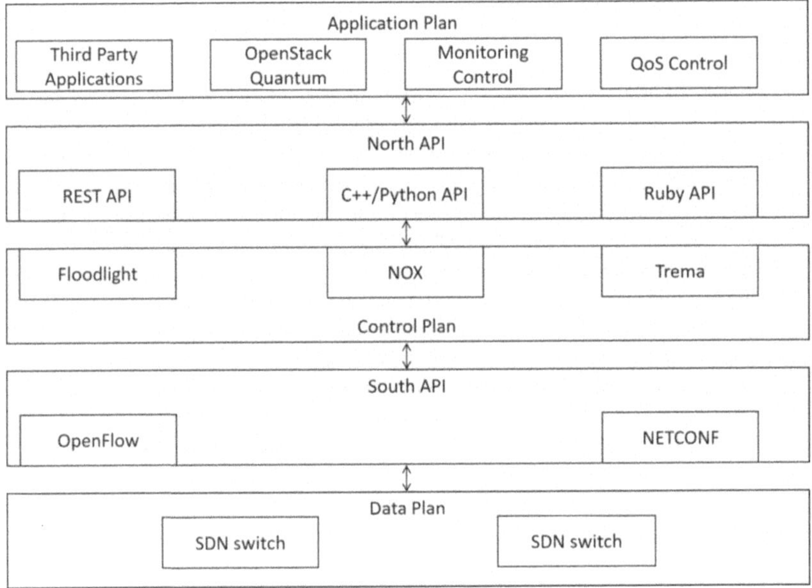

Fig. 1. SDN general architecture

To address these challenges, this study proposes a multi-agent security testing framework for software-defined space-based networks. First, an analysis of the architecture of software-defined space-based networks is conducted. Subsequently, the security of software-defined space-based networks is formally described using an attack graph model. Building upon this, a multi-agent security testing framework for software-defined space-based networks is designed. In the system implementation section, the environmental configuration, implementation algorithms, and workflow of this framework are explained in detail. Within the implementation algorithms, three algorithms are proposed: a Topology Construction Algorithm, a Routing Prediction Algorithm, and an Attack Propagation Analysis Algorithm. The Topology Construction Algorithm dynamically generates a risk-aware topology by integrating a five-tuple attack graph with the physical composition architecture. The Routing Prediction Algorithm avoids high-risk paths and optimizes secure transmission paths. The Attack Propagation Analysis Algorithm quantifies the cascading effects of vulnerabilities in real-time and generates repair strategies. Finally, regarding how risk detection and assessment are performed within the framework workflow, a "trigger principle-affected component-trigger effect" triplet mapping model for flow risks is designed by classifying four types of flow risks, thereby achieving standardized and observable risk characterization.

This study has two main contributions:

1. It proposes implementation algorithms for a multi-agent security testing framework, overcoming the bottlenecks of long latency and dynamic topology in space-based networks. These algorithms enable dynamic topology construction, path prediction, and attack determination, providing an algorithmic description for the practical implementation of the testing framework.
2. It designs a triplet mapping model for four types of flow risks. This model enables standardized and observable risk characterization, supporting the security risk assessment of software-defined space-based networks.

The subsequent structure of the article is arranged as follows: Sect. 2 introduces the current state of SDN-based security testing and reviews space-based network simulation technologies; Section 3 introduces the system framework design, including the composition architecture of software-defined space-based networks and the test case generation method based on the attack graph model; the chapter concludes by introducing the composition of the multi-agent security testing framework; Section 4 details the environmental configuration and core algorithm implementation of the multi-agent testing framework, and based on this, introduces the framework workflow; Section 5 details the impact of the system's four types of risks on space-based components; Section 6 provides a summary of the entire paper.

2 Related Work

Currently, software-defined network security testing technology has matured, while research on software-defined space-based network security testing is still under in-depth exploration. In the field of terrestrial SDN, Naresh et al. [7] proposed a privacy-preserving intrusion detection framework integrating homomorphic encryption and deep neural networks to ensure data confidentiality by encrypting traffic; the Medjadba team [8] used Bayesian ensembles to improve threat detection accuracy, combining convolutional neural networks and Monte Carlo Dropout to quantify prediction uncertainty; Dadhania et al. [9] used the GraphSAGE algorithm to enhance DoS attack detection, integrating four anomaly detection technologies to achieve accurate threat identification. These achievements provide efficient security mechanisms for ground networks.

In contrast, research on space-based network simulation has evolved through three stages:

Infrastructure verification stage: Focused on the feasibility of the SDN architecture, such as OpenSAN proposed by Bao et al. [10] to port the satellite SDN protocol stack, and the SERvICE framework by Li et al. [11] which broke through the space-ground interface differences, but static modeling struggled to meet the challenge of orbital dynamics. Dynamic environment adaptation stage: Focused on the collaborative optimization of the physical layer and control layer. Zhang et al. [12] developed an air-ground integrated platform to simulate orbital perturbations and channel attenuation, and Torkzaban [13] proposed a hierarchical control architecture to optimize LEO constellation response, but shortcomings remained in long-delay interface stability and on-board resource modeling. Multi-dimensional intelligent verification stage: Minardi [14] built a collaborative detection framework to improve anomaly capture capability, Jiang [15] designed a distributed learning framework to enhance bandwidth adaptability, and the Qin team [16] explored a quantum security fusion mechanism, but the problem of dynamic injection of risk attacks remains unsolved.

From the above research, firstly, high delay and resource bottlenecks severely constrain the real-time performance of testing methods. The inter-satellite link delay in space-based networks can reach hundreds of milliseconds, while software-defined network testing methods are typically assumed to be implemented on the ground. Simultaneously, dynamic topology changes lead to test scenario mismatches. The topology switching frequency in space-based networks is very high, whereas testing methods for software-defined networks are mostly based on static topology design. These limitations highlight the lack of adaptability of software-defined network testing methods in space-based networks, urgently necessitating the development of specialized security testing methods for software-defined space-based networks.

3 System Framework Design

This chapter aims to design a multi-agent security testing framework for software-defined space-based networks to address the unique challenges of highly dynamic topologies and long-delay links.

3.1 Software-Defined Architecture of Space-Based Network

To better test the security of software-defined space-based networks, we should first understand their architecture. As shown in Fig. 2, the software-defined space-based network adopts a hierarchical collaborative architecture, divided into a control plane, data plane, and application management plane. The control plane is composed of geosynchronous orbit satellites, a ground control center, and distributed nodes, achieving network scheduling through a centralized optimization and distributed execution mechanism. The data plane relies on the programmable forwarding capability of satellites in low and medium earth orbit to ensure efficient inter-satellite transmission; the application management plane performs global policy arrangement and security collaboration through the security management center and the multi-task scheduling platform.

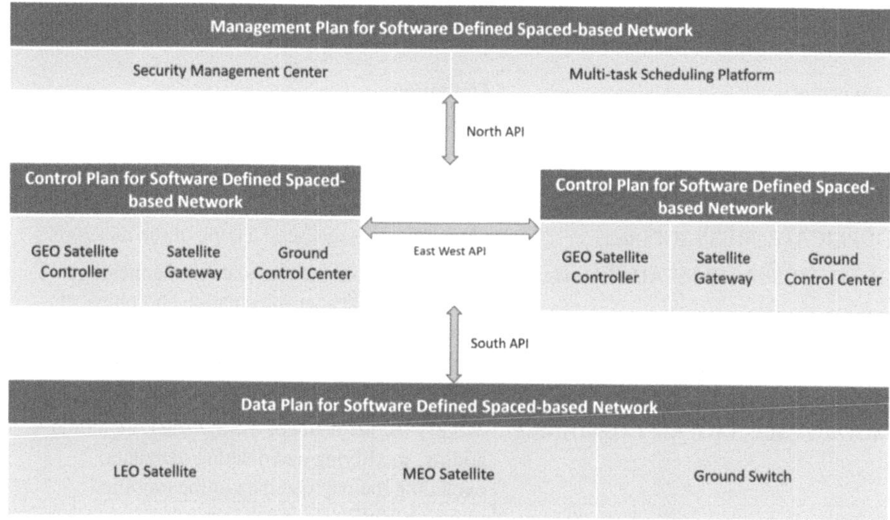

Fig. 2. Architecture diagram of space-based network based on SDN

3.2 Test Case Generation Method for Software-Defined Space-Based Network Based on Attack Graph Model

Aiming at the defect that vulnerability scanning tools and risk matrices are difficult to adapt to the dynamic topology of space-based networks, this study proposes a test case generation method based on a five-tuple attack graph model, including system model, capability model, risk model, initial state, and target state, denoted as AG = (S, C, R, S_0, S_t).

The System model S, as the physical basis for attack path construction, completely defines five elements of the space-based network: the controller set is responsible for centralized policy generation; the switch set performs data forwarding; the end node set constitutes the network edge; the data plane describes the device connectivity relationship with the topological graph $G_d = (V_d, E_d, A_d)$; and the control plane establishes the coordination mechanism between the controller and the switch through a many-to-many TCP connection set.

The Capability model C quantifies threat behavior through nine types of attack operations: the attack capability on the control plane connection indicates the degree to which an attacker understands and modifies control information. The basic capabilities are as shown in Table 1; the attacker's capability can be expressed as the collection of capabilities listed in Table 1.

Table 1. List of attacker capabilities for control plane connections

Competence	Definition
DROP_MESSAGE(msg)	Discard the message, thus preventing it from being sent and received.

(continued)

Table 1. (*continued*)

Competence	Definition
PASS_MESSAGE(msg)	Allow messages to be sent and received normally.
DELAY_MESSAGE(msg)	Send and receive messages after a specified time delay.
DUPLICATE_MESSAGE(msg)	Copy the message, send a copy of the message.
READ_MESSAGEMETADATA(msg)	Read and record the metadata of the message, including the header information and physical timestamp of Layer 2, Layer 3 and Layer 4, excluding the payload data of the read information itself.
MODIFY_MESSAGEMETADATA(msg)	Modify the metadata of the message, including adding, modifying and deleting metadata, excluding the payload data of the modified message itself.
FUZZ_MESSAGE(msg)	Randomly modify the metadata or payload data bits of the message in a semantic-free way.
READ_MESSAGE(msg)	Read or record the message payload in a semantic way, so that it conforms to OpenFlow protocol, excluding the message payload that cannot be decrypted.
MODIFY_MESSAGE(msg)	Modify the message payload in a semantic way to make it conform to OpenFlow protocol, including adding, modifying and deleting data from the message payload.
INJECTNEW_MESSAGE(msg)	Inject new and semantic messages into the control plane connection.

As for the Risk model R, the security risk of the software-defined space-based network architecture focuses more on the control plane, and its core hub position makes its interactive state central to risk monitoring. By deconstructing the lifecycle of control flows, risks are classified into four categories: symmetric control flow risk, asymmetric control flow risk, internal control flow risk of the controller, and non-flow operation risk. The risk classification corresponding to flow types is shown in Table 2.

Table 2. Risk classification of stream types in software-defined space-based networks

Operation flow type	Risk number	Risk name
Symmetric control flow risk (Symmetric Flows)	SF-1	Replay attack risk
	SF-2	Risk of resource exhaustion
	SF-3	Risk of agreement inconsistency

(*continued*)

Table 2. (*continued*)

Operation flow type	Risk number	Risk name
Asymmetric control flow risk (Asymmetric Flows)	AF-1	Control the risk of message dropping
	AF-2	Unlimited cycle attack risk
	AF-3	Packet flood attack risk
	AF-4	Flood attack risk of flow rule
	AF-5	Risk of man-in-the-middle attack
Internal control flow risk of controller (Intra-Controller Flows)	CF-1	Internal storage abuse risk
	CF-2	Risk of application eviction attack
	CF-3	Event Listener Unsubscribes Attack Risk
Non Flow Operations risk	NF-1	Risk of system command execution attack
	NF-2	Risk of resource exhaustion
	NF-3	System time manipulation risk

The initial state S_0 of the attack graph is the state when the software-defined space-based network is not attacked, and the target state S_t is the final state of the attack graph after the attack is completed.

3.3 Security Testing Framework Based on Multi-agent

As shown in Fig. 3, for the method of generating test cases for software-defined space-based networks based on the attack graph model, this study designs a multi-agent security test framework. Its core goal is to achieve automatic coverage of four types of risk scenarios through modular collaboration and adapt to the dynamic topology and long delay characteristics of space. The framework consists of five core modules: agent management, application agent, host agent, channel agent, and space-based agent.

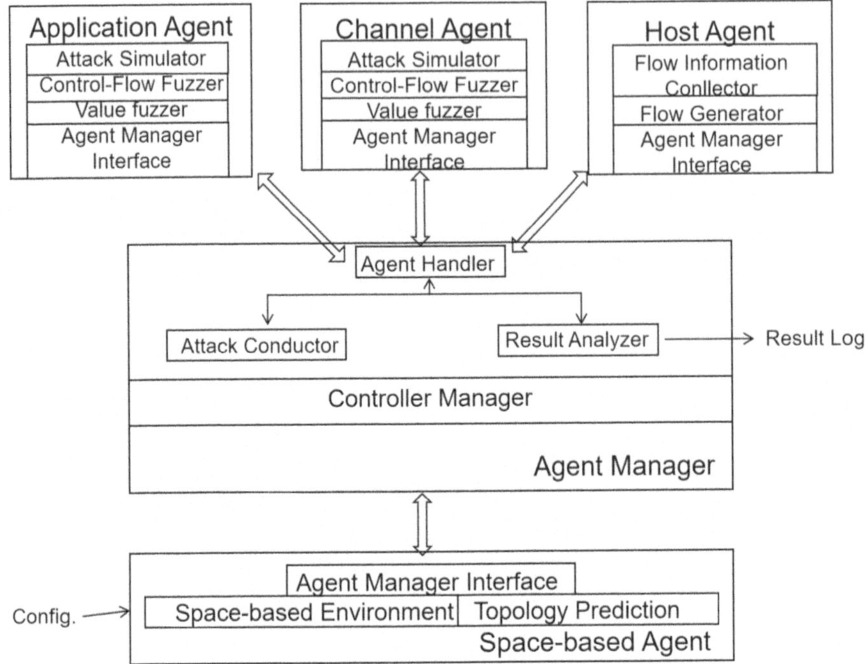

Fig. 3. Architecture diagram of software-defined space-based network testing framework

As the core control unit of the test framework, the agent management module coordinates task scheduling, execution monitoring, and result analysis for all agent components to ensure the coordinated operation of the entire system. The application agent module simulates malicious application behavior within the test framework and directly intervenes in the controller to manipulate control flow and input variables to trigger security vulnerabilities. The host agent module is primarily used to simulate the behavior characteristics of terminal equipment and generate network traffic conforming to specific attack scenarios to verify the ability to identify abnormal traffic. The channel agent module intercepts and modifies control messages between the controller and the data plane, focusing on attack simulation for unencrypted OpenFlow channels. As a special adaptation component for space-based networks, the space-based agent module integrates orbit prediction and inter-satellite link monitoring capabilities.

To clarify the functional boundaries and collaboration methods of each agent module, the interaction process follows the architectural flow illustrated in Fig. 3. The entire procedure begins with the task initialization phase: the Agent Management module receives the test strategy and issues orbit prediction instructions to the Space Agent. The Space Agent invokes high-precision ephemeris data to calculate real-time satellite orbital parameters, forwards the generated link state information to the Channel Agent, thereby ensuring the accurate construction of the dynamic network topology before security testing commences.

Subsequently, the process advances to the attack execution and risk analysis phase. The Agent Management module, based on the risk model, directs the Application Agent to generate specific attack vectors. The Application Agent immediately injects simulated attack traffic into the network and simultaneously notifies the Host Agent to initiate collaborative verification. Meanwhile, the Channel Agent performs real-time network monitoring leveraging the link state information provided by the Space Agent, computes weight metrics through a risk quantification algorithm, and reports the evaluation results to the Agent Management module to form global situational awareness.

The final phase achieves closed-loop control and response. The Host Agent conducts in-depth analysis of network traffic, verifies the actual impact of attacks, generates a detailed detection report, and feeds it back to the Agent Management module. The Agent Management module synthesizes the risk weight analysis results from the Channel Agent and the verification data from the Host Agent, formulates the final remediation strategy, and outputs the response plan. Through this structured multi-agent collaboration mechanism, efficient and automated security assessment for space-based networks is realized.

Through the design work in this chapter, the theoretical construction of the security testing framework for software-defined space-based networks has been completed. Specifically, a hierarchical collaborative architecture has been defined as the foundational test object; a five-tuple attack graph model-based test case generation method has been established; and an innovative multi-agent collaborative testing framework comprising agent management, application agents, host agents, channel agents, and space-based agents has been designed.

4 System Implementation

This chapter aims to concretely implement the designed security testing framework for software-defined space-based networks.

4.1 Environment Configuration

To realize the security testing framework based on multi-agent, it is necessary to build a standardized testing environment. The base system adopts Ubuntu 18.04 LTS or a higher operating system to meet the framework's runtime environment requirements, and the core dependency toolchain is installed. The system configuration meets the topology simulation requirements for 8 satellites, 2 ground stations, and 2 ground terminals. An 8-satellite network is configured as a constellation, where two satellites assume the control plane function and six satellites serve as data plane forwarding nodes. Inter-satellite communication adopts laser link interconnection, establishing direct connections between satellites to form a mesh topology. The ground layer is equipped with ground control stations and user terminal nodes to realize space-ground cooperation, as shown in Fig. 4.

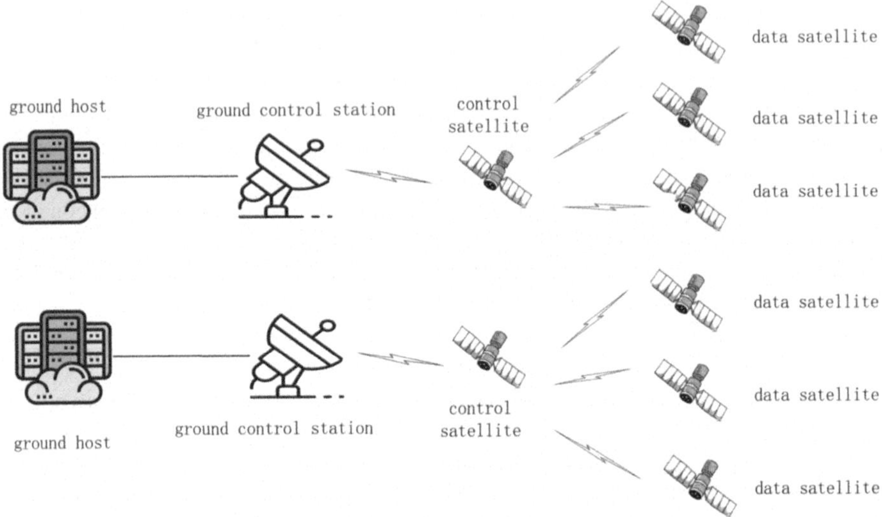

Fig. 4. Topology Diagram of Environment

Regarding environment deployment: Firstly, the SNS-3 orbital service is constructed. The core library is cloned, designated modules are integrated, and standard compilation commands are executed, thus generating the constellation simulation environment. Subsequently, the topology of 8 satellites, 2 ground stations, and 2 ground terminals is started. Then, the multi-agent software defined space-based network framework is configured; initialization scripts are run to create container clusters; and application agents are deployed to on-board controller nodes, channel agents to laser data links, and host agents to user terminal nodes.

At the same time, this study recognizes that real-world space-based network environments exhibit uncertainties such as packet loss and bandwidth jitter caused by atmospheric disturbances and the Doppler effect. To accurately evaluate the core logical efficacy of the proposed security testing framework, the current simulation employs a controlled, simplified channel model. This approach aims to isolate and focus on validating the effectiveness of the algorithms themselves, rather than on high-fidelity replication of physical-layer perturbations. Specifically, when analyzing the framework's robustness, we introduced statistical models in the post-processing phase to assess the potential impact of non-ideal channels on key metrics such as detection rate and false positive rate. The integration of high-fidelity physical layer effects is a priority for future work. Final validation will be conducted through an extended NS-3 SatelliteChannel module to ensure the framework's applicability in real-world space environments.

4.2 Implementation Algorithm

Within the software-defined space-based network security testing framework, dynamic topology adaptation and accurate risk location are achieved through three algorithms: topology construction algorithm, route prediction algorithm, and attack propagation analysis algorithm.

As shown in Fig. 5, the topology construction algorithm dynamically generates the physical architecture based on the five-tuple attack graph. Satellite orbit positions are calculated by a high-precision ephemeris engine; the initial state marks the controlled node; and the target state marks the high-risk attack path, thereby realizing the deep integration of risk and physical topology.

Complexity Analysis: The time complexity is $O(n^2)$, as the process involves nested loops for processing each of the n nodes and their potential neighbors, as depicted in Fig. 5. The space complexity is $O(|V| + |E|)$ for storing the graph topology. This is feasible for onboard computation as the number of nodes within a satellite's communication horizon is limited.

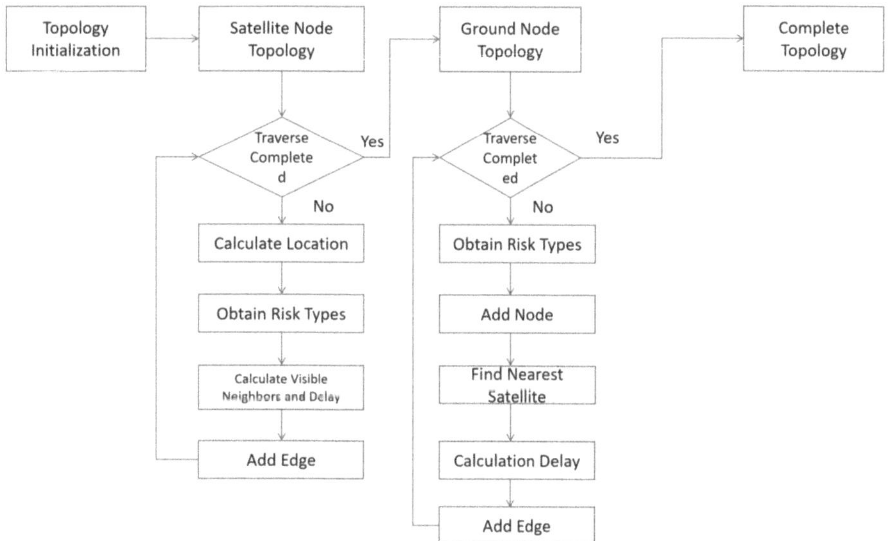

Fig. 5. Diagram representation of topology construction algorithm

As shown in Fig. 6, the route prediction algorithm realizes safe path decisions in the dynamic space environment. The space-based agent performs orbit position prediction, and the channel agent updates the state of the inter-satellite link in real-time to avoid the $S_0 \rightarrow S_t$ high-risk attack path generated by the attack graph. Path optimization integrates link transmission delay, risk type weight, and topological stability parameters, using an improved Dijkstra algorithm to pre-calculate candidate paths and automatically screen transmission schemes that meet the security threshold.

Complexity Analysis: The employed improved Dijkstra algorithm exhibits a time complexity of $O(|E|+|V|\log|V|)$ for computing secure paths, which is efficient for the control layer's onboard processing. Its space complexity is $O(|V|)$, primarily for maintaining the priority queue and path cost arrays.

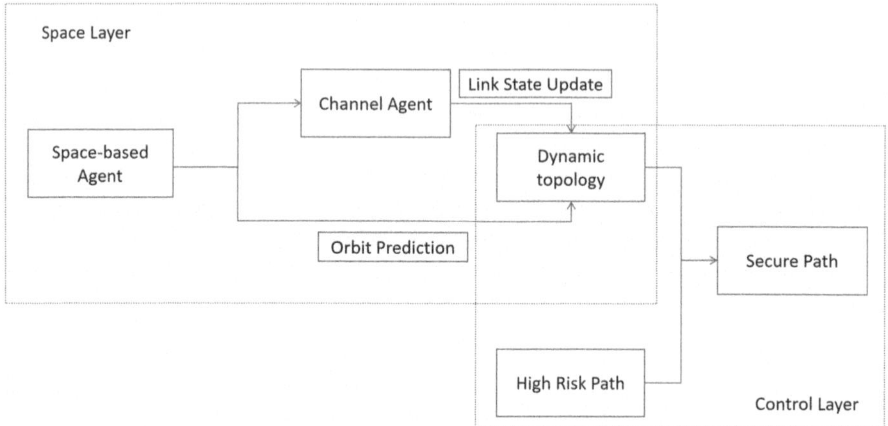

Fig. 6. Topology diagram of route prediction algorithm

The attack propagation analysis algorithm uses breadth-first search (BFS) to quantify the vulnerability cascade effect. It traverses neighboring nodes (depth ≤ 5) from the compromised node, verifies the existence of the 14 types of risks using agents, and dynamically updates the node status in the attack graph. Risk propagation strictly follows the test case generation process to output a list of vulnerable nodes and repair priority suggestions.

Complexity Analysis: The algorithm's core is BFS, yielding a worst-case time complexity of $O(|V| + |E|)$. However, the critical constraint of a maximum search depth ($d \leq 5$) drastically reduces the practical complexity to $O(b^d)$, where b is the average branching factor. The space complexity is $O(|V|)$ for the queue and visited set. This design is highly feasible for resource-constrained space-borne devices, as the depth limit ensures lightweight execution.

```
Algorithm1: Attack Propagation Analysis
Input: Compromised node C, Topology T, AppAgent AA, AttackGraph AG
Output: Impact scope IS
IS ← {C} // Initialize the sphere of influence
queue ← initialize queue (c)//bfs traverse the queue
while not queue.Empty() do
  current ← queue.Dequeue()
// Apply the proxy to verify the existence of the vulnerability.
is _ vulnerable ← aa.verifyrikexistance (current, ag.r _ model)//Table 2 Risk detection
// Update the attack graph status
  AG.UpdateState(current, "COMPROMISED")
  for each neighbor in T.GetNeighbors(current) do
    if neighbor not in IS and is_vulnerable then
      IS.Add(neighbor)
      queue.Enqueue(neighbor)
// Extended attack path
ag.addattackpath (current, neighbor)//Add S0→St path.
    end if
  end for
end while
return IS // Returns the set of affected nodes.
```

4.3 Framework Workflow

The workflow of the framework integrates the synergy between test cases and fuzz tests and is divided into five stages: initialization, agent scheduling, use case execution, result verification, and model iteration. The flow is shown in Fig. 7.

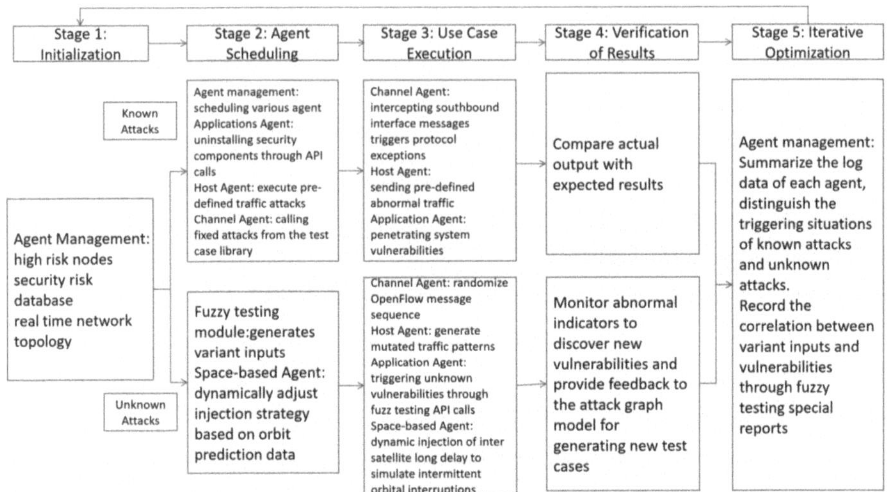

Fig. 7. Software-Defined Space-based Network Framework Process Working Diagram

In the initialization stage, the agent management module loads the five-tuple model of the attack graph and injects satellite constellation parameter. Simultaneously, four types comprising fourteen risk scenarios are analyzed, and a constellation simulation environment is constructed through orbit service.

Entering the agent scheduling stage, intelligent task distribution is realized by integrating the route prediction algorithm. For known attack paths, the channel agent calls the preset attack sequence library, the host agent generates protocol-abnormal traffic, and the application agent unloads security components through the interface; For unknown attack detection, the space-based agent performs orbit prediction to avoid high-risk paths, the channel agent dynamically updates the link state, and the fuzz test module generates an input mutation strategy based on risk weight. Multi-agents pre-calculate safe paths by improving the path search algorithm, integrating transmission delay, risk weight, and topological stability parameters to realize dynamic obstacle avoidance of attack paths.

In the use case execution and verification phase, a dual-path collaboration mechanism is used to perform the test task. When the attack path is known, the channel agent intercepts messages on the southbound interface and triggers protocol exceptions, the host agent sends predefined flood flows, and the application agent exploits controller vulnerabilities; Under an unknown attack path, the channel agent randomizes the message structure, the host agent generates variant traffic patterns, and the space-based agent injects inter-satellite long delays. The attack propagation analysis algorithm verifies the cascading effect of vulnerabilities in real-time, uses agents to detect the existence of risks and mark the state of nodes, and identifies new threats by comparing actual output with expected results.

In the result feedback stage, the attack graph model is dynamically optimized, and response strategies are generated. Detected vulnerability nodes are added to the attack graph, attack paths are expanded, and corresponding test cases are generated. The channel agent updates the state of the inter-satellite link, and the space-based agent recalculates safe transmission paths to avoid high-risk areas. All abnormal indicators are mapped to the risk model, risk weight values are corrected, and a heat map of vulnerable nodes and repair priority suggestions are output to provide a quantitative basis for emergency response.

Finally, in the closed-loop iteration stage, two-way optimization of parameter configuration and the model is realized. The agent management module analyzes log data, distinguishes attack trigger states, and records the mapping relationship between input variation and vulnerability. The orbit prediction window is dynamically adjusted according to link stability, and risk model parameters are revised based on vulnerability coverage. Finally, a security report including topology evaluation, risk propagation paths, and a repair matrix is generated; the probability parameters of the attack graph are updated; and the test cycle is restarted, forming an autonomous optimization system from environment configuration to model iteration.

Through the system implementation work in this chapter, a multi-agent security testing platform for software-defined space-based networks has been successfully deployed. This achievement encompasses two key components: construction of a standardized constellation simulation environment featuring an 8-satellite and 2-ground-station topology using Ubuntu and NS-3; Implementation of three core algorithms overcoming bottlenecks in dynamic topology adaptation and risk quantification.

5 System Risk Detection

According to the security risk model proposed in Sect. 3.2, combined with the multi-agent security testing framework, 14 kinds of security risks within four categories are studied in detail. Their triggering principles, influencing components, and effects after risk triggering are sorted out.

5.1 Symmetric Control Flow Risk

Symmetric control flow risk focuses on the protocol interaction process of the southbound interface between the satellite controller and the ground switch, covering three typical threats: Replay attack risk induces the controller to repeat the authentication process by forging OpenFlow Hello messages, leading to disconnection of the southbound interface; Resource exhaustion risk uses forged handshake messages to continuously occupy the controller's memory resources, triggering service denial; Protocol inconsistency risk causes protocol parsing exceptions by tampering with the version field of control flow messages, causing the ground switch to actively disconnect. These risks directly destroy the cooperative communication ability of controllers, switches, and interfaces, potentially leading to the interruption of telemetry data transmission or paralysis of the control plane. Thus, the risk model impact library for symmetric control flow is established, as shown in Table 3.

Table 3. Impact Library of Symmetric Control Flow Risk Model

Risk number	Risk name	Risk trigger principle	Risk impact component	Risk trigger effect
SF-1	Replay attack risk	Attackers replay legitimate handshake messages (such as OpenFlow Hello messages) to induce satellite controllers to repeat the authentication process.	Satellite controller, satellite switch, ground switch, southbound interface	The satellite controller is disconnected from the ground exchange, the southbound interface returns an error response, and the control plane communication is interrupted.
SF-2	Risk of resource exhaustion	Continuous sending of forged handshake messages (such as version number conflict) occupies the memory resources of the satellite controller.	Satellite controller, satellite switch, ground switch.	The memory usage is abnormally high, and the satellite controller cannot handle new requests due to insufficient resources, resulting in service denial.
SF-3	Risk of agreement inconsistency	Tampering with the version field or the protocol field of the symmetric control flow message triggers a protocol parsing exception.	Satellite controller, satellite switch, ground switch.	The ground switch is disconnected, the satellite controller returns an illegal version error, and the interaction of the southbound interface protocol fails.

5.2 Asymmetric Control Flow Risk

Asymmetric control flow risk focuses on the directional interference of malicious applications with control message delivery, manifested in five types of attack modes: Control message dropping risk blocks the communication link between controller and switch by forging discard flag bits, resulting in loss of telemetry data on the northbound interface; Unlimited cycle attack risk uses malicious rules to trigger infinite loops in the controller CPU, causing traffic processing delays at the ground switch; Packet flooding attack risk inundates the controller's computing resources through massive PACKET_IN messages, causing abnormal forwarding paths at the ground switch; Flow rule flood attack risk injects forged flow entries to overflow the switch's memory capacity, destroying legal forwarding rules; Man-in-the-middle attack risk tampers with inter-satellite link control message fields and hijacks telemetry data transmission paths. This category of risk directly threatens data transmission integrity by destroying the dynamic topology cooperation mechanism involving satellite switches, ground switches, and controllers. Thus, the impact library of the asymmetric control flow risk model is established, as shown in Table 4.

Table 4. Impact Library of Asymmetric Control Flow Risk Model

Risk number	Risk name	Risk trigger principle	Risk impact component	Risk trigger effect
AF-1	Control the risk of message dropping	Malicious applications interfere with the message delivery sequence or forge discard flags to block the communication between the satellite controller and the ground switch.	Satellite controller, satellite switch, ground switch and northbound interface.	The control message is lost, the northbound interface cannot obtain telemetry data, and the forwarding path of the ground switch is abnormal.
AΓ-2	Unlimited cycle attack risk	The satellite controller is triggered to execute an infinite loop through malicious rules or events, which consumes CPU resources.	Satellite controller, satellite switch, ground switch.	The utilization rate of CPU increased abnormally, the response delay of satellite controller increased sharply, and the traffic processing of ground switch failed.

(*continued*)

Table 4. (*continued*)

Risk number	Risk name	Risk trigger principle	Risk impact component	Risk trigger effect
AF-3	Packet flood attack risk	Forging massive data packets triggers the satellite controller to process PACKET_IN messages frequently, which takes up computing resources.	Satellite controller, ground switch, northbound interface	The CPU of the satellite controller is overloaded, the forwarding path of the ground switch is delayed, and the response of the northbound interface is overtime.
AF-4	Flood attack risk of flow rule	Inject a large number of flow rules and overflow the anti-radiation memory capacity of the satellite switch.	Satellite switch, ground switch, satellite controller	The number of flow table entries increases abnormally, and the ground switch discards legal rules due to storage overflow, and the forwarding path is wrong.
AF-5	Risk of man-in-the-middle attack	Tampering with the inter-satellite link control message and hijacking the telemetry data transmission path.	Satellite switch, ground switch, satellite controller	Telemetry data is redirected to the attacker's node, the forwarding path of the ground switch is abnormal, and the data integrity is damaged.

5.3 Risk of Control Flow Inside the Controller

The internal control flow risk of the controller originates from the directional destruction of the satellite controller's internal logic by malicious applications, covering three core attack scenarios: Internal storage abuse risk misleads the multi-task scheduling platform by tampering with topological data, resulting in forwarding path errors at the ground switch; Application eviction attack risk dynamically unloads key security applications, weakening the cooperative protection ability of controllers and switches; Event listener unsubscribe attack risk prevents legitimate applications from subscribing to topology change events, causing the ground switch to forward abnormal data because the flow table is not updated. This category of risk directly destroys the decision-making cooperation mechanism involving the orbit prediction module, security management center, and ground switch, potentially leading to loss of telemetry data or missed detection of attack behavior. Thus, the impact library of the internal control flow risk model for the controller is established, as shown in Table 5.

Table 5. Impact Library of Risk Model for Internal Control Flow of Controller

Risk number	Risk name	Risk trigger principle	Risk impact component	Risk trigger effect
CF-1	Internal storage abuse risk	Malicious applications tamper with the internal topology data or flow table cache of the satellite controller, misleading the flow decision logic.	Satellite controller, multi-task dispatching platform, ground switch.	The multi-task scheduling platform cannot generate correct flow rules, the forwarding path of the ground switch is wrong, and the telemetry data is lost.
CF-2	Risk of application eviction attack	Dynamically uninstall key security applications (such as intrusion detection module), which destroys the protection ability of satellite controller.	Satellite controller, security management center, ground switch.	The satellite controller can't implement the security policy, and the ground switch forwards malicious traffic because of the lack of protection mechanism.
CF-3	Event Listener Unsubscribes Attack Risk	Prevent legitimate applications from subscribing to satellite controller events (such as topology change events), resulting in message processing interruption.	Satellite controller, ground control center, ground switch.	The satellite controller can't respond to the topology change, and the ground switch fails to update the flow table, resulting in abnormal data forwarding.

5.4 Non-flow Operation Risk

Non-flow operation risk attacks the system-level functions of the satellite controller, covering three typical threats: System command execution attack risk triggers firewall closure through command injection loopholes, making the ground switch a malicious traffic transit node; Resource exhaustion risk uses infinite threads to seize the controller's CPU resources, causing the ground switch to interrupt forwarding due to resource exhaustion; System time manipulation risk tampers with parameters of time synchronization protocols, causing time-asynchronous packet loss in satellite-ground equipment. This category of risk destroys the cooperative operation mechanism of the on-board operating system, distributed nodes, and ground switches, potentially leading to orbit calculation deviation or invalidation of telemetry data timestamps. Thus, the impact library of the non-flow operation risk model is established, as shown in Table 6.

Table 6. Impact Library of Non-flow Operation Risk Model

Risk number	Risk name	Risk trigger principle	Risk impact component	Risk trigger effect
NF-1	Risk of system command execution attack	Malicious applications use satellite controller vulnerabilities to trigger dangerous operations.	Satellite controller, security management center, ground switch.	The satellite controller is abnormal, and the ground switch forwards malicious traffic due to the failure of security policy.
NF-2	Risk of resource exhaustion	By occupying all memory or CPU resources, the satellite controller is paralyzed.	Satellite controller, distributed node, ground switch.	The satellite controller is restarted frequently, and the ground switch can't handle the traffic due to insufficient resources, and the forwarding path is interrupted.
NF-3	System time manipulation risk	Tampering with satellite controller system time, interfering with orbit calculation or time synchronization protocol.	Time synchronization protocol, satellite switch, ground switch.	The ground exchange lost packets due to time synchronization, the time synchronization protocol failed, and the telemetry data timestamp was abnormal.

Through refined modeling and impact analysis of 14 security risks across four categories in software-defined space-based networks, this chapter systematically establishes a ternary mapping repository correlating risk trigger principles, affected components, and trigger effects. Deeply integrated with multi-agent collaborative mechanisms, this framework achieves observable, quantifiable, and verifiable risk status assessment, thereby establishing a standardized dynamic security evaluation benchmark for software-defined space-based networks.

6 Conclusion

This study proposes a testing framework and risk detection mechanism based on multi-agent collaboration to meet the dynamic security verification requirements of software defined space-based networks. The framework design collaborates with five modules:

proxy management, application proxy, host proxy, channel proxy, and space-based proxy to solve the challenges of satellite ground long latency and topology transient adaptation. Algorithm implementation breaks through three major bottlenecks: topology construction algorithm dynamically integrates risk and physical topology; Route prediction algorithms avoid high-risk paths; Quantify the cascading effects of vulnerabilities in attack propagation analysis algorithms. Risk detection relies on the attack graph quintuple model to generate a triplet relationship mapping covering four types of risks. This framework supports full coverage of risk scenarios and provides a feasible security benchmark for low orbit constellations.

References

1. Lu, X., Wei, W., Fu, L., et al.: Link attributes based multi-service routing for software-defined satellite networks. Comput. Electr. Eng. **119**, 109467 (2024)
2. Wang, F., Jiang, D., Wang, Z., et al.: Fuzzy-CNN based multi-task routing for integrated satellite-terrestrial networks. IEEE Trans. Veh. Technol. **71**(2), 1913–1926 (2021)
3. Zhang, G., Luo, H., Qiao, H., et al.: Research on military application and countermeasures of "Star Chain." Commun. Technol. **58**(2), 164–168 (2025)
4. Zhao, G., Wei, Y., Huang, W., Zhao, P.: Research on the latest progress of software-defined satellites abroad. Int. Space (04), 16–23 (2025)
5. Chen, C., Cai, C., Pan, L., Dai, W.: Comparative analysis of PPP performance of several typical LEO constellations in China. Geodesy Geodyn. (2025). https://doi.org/10.14075/j.jgg.2024.07.345
6. Dooley, S.J.: Typical application of cloud engineering in eight key industries. Sat. Appl. (03), 66–72 (2020)
7. Naresh, V.S., Ayyappa, D.: Enhancing security in software defined networks: privacy-preserving intrusion detection with Homomorphic Encryption. J. Inf. Secur. Appl. **92**, 104084 (2025)
8. Medjadba, Y., Drid, H., Rahouti, M.: Intrusion detection in Software-Defined Networking using hybrid Bayesian model averaging for reliable uncertainty quantification. Comput. Netw. **269**111436 (2025)
9. Dadhania, A., et al.: Software defined network and graph neural network-based anomaly detection scheme for high speed networks. Cyber Secur. Appl. **3**100079 (2025). https://doi.org/10.1016/j.csa.2024.100079
10. Bao, J., Zhao, B., Yu, W., et al.: OpenSAN: a software-defined satellite network architecture. ACM SIGCOMM Comput. Commun. Rev. **44**(4), 347–348 (2014)
11. Li, T., Zhou, H., Luo, H., et al.: SERvICE: A software defined framework for integrated space-terrestrial satellite communication. IEEE Trans. Mob. Comput. **17**(3), 703–716 (2017)
12. Zhang, Y., Wang, B., Guo, B., et al.: A research on integrated space-ground information network simulation platform based on SDN. Comput. Netw. **188**, 107821 (2021)
13. Torkzaban, N., Baras, J.S.: Controller placement in SDN-enabled 5G satellite-terrestrial networks. In: 2021 IEEE Global Communications Conference (GLOBECOM), pp. 1–6. IEEE (2021)
14. Minardi, M., Vu, T.X., Lei, L., et al.: Virtual network embedding for NGSO systems: algorithmic solution and SDN-testbed validation. IEEE Trans. Netw. Serv. Manag. **20**(3), 3523–3535 (2022)
15. Jiang, W., Zhan, Y., Fang, X.: Satellite edge computing for mobile multimedia communications: a multi-agent federated reinforcement learning approach. ACM Trans. Auton. Adapt. Syst. (2025)

16. Qin, X., Ma, T., Tang, Z., et al.: Service-aware resource orchestration in ultra-dense LEO satellite-terrestrial integrated 6G: a service function chain approach. IEEE Trans. Wirel. Commun. **22**(9), 6003–6017 (2023)

NetInno: A Multi-Agent-Based LLM Framework for Network Research Innovation

Hongyu Du[1], Qingyu Song[1], Congming Gao[1], Rongxin Wu[1], Zhirong Shen[1], Yuanxun Kang[2], Fei Yuan[1], and Qiao Xiang[1](✉)

[1] Xiamen University, Xiamen, China
xiangq27@gmail.com
[2] Yealink, Xiamen, China

Abstract. In the field of computer networks, innovation is crucial for both the academic and industrial sectors. As more researchers engage in this important research area, peer competition intensifies. However, traditional methods of innovation are hindered by personal biases, knowledge boundaries, time costs and resource constraints, which impede scientific breakthroughs in the network domain. In this paper, we introduce NetInno, a multi-agent cyclic framework. NetInno is based on Large Language Models (LLMs) and is capable of autonomous innovation. It utilizes feedback to further optimize results, thereby reducing the need for human intervention. Each agent employs tailored prompting strategies to enhance expertise, eliminating the need for extensive initial setup and model training. Human review ensures the professionalism of the feedback, addressing potential "hallucination" issues of LLMs. Our initial experiments and case studies validate the effectiveness and applicability of NetInno, demonstrating its potential to automate innovation through iterative frameworks and tailored strategies. We believe this represents the first step towards developing fully automated systems for research innovation in the future of networking.

Keywords: LLMs · Innovation

1 Introduction

In the field of computer networks, innovation is essential. Academically, innovation drives the improvement of network performance, security, and reliability, as well as optimizing network operations. A study from SIGCOMM '23 proposed the Klotski system for safely and efficiently generating network service migration plans. The system uses the A* algorithm and domain-specific priority-based intelligent solving, and leverages data center network locality and compressed topology representations to speed up the solving process. Compared to existing methods, Klotski achieves higher planning efficiency while adhering to operational constraints [1]. From the perspective of business competitiveness, innovation enhances market competitiveness, improves operational efficiency, and

T. Qiu et al. (Eds.): CCF ChinaNet 2025, CCIS 2810, pp. 89–99, 2026.
https://doi.org/10.1007/978-981-95-8450-5_7

provides differentiated competitive advantages. Empirical research indicates that China is entering an era shifting from secondary innovation to independent innovation, and Chinese high-tech companies should focus on independent innovation [2]. Moreover, competition among peers is increasingly intense. A recent report shows that the acceptance rate for the top computer networking conference INFOCOM '24 is only 19.5%, highlighting the urgent need to change this traditional innovation model.

The formulation of superior research strategies for tackling scientific challenges is the cornerstone of innovation. The process of conceptualizing research designs in scientific inquiry, primarily a cognitive task performed by researchers, is complex and intricate. This intellectual exercise is subject to individual biases and preconceived notions, which can inadvertently skew the objectivity of the research direction. The personal nature of the ideation process can lead to knowledge silos, where researchers might fail to fully grasp the broader context or interdisciplinary connections, further hindering innovation potential by adhering to established paradigms, thereby reducing the likelihood of exploring new and unknown research areas. Furthermore, generating novel and viable research ideas can be time-consuming, often requiring exhaustive literature reviews and extensive brainstorming, delaying the commencement of empirical work. This brainstorming process is also constrained by the availability of resources such as funding, equipment, and skilled personnel, which can limit the scope and depth of the proposed research.

With the substantial increase in the size of language models (e.g., from 220 million parameters in BERT to 175 billion parameters in ChatGPT) and the enhancement of their capabilities, the paradigm for using LLMs has shifted towards pre-training and prompting due to the high cost of fine-tuning the entire model [3]. More importantly, LLMs possess a powerful knowledge [5] base necessary for research innovation. Intuitively, LLMs are expected to cost-effectively assist in research innovation within the field of computer networks. However, in this paper, we should also consider how we should also consider how to enable LLMs to simulate the research and innovation processes of network researchers.

To address these challenges, we introduce NetInno, an LLM-based framework for research innovation. This framework employs a multi-agent cyclic strategy to simulate the general process of scientific innovation, comprising three core modules: Planner, Analyzer, and Evaluator. Specifically, the Planner formulates research plans targeting specific innovation needs in the networking domain [4]. The Analyzer conducts analyses based on the research plan and concurrently generates multiple innovative proposals. The Analyzer refines these proposals in each iteration according to feedback from the Evaluator and ongoing guidance from the Planner. The Evaluator assesses the innovative proposals in conjunction with the research plan and provides constructive feedback to guide the research in the next cycle of NetInno. Additionally, we incorporate human review to ensure the professionalism of the proposals and feedback, further mitigating issues related to LLM hallucinations [6]. Notably, we have designed tailored prompting strategies for each agent to enhance their expertise. Our experimental results using various innovation needs have verified the capability of our framework to provide research proposals and expand research directions. We position NetInno as a pioneering and significant advancement in the development of future autonomous network innovation systems.

2 Background and Motivation

2.1 Background

Researchers face a variety of challenges when innovating. Innovation is often hindered by the personal biases of researchers, which can affect the selection of research topics, interpretation of data, and acceptance of novel ideas. Recognizing and mitigating these biases is essential for fostering genuine innovation. When conceiving research solutions, researchers initially confront the task of exploring the boundaries of existing knowledge. This requires a deep understanding of established theories as well as the capacity to identify and question prevailing assumptions and limitations. The pursuit of innovation is time-intensive, demanding significant periods for brainstorming, developing, and testing new ideas. This time commitment can strain resources and delay the progression of research projects, making efficient time management crucial. *Resource constraints.* Researchers often face limitations in terms of funding, equipment, and human resources, which can restrict their ability to pursue innovative ideas. Overcoming these constraints requires strategic resource allocation and the pursuit of alternative funding or partnerships.

In summary, the personal biases, limited knowledge, time pressure, and resource constraints challenges that researchers face when formulating research proposals collectively create a complex environment that can render the innovation process inefficient and of lower quality. These factors indicate that, despite researchers' high levels of expertise and creativity, their innovation processes are often inefficient and constrained by human cognitive limitations.

2.2 Motivation

Recently, LLMs like ChatGPT and Kimi in the field of Natural Language Processing (NLP) [8,9]have become popular, with billions of pre-trained parameters [17]. These models absorb extensive knowledge through vast amounts of data and have demonstrated extraordinary capabilities in dialogue, code generation [18], reasoning, and text generation within NLP [10,11]. Importantly, the activation of LLMs' abilities relies on prompts [12], which are usually in the form of text templates [13]. Advanced prompting strategies [14–16] can significantly enhance the performance of LLMs [3]. Inspired by these outcomes, we believe that LLMs can serve as foundational models for assisting with innovations in networking because many network innovation tasks can also benefit from their extensive knowledge and reasoning abilities. For instance, in the topic of Data Plane Validation (DPV), the comprehensive knowledge base of LLMs can be leveraged to unearth methods for better accelerating DPV, thereby significantly speeding up validation. Additionally, their reasoning capabilities can be utilized to analyze the current state of previous research, identifying innovation points that might be overlooked by human innovation. Therefore, we envision LLMs as a key to realizing networking innovation tasks. They not only explore this new paradigm of automated innovation but also do so at low cost, without the need for extensive initial setup and model training [7].

The current challenge is how to harness the vast knowledge base of LLMs to maximize their innovative potential, ensuring alignment with the research practices of professional computer networking researchers, ultimately meeting research needs. We need a carefully designed framework to achieve this goal. For example, utilizing multiple LLM agents to embody different roles of researchers and simulate their behaviors, thereby reconstructing the actual research and innovation workflow.

3 Design Overview

To enable LLMs to assist in scientific research and innovation within the networking domain, we propose NetInno, an LLM-based multi-agent iterative framework. To achieve this goal, NetInno is built around three core components: Planner, Analyzer, and Evaluator. As shown in Fig. 1.

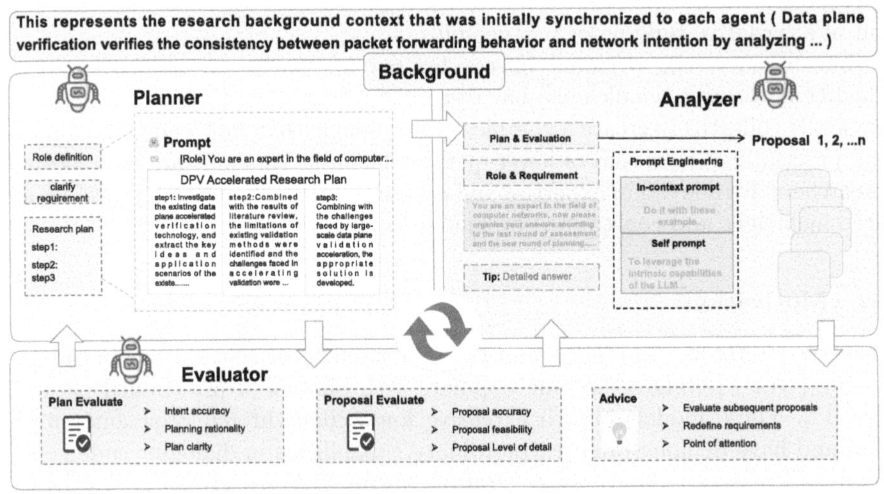

Fig. 1. Framework overview.

Planner formulates feasible research plans tailored to specific scientific research needs, helping the Analyzer develop innovative proposals that align with the research needs of scientists.

The Analyzer conducts research according to the research plan designed by the Planner based on specific innovation requirements, concurrently providing multiple innovation solutions. In the next round of research, the Analyzer can refine its innovative solutions based on the feedback from the Evaluator and the updated research plan from the Planner to meet specific research needs. Once the analysis is complete, the research recommendations proposed by the Analyzer and the research plan provided by the Planner will be forwarded to the Evaluator.

The Evaluator evaluates them and generates constructive feedback for further improvement. The evaluation criteria can be flexible, determined by the Evaluator or restricted by prompts. It is important to emphasize that we have proposed a preliminary automated innovation framework, which offers researchers considerable flexibility in adjusting their innovation process. Specifically, researchers can choose whether to forward the evaluator's feedback to the analyzer or to both the analyzer and the planner simultaneously. The criterion for this decision is the complexity of the innovation demand analysis: if the demand is complex, the feedback will be forwarded to both, allowing the planner to first provide a plan, followed by the analyzer conducting the analysis based on that plan.

In addition, to accurately formulate research proposal for scientific needs, it is important to ensure that all agents share the same context. Therefore, if it does not exceed the LLM token limit, provide an initial description of the research context to the agents, ensuring that all agents conduct research within the same context.

3.1 Prompt Engineering

A key factor in implementing NetInno is the use of appropriate strategies to construct prompt prefixes. We designed three different strategies to build prompt prefixes, each based on a unique fundamental principle: (1) *self-prompt,* which aims to leverage the intrinsic capabilities of the LLM to generate pertinent prompt candidates for innovation tasks; (2)*chain-of-thought (CoT) prompt,* which emphasizes a systematic, step-by-step reasoning process by compelling the LLM to address innovation tasks through a sequence of intermediate steps, both explicitly and implicitly; (3) *in-context prompt,* which supplies multiple research examples to establish a contextual understanding for the innovation tasks.

In addition, we have carefully designed the following aspects for the prompt templates. A brief explanation is provided below.

1. Define the agent's role as an expert in the field of computer networking, required to research scientific innovation in the field of networking.
2. Clarify the thematic requirements, such as providing a research plan, analyzing research proposals, or feedback.
3. Guide the agent by inserting tips to enhance the agent's research capabilities and prevent the generation of erroneous analysis.

4. We meticulously prepared relevant background descriptions for each research requirement. They serve as crucial components of prompt prefixes, shared across all agents. Consistent prompt design ensures agents operate within the same context, yielding consistent outputs. This consistency helps improve NetInno in iterative research needs.

3.2 Implementation Details

We provide more details on each component and clarify our design motivations.

Comprehensive background knowledge is the foundation of research innovation. A planner first needs to fully understand the background knowledge related to the innovation requirements before providing a detailed research plan. Therefore, besides clearly understanding the requirements, it is crucial that our initial prompt content is closely related to the innovation needs.

Fortunately, if background prompts are used, the planning agent can understand the task by incorporating additional background information into the input. Apart from background prompts, we do not need to construct other complex prompt prefixes, as the planning agent can generate a research plan aligned with our research intentions. For example, within the context of DPV acceleration, by providing explanations of DPV tasks and research requirements, agents can understand our research intent and develop a sound research plan for the subject. It should be emphasized that in the next round of research, research requirements will be replaced by advice provided by evaluator. Therefore, this paper proposes a prompt template with two slots for generating a reasonable research plan.

Template for prompts to generate a research plan

{subject background}

The above is a description of the subject background. You are an expert in the field of computer network. You want to {research need/advice} Please define the steps for this goal.

After receiving the planner's plan or the evaluator's feedback, the analyzer will formulate a more detailed innovative plan based on the latest instructions. This plan will then be submitted to the evaluators for assessment. Typically, issues such as drafting rough plans may arise. In NetInno, we use manual review to enhance the framework's continuous research capabilities, ensuring the smooth progress of the research.

Unlike interactions with the planning agent, when interacting with the analyzing agent, we construct a contextual prompt prefix. This allows the analyzer agent to learn within the context by reflexively responding to a few input-output pairs (demonstrations). Therefore, this paper proposes a three-slot prompt template to generate reasonable innovative proposal.

Template for prompts to generate a research proposal

{subject background}
The above is a description of the subject background.
You are an expert in the field of computer network. Below is an example of a research requirement and its corresponding program or research direction.
{example research need + example research proposal}
You want to {research need/advice} Please follow the analysis of the research plan and develop a research proposal to address the research need.
Note that yourproposal should be as comprehensive and detailed as possible.

We aim to automate the process as much as possible to stimulate the analyzer's innovative capacity, allowing the agent to concurrently draft different research propoals from multiple perspectives. Inspired by the study of Jiao et al. [17], we attempt to create prompts that can activate ChatGPT's innovative capabilities by directly soliciting suggestions from ChatGPT itself (i.e., self-prompting), as illustrated in the figure. Our experience indicates that self-prompting works best when used after the analyzer has completed a round of responses to research propoals.

Here are some prompts that could be used to make scheme:

1. Develop a research proposal by dissecting the research plan to meet the specified research requirements.
2. Craft a research proposal based on a thorough analysis of the existing research plan to address the research demands.
3. Formulate a research proposal by scrutinizing the research plan in alignment with the research needs.
4. Create a tailored research proposal through an in-depth examination of the research plan to satisfy the research objectives.
5. Design a research proposal by evaluating the research plan to ensure it aligns with the research necessities.

The evaluator will collect all the results from the previous round and provide feedback and suggestions to the analyzer and the planner. This approach has two main benefits. First, the analyzer can clearly understand the specific context of the proposed innovative plan without being misled by other modifications. Second, the analyzer can grasp the strengths and weaknesses of the existing plan, providing guidance for further improvements.

Our preliminary experiments show that when using simple prompts, agents often make confused evaluations based on hallucinatory content (e.g., the analyzer suggests using a distributed architecture for network validation, while the evaluator simply assesses the pros and cons of the distributed architecture, ignoring the evaluation of the solution's completeness). Therefore, we construct the prompt prefix using refined research needs to clarify the agent's intent. Meanwhile, the agent is implicitly required to create a reasonable chain of thought to make more logical decisions. Consequently, we propose an evaluation template consisting of four slots, structured as follows:

Template for prompts to evaluate

{subject background}
The above is a description of the subject background.
My research needs are{research need}
{research plan and proposal}
The above is the research plan and proposal based on my research need. You are an expert in the field of computer networking. You are asked to evaluate the research plan and program in light of the research needs, and you need to assess {assessment metrics}Briefly explain the reason for each logging.

4 Experiment

We detail experiments on the subject of data plane validation to illustrate how NetInno assists researchers in conducting innovative research. In the first round of research, we focused on a distributed validation method proposed by NetInno.

Preliminary scheme

The verification task is decomposed and distributed to multiple nodes for parallel processing, thus meeting the challenge of large-scale network verification. This approach distributes complex verification tasks to multiple nodes to improve processing speed and scalability.

In the new round of research, NetInno suggested a key point proposed in this paper: representing the network as a directed acyclic graph (DAG). Surprisingly, NetInno also explained why the network should be modeled as a DAG. Additionally, NetInno proposed that the task scheduler and validator need to be designed to accomplish distributed validation, which aligns with the basic framework introduced in this paper.

Basic framework

Directed acyclic graph: In most traditional local area networks (Lans) and wide area networks (Wans), while communication is usually two-way, data can flow in both directions. However, **directed graphs can clearly represent the direction of packet forwarding. The structure of acyclic graph is not only suitable for distributed processing, but also conforms to the expectation of packet forwarding.**

- **Task scheduler:** Responsible for assigning subtasks to different nodes
- **Validator:** Completes the tasks specified by the validation scheduler

In the third round of research, we prompted NetInno to analyze the operations of the data plane using reachability verification as an example. NetInno presented a detailed plan for distributed validation based on the DAG data structure, as shown in the figure below.

Key insights

The data plane typically involves examining forwarding tables, routingtables, and access control lists (ACLs) to determine the forward pathof packets. Directed acyclic graph can represent the forward path ofdata packet. Reachability verification needs to be combined with theactual operation of network devices such as routers and switches. Each node calculates the information to be synchronized to theneighboring devices based on the data plane information on its owndevice and the synchronization information received from theneighboring devices. Lightweight communication protocol is designedto reduce the overhead of inter-node communication.

In just three cycles, NetInno, under the operation of a mid-level researcher, analyzed the core design of Croal, a paper from SIGCOMM'23. This demonstrates that our proposed NetInno is highly valuable for innovation in the networking domain. Although NetInno did not abstract DPV (Data Plane Validation) as a counting problem on a DAG in the three rounds of research, NetInno identified that the essence of DPV is to verify whether packet forwarding on the acyclic graph is as expected, which aligns with Croal's insights. Furthermore, NetInno provided more advanced insights into designing lightweight communication protocols and optimizing data structures for node storage and synchronization information in Croal. It should be emphasized that this part of our experiment is based on Kimi. Kimi's literature list for answering questions did not include content related to Croal. Instead, Kimi conducted research through our designed framework, leading to the analysis we needed.

5 Conclusion

This paper presents NetInno, the framework adopts a cyclic strategy to simulate the general process of scientiffc innovation and consists of three core modules: Planner, Analyzer, and Evaluator. It proposes and implements novel research ideas through collaboration between the Planner and Analyzer. the Planner's reasoning quality is signiffcantly enhanced.

In the future, our goal is to explore whether NetInno can support interdisciplinary research. Currently, our framework and prompt strategies are speciffcally tailored for the networking domain. We plan to investigate the applicability of NetInno to other ffelds and explore how to adapt it to various research directions. This includes evaluating the framework's ffexibility and scalability, and identifying new research opportunities through interdisciplinary collaboration.

References

1. Zhao, Y., et al.: Klotski: efficient and safe network migration of large production datacenters. In: Proceedings of the ACM SIGCOMM 2023 Conference, pp. 783–797 (2023)
2. Cao, B., Han, Z., Liang, L., Liu, Y., Wang, J., Xie, J.: Independent innovation or secondary innovation: the moderating of network embedded innovation. Sustainability **14**(22), 14796 (2022)
3. Liu, P., Yuan, W., Fu, J., Jiang, Z., Hayashi, H., Neubig, G.: Pre-train, prompt, and predict: a systematic survey of prompting methods in natural language processing. ACM Comput. Surv. **55**(9), 1–35 (2023)
4. Zhang, T., Huang, X., Zhao, W., Bian, S., Du, P.: LogPrompt: a log-based anomaly detection framework using prompts. In: 2023 International Joint Conference on Neural Networks (IJCNN), pp. 1–8 (2023)
5. Wu, D., et al.: Large language model adaptation for networking. arXiv preprint arXiv:2402.02338 (2024)
6. Zhang, M., Press, O., Merrill, W., Liu, A., Smith, N.A.: How language model hallucinations can snowball. arXiv preprint arXiv:2305.13534 (2023)
7. Zhuang, S., Ma, X., Koopman, B., Lin, J., Zuccon, G.: PromptReps: prompting large language models to generate dense and sparse representations for zero-shot document retrieval. arXiv preprint arXiv:2404.18424 (2024)
8. Feng, S., Park, C.Y., Liu, Y., Tsvetkov, Y.: From pretraining data to language models to downstream tasks: tracking the trails of political biases leading to unfair NLP models. arXiv preprint arXiv:2305.08283 (2023)
9. Kocmi, T., Federmann, C.: Large language models are state-of-the-art evaluators of translation quality. arXiv preprint arXiv:2302.14520 (2023)
10. Peng, K., et al.: Towards making the most of chatgpt for machine translation. arXiv preprint arXiv:2303.13780 (2023)
11. Kung, T.H., et al.: Performance of ChatGPT on USMLE: potential for AI-assisted medical education using large language models. PLoS Digit. Health **2**(2), e0000198 (2023)
12. Zhou, Y., Muresanu, A.I., Han, Z., Paster, K., Pitis, S., Chan, H., Ba, J.: Large language models are human-level prompt engineers. arXiv preprint arXiv:2211.01910 (2022)

13. White, J., et al.: A prompt pattern catalog to enhance prompt engineering with chatgpt. arXiv preprint arXiv:2302.11382 (2023)
14. Wei, J., et al.: Chain-of-thought prompting elicits reasoning in large language models. Adv. Neural. Inf. Process. Syst. **35**, 24824–24837 (2022)
15. Yao, F., et al.: Thinking like an expert: multimodal hypergraph-of-thought (hot) reasoning to boost foundation modals. arXiv preprint arXiv:2308.06207 (2023)
16. Braden, R., Zhang, L., Berson, S., Herzog, S., Jamin, S.: Resource ReSerVation protocol (RSVP) – version 1 functional specification. RFC 2205 (1997)
17. Khan, S.A., Dang-Nguyen, D.-T.: CLIPping the deception: adapting vision-language models for universal deepfake detection. In: Proceedings of the 2024 International Conference on Multimedia Retrieval, pp. 1006–1015 (2024)
18. Xiang, Q., et al.: Toward reproducing network research results using large language models. In: Proceedings of the 22nd ACM Workshop on Hot Topics in Networks, pp. 56–62 (2023)
19. Xiang, Q., et al.: Beyond a centralized verifier: scaling data plane checking via distributed, on-device verification. In: Proceedings of the ACM SIGCOMM 2023 Conference, pp. 152–166 (2023)

A Deep Reinforcement Learning Framework for Sensor Network Deployment in Urban Power Grid Monitoring Optimization Analytics

Cheng Su[1,2], Dachuan Xu[1,3], Shijie Li[4], Hao Wang[5], Xiaohan Jiang[6], Chang Liu[1,2], and Shaohua Wang[1,2](✉)

[1] State Key Laboratory of Remote Sensing and Digital Earth, Aerospace Information Research Institute, Chinese Academy of Sciences, Beijing 100094, China
wangshaohua@aircas.ac.cn

[2] College of Resources and Environment, University of Chinese Academy of Sciences, Beijing 100049, China

[3] Faculty of Geomatics, Lanzhou Jiaotong University, Lanzhou 730070, China

[4] China Southern Power Grid Company Limited, Guangzhou, China

[5] Henan Key Laboratory of Big Data Analysis and Processing, Henan University, Kaifeng 475004, China

[6] School of Architecture and Urban Planning, Lanzhou Jiaotong University, Lanzhou 730070, China

Abstract. As urban power grids grow in scale and complexity, rational deployment of sensor networks is critical to ensure operational security and stability. This study proposes a Deep Reinforcement Learning (DRL) framework for sensor network deployment optimization, integrating cluster-based spatial priority scoring. A case study involving 352 transmission towers in Tianhe District, Guangzhou, is presented. The framework incorporates commercial mathematical programming (Gurobi), Genetic Algorithm, and DRL approaches to systematically compare performance under varying deployment budgets. Experimental results demonstrate that the DRL method achieves high coverage and redundancy with superior computational efficiency and adaptability, effectively addressing complex sensor placement challenges in urban environments. This study offers an efficient and scalable decision-support tool for smart grid maintenance with significant theoretical and practical implications.

Keywords: Deep Reinforcement Learning · Sensor Network Deployment · Power Grid Monitoring · Cluster Analysis · Geospatial Optimization Analytics

1 Introduction

With the rapid acceleration of global urbanization and the advancement of information and communication technologies, smart cities have emerged as the primary trajectory for future urban development [1]. By integrating technologies such as the Internet of Things (IoT), big data, and artificial intelligence (AI), smart cities aim to enable intelligent

T. Qiu et al. (Eds.): CCF ChinaNet 2025, CCIS 2810, pp. 100–113, 2026.
https://doi.org/10.1007/978-981-95-8450-5_8

management of urban infrastructure, thereby fostering livable, efficient, and sustainable urban environments [2]. Among the foundational components of a smart city, the power system plays a pivotal role. A reliable power grid not only underpins industrial production and economic stability but also ensures the continuity of residents' daily lives [3]. However, as energy demands grow increasingly complex and the integration of renewable energy sources continues to rise, urban power grids face unprecedented challenges. These include aging infrastructure [4], heightened vulnerability to extreme weather events [5], and increased risks of cascading failures [6]. In this context, routine and sustained power grid inspection becomes crucial for maintaining the operational stability of urban electricity networks. Effective monitoring can facilitate the timely detection of grid anomalies and safeguard the reliable operation of the power system [7].

In recent years, intelligent multimodal data acquisition sensors integrated with multiple perception modules have been widely deployed and applied in the field of urban environmental monitoring [8]. These sensor systems typically enable the synchronous monitoring of multidimensional environmental variables such as temperature, humidity, atmospheric pollutant concentrations, noise levels, and light intensity. Additionally, they are equipped with high-resolution imaging units and infrared sensing components, facilitating the acquisition of visual information in complex urban scenarios [9]. Perception platforms based on multi-sensor fusion not only offer significant advantages in terms of system construction and operational costs, but also demonstrate strong capabilities in data integration and information extraction [10]. These features highlight the promising application prospects and technical feasibility of such systems for real-time perception and fine-grained monitoring of smart grid operational states.

The deployment of sensor monitoring networks in urban power grids constitutes a complex configuration and optimization problem [11]. The layout of sensors directly impacts the monitoring coverage, cost-effectiveness, and operational reliability of the power grid. Different application scenarios impose varying requirements on sensor deployment, necessitating a comprehensive consideration of factors such as geographic environment, monitoring objectives, resource constraints, and maintenance accessibility [12]. Poorly designed sensor configurations may not only result in resource inefficiencies but also create blind spots in monitoring, thereby compromising the system's ability to detect and respond to critical events in a timely manner.

In power grid condition monitoring systems, the location and deployment strategy of sensor networks is of paramount importance. A key challenge lies in determining the optimal number and placement of sensors under constrained resources to ensure redundant coverage of critical power infrastructure—thereby supporting the stable operation and effective situational awareness of the grid [13]. Existing research has primarily focused on optimizing sensor deployment in transmission and distribution networks, aiming to balance monitoring accuracy and coverage efficiency within budgetary limitations. For instance, Paruta et al. proposed a greedy placement method for distribution network state estimation based on an improved DistFlow model. This approach first estimates voltage and line current state variables at each node in the network, and then applies a heuristic strategy to select an optimal set of measurement points—minimizing sensor count while maintaining estimation errors within acceptable limits [14]. Buason et al.

developed a two-level optimization framework to address sensor deployment for monitoring voltage violations in distribution grids. The upper-level model minimizes sensor investment costs under budget constraints, while the lower-level model employs linear approximations and scenario-based simulations to assess the adaptability and accuracy of the selected layout under diverse operational conditions [15].

Recently, deep learning approaches have also been introduced to deployment optimization task. For instance, DeepMCLP employs graph neural networks to model the Maximum Coverage Location Problem, capturing complex spatial dependencies and feature distributions to achieve fast approximate solutions for large-scale combinatorial optimization tasks [16]. Building on such advances, the incorporation of Deep Reinforcement Learning (DRL) enables the sensor deployment strategy to dynamically adapt and improve through continuous interactions with the environment, effectively addressing complex constraints and sequential decision-making challenges in power grid monitoring [17].

At present, research specifically addressing the optimization of sensor deployment for power grid condition monitoring remains limited. Existing approaches to sensor network optimization in power grids often lack generalizability and are insufficiently adaptable to the complexity of real-world operational scenarios. To address this gap, we develop a mathematical optimization model for sensor deployment tailored to power grid condition monitoring, aiming to achieve an optimal balance between coverage efficiency and dynamic adaptability under resource constraints. Specifically, we introduce a DRL framework to solve the model, enabling the sensor deployment strategy to continuously adjust and improve through interactions with the environment. This data-driven intelligent optimization approach overcomes the limitations of traditional heuristic algorithms in adapting to complex grid environments. It holds significant research value and practical potential, offering meaningful contributions to the construction of resilient and stable urban power grids.

2 Methodology

2.1 Overall Framework

The proposed framework consists of three modules: data preprocessing, optimization modeling, and solving. In the preprocessing stage, spatial features including building density, population density, and road density are extracted and normalized. KMeans clustering is applied, and cluster-based scores are assigned to generate deployment priority indices.

The optimization model takes demand points, candidate deployment points, and priority scores as input. It formulates a sensor deployment problem under coverage constraints.

To solve the model, we implement three methods: Gurobi solver, Genetic Algorithm, and DRL, and visualize the deployment results for comparative analysis (Fig. 1).

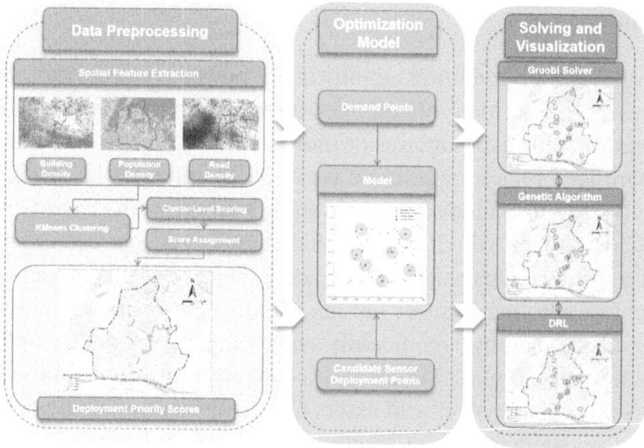

Fig. 1. Overall Framework.

2.2 Cluster-Based Deployment Priority Scoring

To quantify the spatial deployment importance of each monitoring unit, a cluster-based scoring method was designed using normalized urban structure features. Let each monitoring unit i be represented by a three-dimensional feature vector:

$$x_i = \left[population\_density_i, building\_density_i, road\_density_i\right] \in \mathbb{R}^3 \quad (1)$$

These features were normalized to the range [0, 1] to ensure comparability across indicators. A KMeans clustering algorithm was then applied to partition all monitoring units into K groups:

$$\mathcal{C} = \{C_1, C_2, ..., C_K\}, \mathrm{x}_i \in C_k \quad (2)$$

For each cluster C_K, we compute its centroid μ_k, and define its deployment priority score s_k as the Euclidean distance from the origin in the normalized feature space:

$$s_k = \|\mu_k\|_2 = \sqrt{\sum_{j=1}^{3} \mu_{k,j}^2} \quad (3)$$

This score reflects the cumulative intensity of urban activity associated with the cluster. Each monitoring unit i inherits the score of its corresponding cluster:

$$a_i = s_k \text{ if } x_i \in C_k \quad (4)$$

Finally, the scores a_i are normalized to the range [0, 1] to obtain the final deployment priority coefficient a_i^{norm}, which is used as an importance weight in subsequent optimization and decision-making modules:

$$a_i^{\mathrm{norm}} = \frac{a_i - min(a)}{max(a) - min(a)} \quad (5)$$

This method provides a fast, scalable, and spatially interpretable way to incorporate urban heterogeneity into the deployment model without relying on external weights or manually defined classes.

2.3 Optimization Model

In the process of real-time condition monitoring of power grids, the rational deployment of sensor networks is a critical component for achieving automated inspections and early fault detection. However, failures of individual sensors are common due to signal interference, hardware issues, or extreme weather. To enhance the resilience and reliability of transmission tower monitoring, this study introduces the Dual-Coverage Sensor Placement (DCSP) model, which ensures that standby sensors can maintain coverage in the event of a primary sensor failure. The core concept of this model is to guarantee that, in the event of a primary sensor failure, standby sensors can seamlessly take over the monitoring tasks, thereby significantly enhancing the reliability and resilience of the monitoring network. Figure 2 illustrates a conceptual example of the DCSP model: blue dots represent critical power grid assets (e.g., transmission towers), while red stars indicate selected sensor deployment locations. Each sensor has an effective monitoring radius (depicted by red circles), ensuring coverage of nearby assets. In Fig. 2(a), when the primary sensor is operational, both primary and standby sensors function concurrently. In Fig. 2(b), if the primary sensor becomes disconnected, standby (backup) sensors can still provide continuous monitoring.

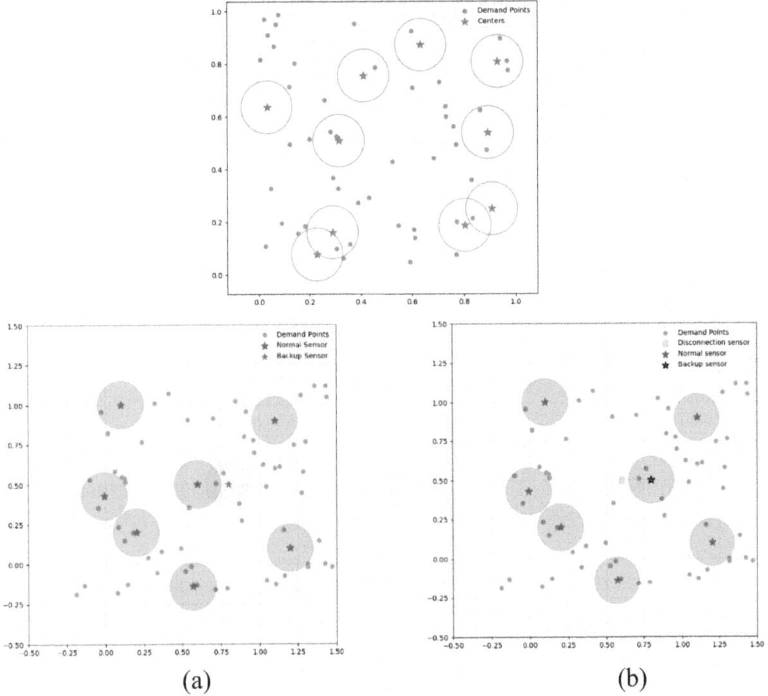

Fig. 2. An example of the DCSP method, where (a) illustrates the normal operational state of the sensors, and (b) depicts the scenario in which one sensor is in a disconnected state.

Optimal sensor deployment in power grid monitoring seeks to determine the optimal number and placement of sensors within a constrained budget, effectively balancing comprehensive monitoring coverage with redundant reliability. This study formulates the problem as a DCSP, aiming to maximize the weighted coverage of critical power grid assets. The model thoroughly accounts for the synergistic interactions between newly deployed and existing sensors to enhance overall system performance.

Objective Functions:

$$MaximizeZ_1 = \sum_i y_i demand_i \tag{6}$$

$$MaximizeZ_2 = \sum_i c_i demand_i \tag{7}$$

Subject to:

$$\sum_{j \in N_i} x_j \geq y_i, \forall i \tag{8}$$

$$\sum_{j \in N_i} x_j - y_i \geq ui, \forall i \tag{9}$$

$$\sum_{j \in N_i} x_j - y_i \geq ui, \forall i \tag{10}$$

$$u_i \leq y_i, \forall i \tag{11}$$

$$\sum_j x_j = p_1 + p_2 \tag{12}$$

$$p_2 = \sum_{c \in C} x_c, c \in C, x_c = 1 \tag{13}$$

$$p_1 + p_2 \leq P, p_1 \geq 0 \tag{14}$$

$$x_j, y_i, c_i \in \{0,1\}, \forall i, j \tag{15}$$

i: A critical power grid asset, such as a transmission tower, transformer, or switch station.

j: A candidate site for sensor deployment.

C: : The set of pre-installed (existing) sensors.

x_j: Binary decision variable; $x_j = 1$ if a sensor is deployed at site j, otherwise 0.

y_i: Binary state variable; $y_i = 1$ if asset i is covered by at least one sensor (primary coverage).

c_i: Binary state variable; $c_i = 1$ if asset i is redundantly covered by at least two sensors (standby coverage).

p_1: Number of new sensors to be deployed.

p_2: Number of pre-installed sensors. In this study,

P: Total budget limit for sensor deployment.

N_i: Set of candidate locations capable of effectively monitoring asset i.

$demand_i$: Importance weight of asset i, which can be determined by factors such as voltage level, topological criticality, failure history, population served, or economic value.

Objective (6) aims to maximize the weighted primary coverage of all critical assets to ensure comprehensive monitoring coverage. Objective (7) seeks to maximize weighted redundant (standby) coverage to enhance network robustness and resilience. Constraint (8) stipulates that an asset is considered primarily covered only if it falls within the range of at least one sensor. Constraint (9) defines redundant coverage: an asset is deemed redundantly covered only when monitored by at least two sensors. Constraint (10) ensures logical consistency by permitting redundant coverage only when primary coverage has already been achieved. Constraints (11) and (12) account for the total number of sensors and mandate the inclusion of all pre-installed sensors in set C. Constraint (13) imposes an overall budget cap. Constraint (14) requires all decision variables to be binary.

In practice, for convenience of calculation, two single objectives are often weighted into a multi-objective optimization function:

$$MaximizeZ = \omega_1 \sum_i y_i demand_i + \omega_2 \sum_i c_i demand_i \tag{16}$$

where ω_1 and ω_2 are weighting coefficients, and $\omega_1 + \omega_2 = 1$. The values of ω_1 and ω_2 are set to 0.2 and 0.8, respectively. This makes our model tend to prioritize ensuring the reliability of coverage for critical assets, emphasizing redundant coverage to enhance the robustness and resilience of the network.

2.4 Deep Reinforcement Learning

DRL has emerged as a promising paradigm for tackling complex combinatorial optimization problems. By enabling an agent to learn through interactions with its environment, DRL autonomously discovers high-quality strategies, particularly for high-dimensional, dynamic, and constraint-heavy decision-making problems. Notably, existing studies have rarely explored how DRL can address location problems like DCSP, where decisions heavily depend on the complex attributes of nodes, such as coverage requirements, redundancy constraints, and budget limitations.

To address the DCSP, we formulate it as a sequential decision-making process solvable by DRL. In this paradigm, an agent learns an optimal policy for deploying sensors by interacting with a simulated power grid environment. The agent's goal is to maximize a cumulative reward signal that reflects the dual objectives of primary and redundant coverage under budget constraints. We model this problem as a Markov Decision Process (MDP) defined by the tuple (S, A, P, R, γ), where the transition probabilities P are determined by the environment dynamics and the discount factor γ is set to 1 for our finite-horizon problem.

State (s_t): At each decision step t, the state s_t must provide the agent with all necessary information to make an informed decision. The state includes: The complete graph structure, including the set of all candidate sites (j), critical assets (i), their importance weights ($demand_i$), and the coverage relationships defined by the sets N_i. The set of sensors selected thus far, $S_t = \{l_1, l_2, \ldots, l_{t-1}\} \cup C$, where C is the set of pre-installed sensors. This also includes the current coverage status y_i and c_i for all assets i) based on S_t, and the remaining budget for new sensors, $P - p_2 - (t - 1)$.

Action (***a***$_t$): An action a_t is the selection of a single new sensor location l_t from the set of available candidate sites that have not yet been chosen. The action space is dynamically masked at each step to exclude already selected sites and to ensure the budget constraint is not violated.

Reward ($\boldsymbol{R}_t$): The reward function is meticulously designed to directly reflect the marginal gain towards the optimization objective defined in Eqs. (17) and (18). Let S_{t-1} be the set of deployed sensors before step t. Let $V(S)$ be the value of the combined objective function for a given set of sensors S:

$$V(S) = \lambda \sum_i y_i(S) \cdot demand_i + (1-\lambda) \sum_i c_i(S) \cdot demand_i \tag{17}$$

where $y_i(S) = 1$ if asset i is covered by at least one sensor in S,and $c_i(S) = 1$ if covered by at least two.When the agent takes action a_t to select location l_t the new sensor set becomes $S_t = S_{t-1} \cup \{l_t\}$. The immediate reward r_t received by the agent is the precise marginal improvement in this value:

$$r_t = V(S_t) - V(S_{t-1}) \tag{18}$$

This dense reward structure provides direct, step-by-step feedback to the agent, guiding it to select sensors that offer the highest immediate contribution to overall coverage.

Our approach leverages a novel encoder-decoder architecture based on the Attention-model framework, specifically tailored for solving combinatorial optimization problems like DCSP. The core innovation lies in replacing conventional Recurrent Neural Networks (RNNs) with a Transformer-based decoder structure in the sequential decision-making process. This design enables the model to more effectively capture complex dependencies among selected nodes when constructing the output sequence.

We employ a Transformer-based encoder to process the entire problem instance, generating powerful contextual embeddings for all candidate locations and critical assets. These embeddings capture the complex spatial and coverage dependencies within the power grid. In the decoder component, a self-regressive Transformer-based decoder generates a sequence of solutions. At each step t, it attends to the encoder's output and the state of previously selected sensors to compute a probability distribution over the set of valid actions. This advanced structure allows the model to effectively reason about the combinatorial nature of the problem and the long-term consequences of each selection.

The model is trained in an episodic manner. In each epoch, batches of DCSP instances are fed to the agent. For each instance, the agent generates a complete solution according to its policy π_θ Rewards and baseline values are computed, and parameters are updated. Performance is periodically checked on a fixed validation set to monitor for generalization and prevent overfitting. Training concludes when validation performance converges, or a maximum epoch limit is reached.

3 Real-World Experiments

3.1 Study Area and Data

This study selects Tianhe District in Guangzhou, China, as a real-world case study area (see Fig. 3). To better support the optimization of transmission tower network monitoring sensor deployment, multiple spatial datasets were integrated for analysis.

The spatial distribution data of transmission towers were obtained from the open-source mapping platform OpenStreetMap (OSM) (https://www.openstreetmap.org, accessed in July 2025), comprising a total of 352 tower locations. The administrative boundary data for Tianhe District were retrieved from the National Geographic Information Resource Directory Service System of China (https://www.webmap.cn/main.do?method=index) to ensure the accurate extraction of tower distributions within the district.

In addition, several supplementary datasets were incorporated to examine the impact of various urban factors on tower placement. The road network data were sourced from OSM, the building footprint data were derived from the dataset published by Zhang et al. [18], and the population grid data were obtained from Chen et al. [19], with a spatial resolution of 100 m × 100 m. All vector data were referenced to the WGS 1984 coordinate system, while the population raster data were projected using the Albers equal-area conic projection to ensure spatial consistency and analytical accuracy.

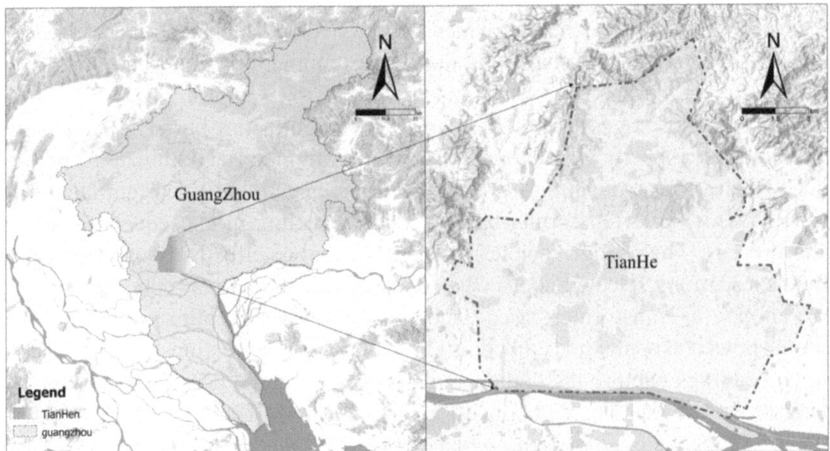

Fig. 3. Study Area.

3.2 Experimental Results

The proposed DRL model is implemented using the PyTorch (v1.11.1) framework in a Python 3.7 environment. All experiments were conducted on a workstation equipped with an Intel Xeon Gold 6530 CPU and an NVIDIA GeForce RTX 4090 GPU with 24 GB of VRAM. To ensure full reproducibility of our experiments, we managed all software dependencies using the Conda environment manager.

In real-world site-selection planning, decision-makers often pre-screen a smaller candidate set from a large pool of potential locations. To simulate this practical scenario, we designed the following data generation strategy: for each problem instance, we randomly sampled 100 candidate sites without replacement from a total of 352 available points to form a new, smaller-scale candidate set. Based on this, we generated synthetic datasets for each task setting, comprising 128,000 training samples, 2,000 validation samples, and 2,000 testing samples.

The core hyperparameters for model training were configured as follows: the total number of epochs was set to 500, and the batch size was 640. We employed the Adam optimizer with a learning rate of 1e−4 to update the model parameters.

To comprehensively evaluate the performance of our DRL model, we benchmarked it against two representative categories of methods:

Exact Solver: We used Gurobi, a state-of-the-art commercial mathematical programming solver. For small- to medium-scale DCSP instances, Gurobi can provide a certifiably optimal solution within a reasonable time. Its output serves as the gold standard for solution quality (Obj_o).

Classic Heuristic Algorithm: We implemented a Genetic Algorithm (GA) as a baseline. The GA is a widely used metaheuristic for combinatorial optimization problems and represents the performance level of traditional optimization techniques.

We adopted the following three core metrics to assess all methods in terms of both solution quality and computational efficiency:

Average Objective Value (Avg-Obj): This metric represents the objective function value of the final solution obtained by a model. It directly reflects the quality of the solution, where a higher value indicates a better solution that covers more asset value.

Optimality Gap (Gap): This metric measures the relative difference between a model's solution and the optimal solution. It is calculated as:

$$Gap = \frac{|Obj_o - Obj_m|}{Obj_o}$$

where Obj_o is the optimal objective value found by Gurobi, and Obj_m is the objective value from the method being evaluated. A smaller Gap indicates that the model's solution is closer to the optimum.

Computation Time (Time): This records the total wall-clock time (in seconds) required for a model or algorithm to produce a final solution from a given input. This metric measures the computational efficiency of the method.

Table 1. Performance Comparison of DRL with Baselines under Different Budgets (M).

Methods	M = 20			M = 25			M = 30		
	Avg-Obj	Time	Gap	Avg-Obj	Time	Gap	Avg-Obj	Time	Gap
Gurobi	217.77	0.21	0.00%	227.25	0.22	0.00%	232.42	0.22	0.00%
GA	210.84	0.45	3.18%	222.45	0.50	2.11%	227.31	0.53	2.20%
DRL	217.68	0.07	0.04%	226.45	0.07	0.35%	231.92	0.09	0.22%

To validate the efficacy of our model, we conducted a comprehensive performance comparison against the industry-standard exact solver, Gurobi, and the classic Genetic Algorithm (GA). As presented in Table 1, the experimental results under various budget scales (M = 20, 25, 30) clearly demonstrate the following:

The most outstanding contribution of our DRL model is its ability to approximate the theoretical optimum with extremely high precision. The data in Table 1 shows that the average optimality gap between our model's solutions and the optimal solutions found by Gurobi was consistently controlled within 0.4% across all test scenarios. Notably, under the M = 20 setting, this gap was a mere 0.04%, achieving a level of quality virtually indistinguishable from the optimum and far superior to the traditional Genetic Algorithm.

While ensuring top-tier solution quality, our DRL model exhibited remarkable computational efficiency. The data reveals that our model's computation time was 2–3 times faster than Gurobi and 5–7 times faster than the Genetic Algorithm. Specifically, in the M = 30 setting, our model required only 0.09 s to find a solution, making it the fastest among all compared methods.

This research successfully demonstrates that DRLearning provides an efficient and precise paradigm for solving combinatorial optimization problems like the DCSP. Our DRL model not only overcomes the shortcomings of traditional heuristics like GA in terms of accuracy and efficiency but also breaks through the bottleneck of exact solvers like Gurobi, which, despite guaranteeing optimality, are relatively time-consuming. Our model strikes an exceptional balance between solution quality, speed, and scalability, offering a powerful decision-support tool for real-world applications that demand the rapid formulation of high-quality deployment plans.

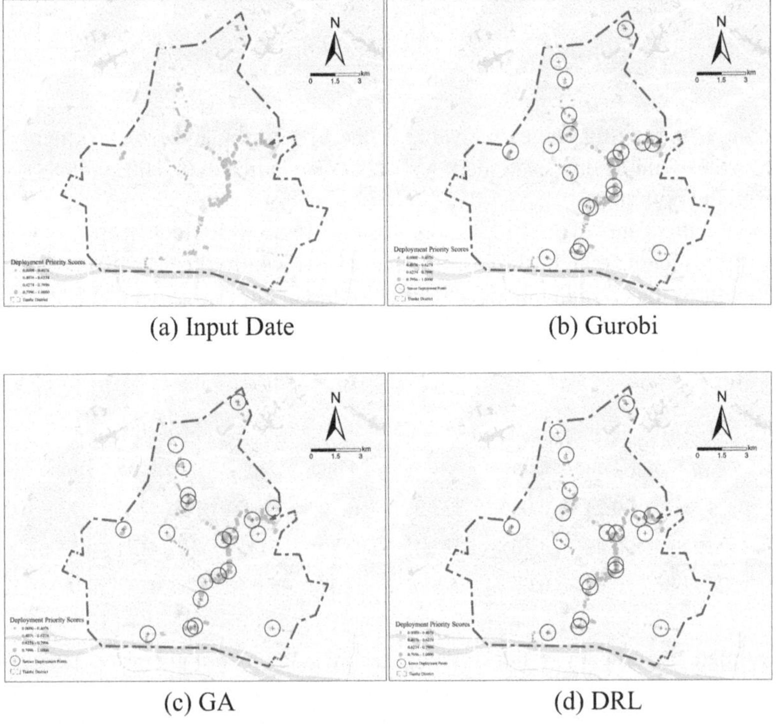

(a) Input Date (b) Gurobi

(c) GA (d) DRL

Fig. 4. Benchmark results of sensor deployment strategies using different optimization methods (a) Input Data, (b) Gurobi, (c) GA, (d) DRL.

By analyzing the varying inspection demands across different locations, the model aims to optimize the sensor deployment strategy to effectively address the complex operational requirements of power grid monitoring in the region. In the visualization of the real-world application, Fig. 4 compares the 20 sensor deployment solutions generated by Gurobi, GA, and DRL, further highlighting the unique advantages of DRL in tackling complex spatial deployment problems and its broad potential in facility location optimization tasks.

4 Conclusion and Discussion

4.1 Conclusion

This study proposed a DRL-based optimization framework for sensor deployment in urban power grid inspection, using Tianhe District in Guangzhou—with 352 transmission towers—as a real-world case study. The framework integrates three solving approaches: a commercial solver (Gurobi), a classic metaheuristic (Genetic Algorithm), and a deep reinforcement learning method.

To incorporate spatial heterogeneity into the deployment process, a cluster-based scoring strategy was designed using normalized urban structure features (population, building, and road densities). This scoring method guided the prioritization of transmission towers during the optimization process, enabling the model to emphasize areas with greater monitoring demand while maintaining overall coverage balance.

Experimental results across various budget constraints (deployment counts of 20, 25, and 30) show that while Gurobi guarantees optimal solutions for small instances, it becomes computationally limited for larger problems. The Genetic Algorithm achieves reasonably good solutions but is sensitive to hyperparameter tuning. The DRL approach, in contrast, achieves near-optimal solutions with minimal computation time, demonstrating superior adaptability and scalability for complex spatial deployment tasks.

Overall, the proposed method proves effective in generating reliable, high-quality deployment plans for power grid monitoring. It achieves a desirable trade-off between primary coverage and redundancy, offering a robust solution for practical infrastructure monitoring in smart city environments.

4.2 Discussion

The presented research addresses the sensor placement challenge in power grid inspection by introducing a reinforcement learning framework capable of learning deployment strategies from complex spatial data. By incorporating cluster-based deployment priority scoring, the framework can dynamically adjust to spatial demand variations without relying on manual weighting or external risk models.

The DRL model demonstrated strong generalization ability across different deployment budgets and consistently produced results with a minimal optimality gap compared to exact solutions. Moreover, its ability to handle large candidate sets and provide fast decisions makes it especially suitable for real-world planning scenarios where both accuracy and efficiency are required.

These findings suggest that DRL-based optimization can serve as a practical and scalable tool for sensor network design in power grid monitoring, supporting preventive maintenance strategies and enhancing system resilience under resource constraints.

Acknowledgments. This research was supported by the China Southern Power Grid Company Limited Science and Technology Project (ZBKJXM20240174), Guangzhou Energy Institute Project, grant number: E4C1020301; the National Key R&D Program of China, grant number: 2023YFF0805904; Talent introduction Program Youth Project of the Chinese Academy of Sciences, grant number: E43302020D, E2Z105010F; the National Natural Science Foundation of China, grant number: 42471495; Deployment Program of AIRCAS, grant number: E4Z202021F.

Disclosure of Interests. The authors have no competing interests to declare that are relevant to the content of this article.

References

1. Yigitcanlar, T., et al.: Understanding 'smart cities': intertwining development drivers with desired outcomes in a multidimensional framework. Cities **81**, 145–160 (2018)
2. Yao, Y.: A review of the comprehensive application of big data, artificial intelligence, and internet of things technologies in smart cities. J. Comput. Methods Eng. Appl. **2**(1), 1–10 (2022)
3. Ghanem, D.A., Mander, S., Gough, C.: "I Think We Need to Get a Better Generator": household resilience to disruption to power supply during storm events. Energy Policy **92**, 171–180 (2016)
4. Smart, I., Nwatu, C.E., Adim, E.M., Okwesa, I.J.: Predictive analytics for aging U.S. electrical infrastructure: leveraging machine learning to enhance grid resilience and reliability. World J. Adv. Res. Rev. **19**(2), 1595–1622 (2023)
5. Dumas, M., Kc, B., Cunliff, C.I.: Extreme weather and climate vulnerabilities of the electric grid: a summary of environmental sensitivity quantification methods. ORNL/TM-2019/1252, 1558514. Oak Ridge National Laboratory, Oak Ridge (2019)
6. Dai, Y., Preece, R., Panteli, M.: Risk assessment of cascading failures in power systems with increasing wind penetration. Electr. Power Syst. Res. **211**, 108392 (2022)
7. Wu, Y., Zhang, P.: Common-Mode (CM) current sensor node design for distribution grid insulation monitoring framework based on multi-objective optimization. IEEE Trans. Ind. Inform. **17**, 3836–3846 (2021)
8. Al-Fuqaha, A., Guizani, M., Mohammadi, M., Aledhari, M., Ayyash, M.: Internet of things: a survey on enabling technologies, protocols, and applications. IEEE Commun. Surv. Tutor. **17**, 2347–2376 (2015)
9. Zheng, K., Zhao, S., Yang, Z., Xiong, X., Xiang, W.: Design and implementation of LPWA-based air quality monitoring system. IEEE Access **4**, 3238–3245 (2016)
10. Liu, Y., Liu, J., Wang, Y., Shi, Y.: Discussion on theory and technology of building robust intelligent power grid in coal mine of China. J. China Coal Soc. **45**(9), 2296–2307 (2020)
11. Zhong, Y., et al.: ReCovNet: reinforcement learning with covering information for solving maximal coverage billboards location problem. Int. J. Appl. Earth Obs. Geoinformation **128**, 103710 (2024)
12. Kumar, S.A., Ovsthus, K., Kristensen, L.M.: An industrial perspective on wireless sensor networks—a survey of requirements, protocols, and challenges. IEEE Commun. Surv. Tutor. **16**, 1391–1412 (2014)

13. Abdulwahid, A.H.: Power grid surveillance and control based on wireless sensor network technologies: review and future directions. J. Phys. Conf. Ser. **1773**, 012004 (2021)
14. Paruta, P., Pidancier, T., Bozorg, M., Carpita, M.: Greedy placement of measurement devices on distribution grids based on enhanced distflow state estimation. Sustain. Energy Grids Netw. **26**, 100433 (2021)
15. Buason, P., Misra, S., Talkington, S., Molzahn, D.K.: A data-driven sensor placement approach for detecting voltage violations in distribution systems. Electr. Power Syst. Res. **232**, 110387 (2024)
16. Liang, H., et al.: Sponet: solve spatial optimization problem using deep reinforcement learning for urban spatial decision analysis. Int. J. Digit. Earth **17**(1), 2299211 (2024)
17. Wang, S., Liang, H., Zhong, Y., Zhang, X., Su, C.: DeepMCLP: solving the MCLP with deep reinforcement learning for urban facility location analytics. SDSS **10** (2023)
18. Zhang, Y., Zhao, H., Long, Y.: CMAB: a multi-attribute building dataset of China. Sci. Data **12** (2025)
19. Chen, Y., Xu, C., Ge, Y., Zhang, X., Zhou, Y.: A 100 m gridded population dataset of china's seventh census using ensemble learning and big geospatial data. Earth Syst. Sci. Data **16**, 3705–3718 (2024)

Corner Navigation Algorithm Design with NLOS Sensing for Mobile Robots

Beichen Yu, Haiming Jin, and Guiyun Fan(✉)

Shanghai Jiao Tong University, Shanghai, China
{polariybc,jinhaiming,fgy726}@sjtu.edu.cn

Abstract. In order to achieve efficient and reliable destination reaching for indoor navigation, mobile robots must accurately perceive their surroundings utilizing multi-modal sensors, dynamically avoid various obstacles, and plan optimal trajectories. In practice, there usually exist obstacles (e.g., walls, cabinets) blocking the sight of mobile robots when they reach the corner or the intersections. Sensors equipped on mobile robots like LiDAR and depth cameras often fail to detect occluded pedestrians and obstacles, potentially leading to suboptimal path planning. Therefore, enabling around-corner sensing can help prevent potential collision by triggering better path planning. For various sensors equipped on mobile robots, mmWave radar provides the opportunity to perceive conditions of around-corner obstacles via multi-bounce signal reflection through wall. In this paper, we achieve the non-line-of-sight (NLOS) sensing by utilizing mmWave Radar with LiDAR assistance. Furthermore, we propose an obstacle-aware corner navigation algorithm based on reinforcement learning (RL) methods, which leverages the NLOS sensing results for corner navigation. Besides, in order to address the challenge that the position and orientation of the mmWave radar significantly influence the performance of NLOS sensing, we design a specialized RL architecture where mmWave radar's instant observations are embedded into the optimization objective for path planning. Experiments show that our proposed method enables more accurate NLOS sensing for mobile robot corner navigation, and significantly outperforms the baseline method with respect to the navigation success rate.

Keywords: indoor navigation · millimeter-wave radar · non-line-of-sight sensing · reinforcement learning

1 Introduction

With the remarkable progress in artificial intelligence (AI) and robotics technologies, indoor mobile robot navigation algorithms have achieved significant maturity. A key challenge in this field is enabling mobile robots to navigate safely among pedestrians by utilizing sensors such as LiDAR and depth cameras for environmental perception and collision-free path planning. While existing

T. Qiu et al. (Eds.): CCF ChinaNet 2025, CCIS 2810, pp. 114–129, 2026.
https://doi.org/10.1007/978-981-95-8450-5_9

algorithms [1–3] achieve satisfactory performance in open spaces, they face significant limitations at corridor corners and intersections. Due to occlusion by objects such as walls and cabinets, pedestrians and obstacles around the corner remain undetected by conventional vision-based sensors, often leading to suboptimal planning and potential collisions.

To overcome this challenge, NLOS sensing technologies present a viable and innovative solution. Recent studies in intelligent sensing [4–6] have demonstrated that Frequency-Modulated Continuous-Wave (FMCW) millimeter-wave (mmWave) radar can detect NLOS targets by leveraging the multi-bounce signal reflection through wall. This capability is critical for navigating complex indoor corners where occlusions are prevalent. Building upon this foundation, our research employs FMCW millimeter-wave radar to enable mobile robot navigation systems to detect obstacles concealed around corners, facilitating proactive and adaptive path planning adjustments. Furthermore, since radar performance is highly sensitive to the robot's pose (position and orientation), our approach requires tight coordination between global path planning and local motion control to maximize the NLOS sensing quality of radar.

Based on the NLOS sensing technology, we formulate the corner navigation problem as a *partially observable markov decision process (POMDP)* [7], with carefully designed observation and action spaces, along with a reward function to explicitly optimize sensing performance. In order to solve the POMDP, we apply the proximal policy optimization (PPO) algorithm [8] with a dedicated actor-critic neural network architecture to train the navigation policy. Our proposed method enables the mobile robots to simultaneously enhance the NLOS sensing performance and make wiser navigation decisions to traverse corners safely.

For the experiments, we first integrates the custom-developed mmWave radar simulation module in Webots in order to perform NLOS sensing. We validate that the FMCW mmWave radar could achieve accurate NLOS detection with the assistance of LiDAR. Then, we carry out the training and testing algorithms in the Webots simulation environment. Comparative results against baseline methods demonstrate the superiority of our algorithm in corner navigation scenarios. Experimental results demonstrate that our method achieves up to a 43% improvement for the navigation success rate compared to baseline approaches.

The main contributions of this work are summarized as follows.

- We achieve NLOS sensing by utilizing mmWave Radar with LiDAR assistance and propose the obstacle-aware corner navigation algorithm based on RL methods.
- We design a specialized RL framework that optimizes radar sensing quality to improve navigation performance, leveraging mutual interactions between robot actions and observations for path planning.
- We validate our method through both real-world experiments and simulations. Experiments show that our proposed method significantly outperforms the baseline method with respect to the navigation success rate.

2 Related Works

NLOS Perception at Corners. Indoor mobile robot navigation struggles at corners where conventional sensors fail to detect occluded obstacles and pedestrians, making NLOS perception a key focus to tackle such limitations. Recent NLOS techniques detect occluded objects via wall-reflected signals, typically using optical, radio-frequency, or acoustic methods. Optical approaches, such as ultrafast time-of-flight imaging, offer high precision. Velten et al. [9] use pulsed lasers and scanning cameras for 3D reconstruction, and Seidel et al. [10] introduce an active corner camera for NLOS snapshots. However, these methods suffer from prohibitive computational costs and latency issues that preclude real-time navigation performance. Compared to them, radio-frequency methods are more practical. FMCW mmWave radar [11] enables NLOS detection by analyzing reflected intermediate frequency signals to extract position and velocity. WiFi-based systems, such as Choi et al. [12], offer low-cost NLOS detection via deep learning but lack velocity resolution. RIS-enhanced radar [13] improves weak multipath signals but requires additional hardware. Acoustic methods like Boger et al. [14] use broadband noise and microphone arrays for passive localization, but are vulnerable to noise and cannot estimate velocity. In summary, existing NLOS approaches, i.e., optical [9,10], WiFi-based [12], acoustic [14], and RIS-aided radar [13], primarily address detection and tracking tasks, yet remain largely decoupled from integrated indoor navigation frameworks. Our work advances this line by combining FMCW mmWave radar, as in [4], with RL-based planning to achieve real-time, velocity-aware navigation through occluded corners, without relying on additional hardware.

RL for Indoor Navigation. RL has emerged as a promising paradigm for indoor robot navigation, offering better adaptability and real-time decision-making than traditional planning algorithms. However, few studies explore RL navigation based solely on radar sensing. Leiva et al. [15] train a neural network on 2D LiDAR data, achieving high success rates in static simulations. Kästner et al. [16] integrate RL into ROS by replacing conventional local planners (e.g., dynamic window approach [17] or timed elastic band [18]), and later introduce a policy switcher for adaptive strategy selection [19]. Yet, these methods are not specialized for corner scenarios, where occlusions limit LiDAR effectiveness, nor do they incorporate perception-quality-aware planning or account for dynamic, pedestrian-rich environments. Meanwhile, RL-based crowd navigation has also been explored. Monaci et al. [1] combine RL with imitation learning in a vision-based framework; Yao et al. [2] fuse LiDAR and depth data in a map-aware model; Matsuzaki et al. [3] employ distributed RL for pedestrian behavior modeling. These methods rely on visual or multi-sensor input [1,2], operate in less constrained spaces, and lack perception-quality optimization. Corner navigation remains underexplored: Perez et al. [20] study confined-space navigation, but their method offers limited innovation. In contrast, our work directly addresses corner-specific challenges through FMCW mmWave radar and a perception-aware RL framework, enabling occlusion-robust, velocity-informed planning in dynamic indoor environments.

3 System Overview

3.1 Overall Framework

The proposed corner navigation system for mobile robots consists of two core components: a LiDAR-aided mmWave radar NLOS sensing module and a RL based corner navigation algorithm. These components work synergistically to enable safe and efficient corner navigation for mobile robots.

The first component, LiDAR-aided mmWave radar NLOS sensing module, leverages the complementary strengths of LiDAR and FMCW mmWave radar. LiDAR provides reliable detection of line-of-sight (LOS) obstacles (e.g., visible walls and nearby static/dynamic obstacles) within its field of view. In contrast, mmWave radar extends environmental awareness to NLOS regions by utilizing multiple reflections of millimeter-wave signals between walls and occluded targets, enabling the detection of pedestrians and obstacles on the other side of corners. The raw point clouds from both sensors are preprocessed into a unified $8\,\text{m}\times 8\,\text{m}$ grid map centered on the robot, fusing LOS and NLOS obstacle information to form a comprehensive environmental representation.

The second component, RL based corner navigation algorithm, is designed to optimize the robot's navigation policy while enhancing NLOS sensing quality. The problem is formulated as a partially observable markov decision process to model the partial observability of NLOS obstacles. A proximal policy optimization algorithm with an actor-critic architecture is employed. The actor network outputs continuous velocity commands (linear velocity v and angular velocity ω) to navigate the robot, while the critic network evaluates state values to guide policy updates. The reward function is specifically designed to balance navigation efficiency, collision avoidance, and NLOS sensing optimization, encouraging the robot to adjust its pose for better radar sensing.

In the proposed framework, PPO training is performed offline, while online inference involves a forward pass through a lightweight neural network, which typically completes within a few milliseconds on embedded GPUs or high-performance CPUs. The mmWave radar signal processing adopts standard FFT-based range-Doppler estimation and Kalman filter fusion, whose end-to-end latency on comparable platforms is generally within tens of milliseconds. This overall processing pipeline is therefore well within the time budget for low-speed indoor navigation tasks, ensuring real-time responsiveness.

3.2 Problem Description

Given the partial observability induced by corner occlusions in indoor environments, the robot must make navigation decisions based on incomplete sensory inputs. The robot operates in a 2D workspace $\mathcal{W}$ with static and dynamic obstacles, where some of which reside in NLOS regions beyond corners. At each timestep t, the robot receives an observation $o_t \in \mathcal{O}$ derived from its onboard sensors, which include both LOS point clouds from LiDAR and partial NLOS information inferred from mmWave radar. Note that the quality and coverage of NLOS sensing depend heavily on the robot's pose $p_t \in \mathcal{P}$.

The core problem this paper investigated is to learn a navigation policy $\pi(a_t|o_t)$ that maps partial observations to continuous control actions $a_t \in \mathcal{A}$, such that the robot reaches its goal $g \in \mathcal{W}$ efficiently while avoiding collisions and actively improving its NLOS perception. Above problem is formulated as a *partially observable markov decision process* (POMDP), and the reward function $R(s_t, a_t)$ is specifically shaped to encourage both navigation performance and enhanced sensing coverage in occluded regions.

4 LiDAR-Aided mmWave Radar NLOS Sensing

In this section, we propose a LiDAR-aided mmWave radar NLOS sensing module for mobile robot corner navigation. Specifically, we first present the real-world feasibility verification experiments, including the validation of NLOS perception capability for static and dynamic obstacles and the analysis of how robot pose affects sensing performance. After that, we detail the data processing pipelines for LiDAR and mmWave radar, covering signal analysis, feature extraction, and noise suppression to ensure reliable LOS and NLOS obstacle perception. Finally, we introduce the spatiotemporal calibration and grid-based fusion methods that integrate multi-sensor data into a unified environmental representation for comprehensive corner obstacle awareness.

4.1 Feasibility Verification

To verify the feasibility of NLOS perception using LiDAR and mmWave radar, and the impact of robot pose on perception quality, we build a real-world experimental platform, and conduct dedicated verification experiments.

We first conduct an experiment to test whether FMCW mmWave radar can effectively detect moving pedestrians behind corners. The experimental setup is configured as shown in Fig. 1(a) and Fig. 1(b). Specifically, the radar is fixed at the corner with a fixed orientation, while a static obstacle (simulating a wall or container) and a pedestrian walking linearly at 0.8 m/s are placed on the occluded side. We collect a total of 100 frames of radar data and process them using Range FFT, Doppler FFT, and CFAR clustering [21]. The processing results show clear detection of static obstacles as stable point clusters in the radar point cloud and continuous trajectory points of the moving pedestrian (Fig. 1(c)).

Another experiment focuses on validating the feasibility of active perception optimization through robot pose adjustments. We test 6 radar positions (A-F) and 3 orientations (0°, 30°, 45° relative to the y-axis) with static obstacles placed at 6 locations, while recording detection success rates. The experimental layout, including radar position distribution, obstacle placement, and orientation

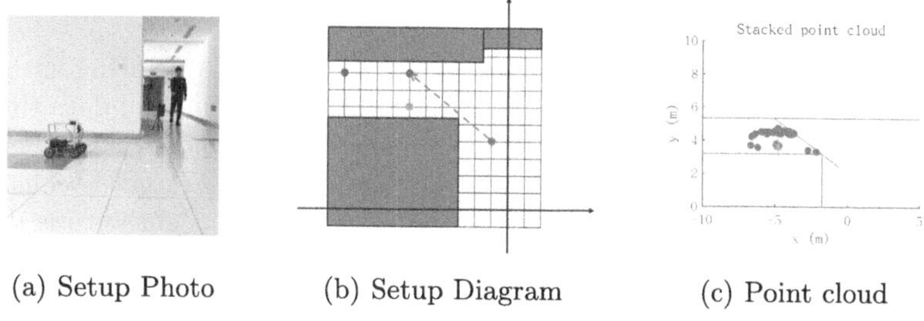

(a) Setup Photo (b) Setup Diagram (c) Point cloud

Fig. 1. Experiment setup and results for NLOS obstacle detection

settings, is illustrated in Fig. 2(a) and Fig. 2(b). Results indicate that obstacles are clearly detected only when the radar is positioned at locations D-F with 30°/45° orientations, as visualized in the valid perception point cloud (Fig. 2(c)). In contrast, no obstacles can be detected when the radar is at positions A-C or in a 0° orientation, which is attributed to blocked reflection paths (Fig. 2(d)). This confirms that robot pose adjustments can effectively influence NLOS perception quality.

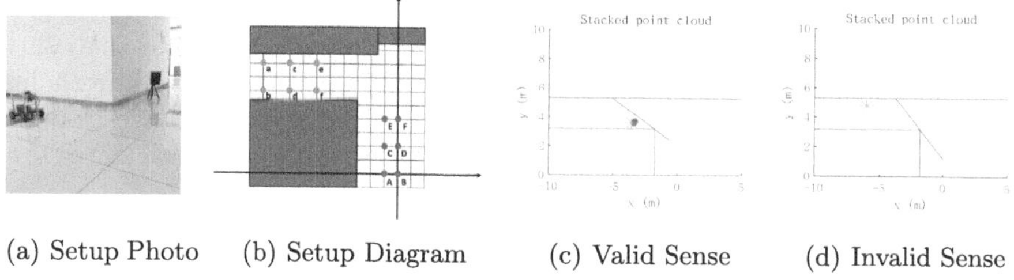

(a) Setup Photo (b) Setup Diagram (c) Valid Sense (d) Invalid Sense

Fig. 2. Experiment setup and results for the impact of radar pose on NLOS sensing

In conclusion, the verification experiments demonstrate that FMCW mmWave radar is capable of effectively achieving NLOS sensing for both static obstacles and moving pedestrians behind corners. The stable point clusters representing static obstacles and the continuous trajectory points of dynamic pedestrians in the processed radar data clearly verify this capability. Additionally, the experiments confirm that robot pose adjustments play a crucial role in optimizing NLOS perception quality. Obstacles could only be detected when the radar is positioned at D - F with 30°/45° orientations, while positions A - C or a 0° orientation lead to no detection due to blocked reflection paths. These findings strongly support the use of mmWave radar for NLOS detection in complex scenarios and highlight the significance of proper robot pose selection for enhancing NLOS perception performance.

4.2 Data Processing

LiDAR Data Processing. The Leishen M10 2D LiDAR, operating with 360° scanning, 10 Hz frequency, and 25 m range, acquires environmental data through laser pulse emission and reflection. For each laser beam, the time delay between emission and reception is measured, and the distance to the target is calculated using the formula $d = \frac{c \cdot t}{2}$ (where c is the speed of light and t is the time delay). Combined with angular resolution data, the 2D coordinates (x, y) in the LiDAR coordinate system are derived as $x = d \cdot \cos(\theta)$ and $y = d \cdot \sin(\theta)$ (where θ is the scanning angle relative to the reference direction). After a full 360° scan, the collected distance, angle, and intensity information (related to surface reflectivity) forms the LOS obstacle point cloud, which undergoes preprocessing steps such as denoising and ground segmentation to filter valid obstacle points.

mmWave Radar Data Processing. The Texas Instruments AWR1843 FMCW mmWave radar (76–81 GHz, 4 GHz bandwidth) processes signals through multi-step operations to generate NLOS perception point clouds. First, the received reflected signals are mixed to produce intermediate-frequency (IF) signals containing distance and velocity information. Range FFT is applied to the IF signals to extract target distance, calculated as $R = \frac{c \cdot f_d}{2 \cdot B}$ (where f_d is the frequency shift, B is the bandwidth). Doppler FFT is then used to derive relative velocity via the Doppler frequency shift $f_D = \frac{2v}{\lambda}$ (where v is target velocity, λ is signal wavelength). Subsequently, CFAR clustering [21] is employed to suppress noise and group valid targets: CFAR dynamically sets detection thresholds based on local noise levels, while clustering aggregates points in range-Doppler space to identify obstacle clusters. Finally, the MUSIC algorithm calculates target coordinates, and the point cloud is mapped from radar coordinates to world coordinates. After filtering based on theoretical NLOS range and reflection path constraints, the final mmWave radar point cloud is generated, containing positions (x_j, y_j) and velocities (v_{xj}, v_{yj}) of NLOS obstacles.

4.3 Data Fusion and Calibration

To integrate perception data from LiDAR and mmWave radar for corner navigation, spatiotemporal calibration and grid-based fusion are implemented, focusing on LiDAR's LOS range perception, mmWave radar's dual perception of NLOS and LOS ranges, and data alignment to distinguish relay reflection point clouds from NLOS object point clouds.

Spatial calibration unifies the coordinate systems of the two sensors mounted on the robot by determining extrinsic parameters (rotation matrix and translation vector) through structural measurements, enabling accurate coordinate transformation for data alignment. Temporal synchronization relies on ROS timestamps to align sampling moments, ensuring time consistency of perception data.

For data fusion, a grid-based approach is adopted. LiDAR point clouds and mmWave radar point clouds are both projected onto an 8 m×8 m grid map centered on the robot. This fused grid map integrates LOS obstacles from LiDAR and NLOS targets from radar, each labeled with position and motion state, serving as input to the RL model for comprehensive environmental perception.

5 RL-Based Corner Navigation Algorithm

The core task of this study is defined as *corner navigation with NLOS sensing*, which requires mobile robots to traverse corridor corners safely while avoiding both LOS and NLOS obstacles (e.g., pedestrians) that are occluded by walls. Traditional navigation algorithms relying on LiDAR or depth cameras often fail in such scenarios due to incomplete environmental perception caused by wall occlusion.

RL is well-suited for this task because it enables robots to learn optimal decision-making strategies through interaction with dynamic environments, even when environmental information is partially observable. Its ability to learn from trial-and-error interactions makes it ideal for navigating corners, where occlusions introduce uncertainties that traditional planning methods struggle to handle. Specifically, we formulate the corner navigation problem as a Partially Observable Markov Decision Process (POMDP) [7], which explicitly models the uncertainty and partial observability inherent in NLOS scenarios.

Unlike existing multi-sensor fusion reinforcement learning approaches that only combine sensor data at the input level, our method also integrates a perception quality metric into the reward function. This dual-level fusion allows the policy to jointly optimize path efficiency and sensing reliability, a design choice that is rarely explored in the literature and that contributes to robust performance across varying indoor layouts.

5.1 Partially Observable Markov Decision Process

The corner navigation problem is formalized as a POMDP defined by the tuple $\langle S, A, T, R, \Omega, O, \gamma \rangle$. This tuple encapsulates core elements of the decision-making process, where S represents the state space, A is the action space, $T(s' \mid s, a)$ is the state transition function, $R(s, a)$ is the reward function, Ω is the observation space, $O(o \mid s, a)$ is the observation probability, and γ is the discount factor. Each component is designed to capture the characteristics of NLOS navigation and defined as follows.

- **State Space (S).** Encompasses the complete environmental state, including the robot's pose (position (x, y), velocity (v_x, v_y), orientation θ), target position (x_g, y_g), and full states (positions and velocities) of all static and dynamic obstacles. This space is partially unobservable due to wall occlusion.
- **Observation Space (Ω).** Integrates multi-sensor data to form perceivable information $o = \{o_{pos}, o_{vel}, o_{rot}, o_{goal}, o_{lidar}, o_{radar}\}$, where $o_{pos}, o_{vel}, o_{rot}$ represent the robot's current position, velocity, and orientation, o_{goal} is the target position, o_{lidar} is the LiDAR point cloud $l_{pcl} = \{p_1, p_2, \cdots, p_m\}$ for LOS obstacles, o_{radar} is the NLOS perception result $l_{nlos} = \{a_1, a_2, \cdots, a_n\}$ with $a_j = \{x_j, y_j, v_{xj}, v_{yj}\}$ from mmWave radar.

- **Action Space (A).** The robot's action space is defined by continuous control signals $a = (v, \omega)$, where $v \in [0, v_{max}]$ is linear velocity and $\omega \in [-\omega_{max}, \omega_{max}]$ is angular velocity. For the Ackermann-steered robot, these velocities are converted to wheel controls using kinematic equations [22] as follows. The turning radius is denoted as $r = \frac{v}{\omega}$, left/right rear wheel speeds are $v_l = v \cdot \frac{r-0.5w}{r}$, $v_r = v \cdot \frac{r+0.5w}{r}$ where w is wheelbase, front wheel angles is $\theta_l = \tan^{-1}\left(\frac{h}{r-0.5w}\right)$, $\theta_r = \tan^{-1}\left(\frac{h}{r+0.5w}\right)$, where h is wheel track. Actions are constrained by the minimum turning radius r_{min}, requiring $|\omega_t| < |v_t|/r_{min}$.
- **Reward Function (R).** The reward function is designed to balance navigation efficiency, safety, and NLOS perception quality. It consists of six components: R_g denotes the target arrival reward, R_p the progress reward, R_c the collision penalty, R_m the stagnation penalty, R_r the smooth movement reward, and R_s the NLOS perception reward. The corresponding definitions are as follows.

$$R_g = \begin{cases} W_g, & \text{if } \|p_t - p_g\|_2 \le D_g, \\ 0, & \text{otherwise}, \end{cases} \quad R_c = \begin{cases} W_c, & \text{if collision occurs}, \\ 0, & \text{otherwise}, \end{cases}$$

$$R_r = w_r \cdot (v_t - w_\omega \cdot \omega_t), \ R_s = w_s \cdot n_t, \ R_p = w_p \cdot (\|p_{t-1} - p_g\|_2 - \|p_t - p_g\|_2),$$

$$R_m = \begin{cases} W_m, & \text{if } \|p_t - p_{t-1}\|_2 \le D_m, \\ 0, & \text{otherwise}. \end{cases}$$

The total reward at time t is the sum of all components:

$$R_t = R_g + R_p + R_c + R_m + R_r + R_s.$$

- **State Transition (T).** The state transition $T(s, a, s')$ defines the probability of transitioning from state s to s' after action a, capturing dynamics like obstacle movement and robot motion noise.
- **Observation Probability (O).** The observation probability $O(o|s, a)$ quantifies the likelihood of obtaining observation o from state s after action a, accounting for sensor noise and NLOS perception uncertainties.
- **Discount Factor (γ).** The discount factor $\gamma \in [0, 1)$ balances immediate and future rewards, with long-term cumulative reward $G_t = \sum_{k=0}^{\infty} \gamma^k R_{t+k+1}$.

5.2 Solution Method

To solve the corner navigation problem formulated as a POMDP, we adopt the Proximal Policy Optimization (PPO) algorithm, which is well-suited for handling continuous action spaces and partial observability in NLOS scenarios. This framework integrates policy learning (Actor) and value estimation (Critic) to enable the robot to learn optimal navigation strategies through interaction with the dynamic environment.

The Actor-Critic architecture consists of two key components with distinct roles. The Actor Network is responsible for generating continuous actions based on environmental observations, mapping inputs to velocity commands $a = (v, \omega)$ where v is linear velocity and ω is angular velocity. Its input includes the fused $8\,\mathrm{m} \times 8\,\mathrm{m}$ grid map o_{map} (integrating LiDAR LOS obstacles and mmWave radar NLOS obstacles), robot state $o_{\text{robot}} = \{o_{\text{pos}}, o_{\text{vel}}, o_{\text{rot}}\}$ (position, velocity, orientation), and target position o_{goal}. The network uses a multi-branch feature fusion structure: convolutional layers process o_{map} to extract spatial obstacle features, while multi-layer perceptrons (MLPs) handle low-dimensional states o_{robot} and o_{goal} with ReLU activation. These features are concatenated and fed into shared fully connected layers, with the Actor head outputting actions via Tanh activation, constrained by the robot's kinematic limits (e.g., minimum turning radius).

The Critic Network shares the same feature extraction backbone as the Actor to ensure consistent environmental understanding, estimating state values $V(o)$ that quantify the expected cumulative reward of the current observation. It evaluates the quality of actions selected by the Actor through advantage estimation $A = R + \gamma V(o') - V(o)$, where R is the immediate reward, o' is the next observation, and γ is the discount factor, providing feedback to guide policy updates.

PPO enhances training stability through its clipped surrogate objective, which limits excessive policy drift during updates. The core loss function for the Actor is:

$$L_{\text{CLIP}} = \mathbb{E}\left[\min\left(r_t \hat{A}_t, \text{clip}(r_t, 1-\epsilon, 1+\epsilon)\hat{A}_t\right)\right], \tag{1}$$

where $r_t = \pi_\theta(a_t|o_t)/\pi_{\theta_{\text{old}}}(a_t|o_t)$ is the ratio of new to old policy probabilities, $\hat{A}_t$ is the generalized advantage estimate (GAE), and $\epsilon = 0.2$ is the clipping threshold. The Critic optimizes via mean squared error loss between predicted values and GAE-based target values $L_{\text{VF}} = \mathbb{E}[(V(o_t) - V_{\text{target}})^2]$.

Training proceeds in iterative episodes where the Actor collects trajectories by interacting with the environment; GAE computes advantages and target values; and the Actor and Critic are updated via mini-batch gradient descent with gradient clipping (threshold = 1.0) to prevent instability. The network architecture is visualized in Fig. 3, illustrating the multi-branch fusion and dedicated Actor/Critic heads.

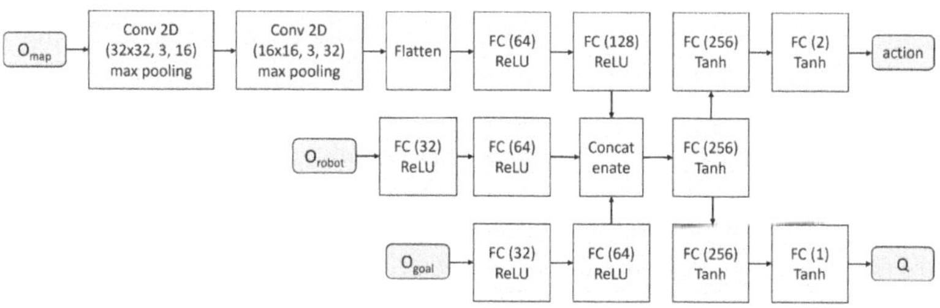

Fig. 3. PPO Actor-Critic network architecture.

6 Experiments

To validate the effectiveness and superiority of the proposed corner navigation algorithm, this section focuses on performance evaluation experiments in simulated environments, including experimental setup, evaluation metrics, design, and result analysis.

6.1 Experimental Setup

For the feasibility verification experiments, the real-world experimental platform is deployed in a corridor corner scenario with the following components:

- *Robot Platform*: Wheeltec R550 (AKM) PLUS Ackermann robot (max speed 1.3 m/s, min turning radius 0.77 m, ROS-controlled).
- *Sensors*: Leishen M10 2D LiDAR (360° scanning, 10 Hz, 25 m range) for LOS obstacle detection; Texas Instruments AWR1843 FMCW mmWave radar (76–81 GHz, 4 GHz bandwidth, 200 m range) for NLOS perception.
- *Environment*: 214.5 cm-wide corridor corner with 60 cm×60 cm positioning tiles. Static obstacles (boxes) and dynamic pedestrians (0.5–1 m/s) are placed on the occluded side of the corner (Fig. 4).

Fig. 4. Experimental setup for indoor Corner Navigation

The mounting position and height of the mmWave radar, as well as its relative placement to the LiDAR, were selected to provide unobstructed sensing coverage and stable fusion geometry, minimizing mutual interference between sensors. Within these typical installation ranges, the sensing coverage and fusion performance remain stable, so the navigation performance is expected to be robust to small variations in these parameters. A systematic sensitivity analysis is left for future work involving broader hardware configurations.

The training and performance evaluation experiments are conducted in the Webots platform, selected for its high-fidelity physics engine and customizable sensor modeling capabilities [23]. A custom mmWave radar module is developed to simulate multi-path reflections, incorporating reflection path calculations (based on wall geometry and obstacle positions) and valid path constraints (no occlusion, within radar field of view) to enable realistic NLOS obstacle perception simulation. Three representative corridor environments are designed: L-shaped single corner, two consecutive L-shaped corners, and a complex scenario with L-shaped and T-shaped corners, each including static obstacles (walls, cabinets) and dynamic pedestrians (moving at 0.3–1 m/s with random trajectories) using the Husarion ROSbot 2.0 robot model (Fig. 5(a)).

Although the real-world experiments were conducted primarily in indoor corridor corner scenarios, the simulation environments covered single-corner, double-corner, T-shaped, and L-shaped layouts with varying obstacle densities. These scenarios exhibit sufficient geometric diversity to demonstrate the robustness of the proposed method and suggest its potential applicability to more complex environments.

The LiDAR-only baseline was chosen as it represents the most widely adopted sensing modality for indoor navigation and provides a clear reference to quantify the contribution of the proposed NLOS sensing fusion. This baseline is implemented using the same RL framework as the proposed method, but without mmWave radar input or NLOS-related reward shaping, so that any performance difference can be attributed to the additional sensing modality and reward design. The PPO algorithm [8] is used with 5000 training epochs, with key parameters including clip threshold $\epsilon = 0.2$, discount factor $\gamma = 0.99$, GAE parameter $\lambda = 0.95$ [24], and Actor/Critic learning rates of 2.5×10^{-4} and 1.0×10^{-3}, respectively. While incorporating additional advanced navigation algorithms or alternative NLOS sensing methods as baselines would provide a broader evaluation, the current LiDAR-only baseline offers a clear and controlled reference for assessing the impact of the proposed NLOS sensing fusion. Expanding the benchmark set remains a meaningful direction for future work.

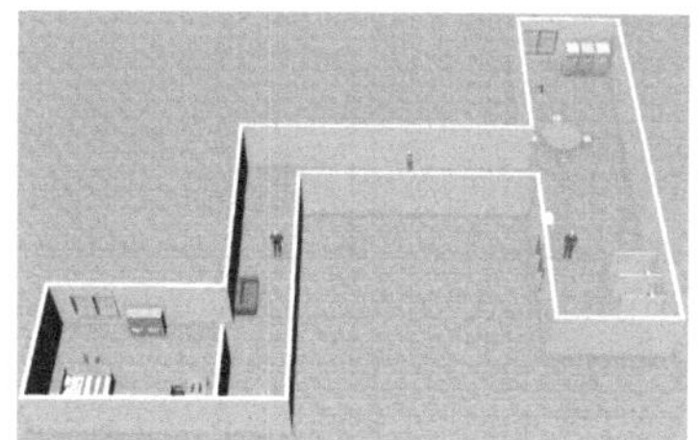

(a) Simulation Environment

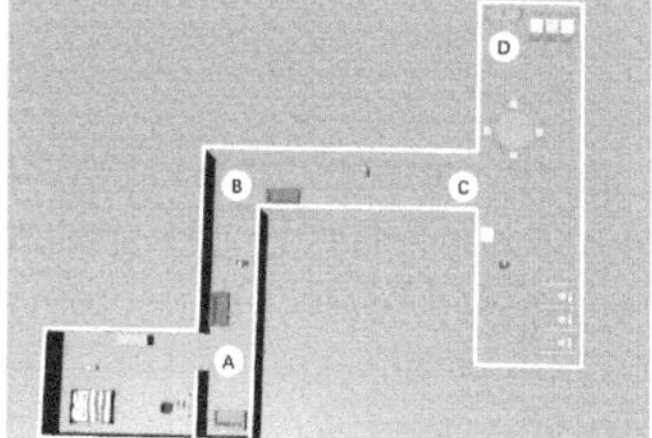

(b) Navigation Target Positions

Fig. 5. Simulation environment

6.2 Performance Evaluation Design

The evaluation metrics include navigation success rate (ratio of trials reaching the target without collision), average navigation time/distance in successful trials (reflecting efficiency), average cumulative reward per trial (indicating alignment with navigation objectives), and all-trial averages (time and distance including failed trials to assess overall robustness).

Four target positions are tested to evaluate performance under varying navigation complexities (Fig. 5(b)): Position A (LOS scenario with no occlusion), Position B (single L-shaped corner with occluded dynamic obstacles), Position C (two consecutive L-shaped corners), and Position D (complex scenario with two L-shaped corners + one T-shaped corner). Each scenario is repeated for 100 trials with both the proposed algorithm and the baseline method.

6.3 Results and Analysis

Performance comparisons across scenarios are summarized in Tables 1, 2, 3 and 4. In the LOS scenario (Position A), both algorithms achieve 100% success, confirming comparable basic navigation capability when obstacles are visible, with the proposed algorithm showing slightly higher efficiency (5.35±0.75 s vs. 5.96±0.48 s).

Table 1. Performance comparison at Position A (LOS scenario)

Metric	Proposed Algorithm	Baseline
Success Rate	100%	100%
Avg. Navigation Time (s)	5.35±0.75	5.96±0.48
Avg. Navigation Distance (m)	5.68±0.87	6.36±0.50
Avg. Cumulative Reward	56.73	61.65
All-Trial Avg. Time (s)	5.35±0.75	5.96±0.48
All-Trial Avg. Distance (m)	5.68±0.87	6.36±0.50

In the single corner scenario (Position B), the proposed algorithm outperform the baseline in success rate (95% vs. 85%), with lower variance indicating greater robustness enabled by NLOS perception for proactive obstacle avoidance, despite marginally longer navigation time (14.57±1.74 s vs. 14.03±0.41 s).

In multiple corner scenarios (Positions C/D), the superiority of the proposed algorithm widen with increasing complexity: at Position C, success rates are 89% vs. 66% as the baseline frequently collide at the second corner; at Position D, the gap is more significant (84% vs. 41%), highlighting the critical role of mmWave radar in early detection of T-shaped corner obstacles – a capability lacking in the baseline.

Trajectory visualizations (Fig. 6) show that the proposed algorithm made deliberate pose adjustments before corners (e.g., approaching walls at 30°-45° angles) to optimize mmWave radar reflection paths, enhancing NLOS detection accuracy.

Table 2. Performance comparison at Position B (single L-shaped corner scenario)

Metric	Proposed Algorithm	Baseline
Success Rate	95%	85%
Avg. Navigation Time (s)	14.57±1.74	14.03±0.41
Avg. Navigation Distance (m)	15.23±1.89	14.86±0.52
Avg. Cumulative Reward	89.64	78.32
All-Trial Avg. Time (s)	13.84±2.15	12.93±1.87
All-Trial Avg. Distance (m)	14.47±2.03	13.61±1.95

Table 3. Performance comparison at Position C (two L-shaped corners scenario)

Metric	Proposed Algorithm	Baseline
Success Rate	89%	66%
Avg. Navigation Time (s)	28.42±2.31	25.17±3.24
Avg. Navigation Distance (m)	29.15±2.56	26.83±3.47
Avg. Cumulative Reward	105.37	82.65
All-Trial Avg. Time (s)	25.30±3.87	19.63±4.12
All-Trial Avg. Distance (m)	25.94±4.02	20.79±4.35

Table 4. Performance comparison at Position D (complex multi-corner scenario)

Metric	Proposed Algorithm	Baseline
Success Rate	84%	41%
Avg. Navigation Time (s)	36.95±2.65	32.68±0.63
Avg. Navigation Distance (m)	37.78±3.43	34.85±0.62
Avg. Cumulative Reward	123.65	103.44
All-Trial Avg. Time (s)	33.31±4.65	23.00±8.63
All-Trial Avg. Distance (m)	34.73±4.01	29.08±8.33

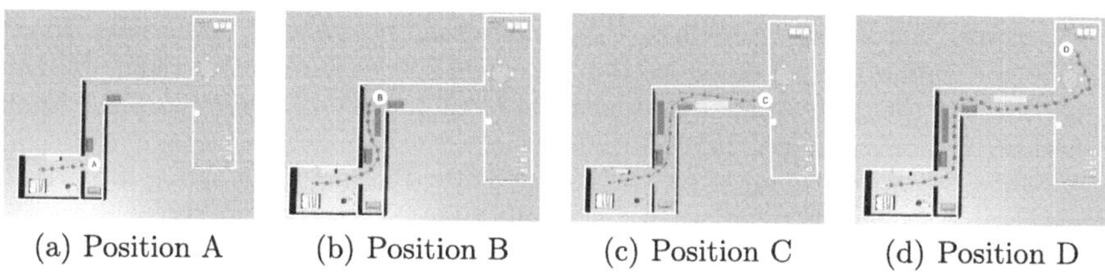

(a) Position A (b) Position B (c) Position C (d) Position D

Fig. 6. Navigation trajectories (A-D)

7 Conclusions

This paper proposes the obstacle-aware RL-based corner navigation algorithm for mobile robots, leveraging the NLOS perception capability of mmWave radar with LiDAR assistance. We find that the robot's pose (position and orientation) critically affects NLOS sensing quality. By deliberately adjusting the radar's pose through planned movements, our method could improve the signal reflection paths, and thus significantly boost hidden obstacle detection rates. We further integrates this principle in our RL framework via a specialized perception optimization reward design, leveraging mutual interactions between robot actions and observations for path planning. Experimental validation confirms that our mmWave radar with LiDAR assistance can effectively detect both static and dynamic obstacles behind corners. Comparative simulations validate the superiority of the proposed algorithm. In scenarios with multiple L-shaped and T-shaped corners, our algorithm achieves up to a 43% improvement for the navigation success rate compared to baseline approaches.

References

1. Monaci, G., Aractingi, M., Silander, T.: Dipcan: distilling privileged information for crowd-aware navigation. In: XVIII Robotics, Science and Systems (RSS) (2022)
2. Yao, S., Chen, G., Qiu, Q., Ma, J., Chen, X., Ji, J.: Crowd-aware robot navigation for pedestrians with multiple collision avoidance strategies via map-based deep reinforcement learning. In: 2021 IEEE/RSJ International Conference on Intelligent Robots and Systems (IROS), pp. 8144–8150. IEEE (2021)
3. Matsuzaki, S., Hasegawa, Y.: Learning crowd-aware robot navigation from challenging environments via distributed deep reinforcement learning. In: 2022 International Conference on Robotics and Automation (ICRA), pp. 4730–4736. IEEE (2022)
4. Scheiner, N., et al.: Seeing around street corners: non-line-of-sight detection and tracking in-the-wild using doppler radar. In: Proceedings of the IEEE/CVF Conference on Computer Vision and Pattern Recognition, pp. 2068–2077 (2020)
5. Yue, S., He, H., Cao, P., Zha, K., Koizumi, M., Katabi, D.: Cornerradar: Rf-based indoor localization around corners. Proc. ACM Interact. Mobile Wearable Ubiq. Technol. **6**(1), 1–24 (2022)
6. Woodford, T., Zhang, X., Chai, E., Sundaresan, K.: Mosaic: leveraging diverse reflector geometries for omnidirectional around-corner automotive radar. In: Proceedings of the 20th Annual International Conference on Mobile Systems, Applications and Services, pp. 155–167 (2022)
7. Kaelbling, L.P., Littman, M.L., Cassandra, A.R.: Planning and acting in partially observable stochastic domains. Artif. Intell. **101**(1–2), 99–134 (1998)
8. Schulman, J., Wolski, F., Dhariwal, P., Radford, A., Klimov, O.: Proximal policy optimization algorithms. arXiv preprint arXiv:1707.06347 (2017)
9. Velten, A., Willwacher, T., Gupta, O., Veeraraghavan, A., Bawendi, M.G., Raskar, R.: Recovering three-dimensional shape around a corner using ultrafast time-of-flight imaging. Nat. Commun. **3**(1), 745 (2012)
10. Seidel, S., Rueda-Chacón, H., Cusini, I., Villa, F., Zappa, F., Yu, C., Goyal, V.K.: Non-line-of-sight snapshots and background mapping with an active corner camera. Nat. Commun. **14**(1), 3677 (2023)

11. Stove, A.G.: Linear fmcw radar techniques. In: IEE Proceedings F (Radar and Signal Processing), vol. 139, pp. 343–350. IET (1992)
12. Choi, J.-S., Lee, W.-H., Lee, J.-H., Lee, J.-H., Kim, S.-C.: Deep learning based nlos identification with commodity wlan devices. IEEE Trans. Veh. Technol. **67**(4), 3295–3303 (2017)
13. Yasmeen, K., Kundu, D., Ram, S.S.: Around-the-corner radar sensing using reconfigurable intelligent surface. In: 2024 IEEE Microwaves, Antennas, and Propagation Conference (MAPCON), pp. 1–4. IEEE (2024)
14. Boger-Lombard, J., Slobodkin, Y., Katz, O.: Non-line-of-sight passive acoustic localization around corners. arXiv preprint arXiv:2211.03453 (2022)
15. Leiva, F., Ruiz-del, J.: Solar: robust rl-based map-less local planning: using 2d point clouds as observations. IEEE Rob. Autom. Lett. **5**(4), 5787–5794 (2020)
16. Kästner, L., et al.: Arena-rosnav: towards deployment of deep-reinforcement-learning-based obstacle avoidance into conventional autonomous navigation systems. In: 2021 IEEE/RSJ International Conference on Intelligent Robots and Systems (IROS), pp. 6456–6463. IEEE (2021)
17. Fox, D., Burgard, W., Thrun, S.: The dynamic window approach to collision avoidance. IEEE Rob. Autom. Mag. **4**(1), 23–33 (1997)
18. Rösmann, C., Feiten, W., Wösch, T., Hoffmann, F., Bertram, T.: Trajectory modification considering dynamic constraints of autonomous robots. In: ROBOTIK 2012; 7th German Conference on Robotics, pp. 1–6. VDE (2012)
19. Kastner, L., Cox, J., Buiyan, T., Lambrecht, J.: All-in-one: a drl-based control switch combining state-of-the-art navigation planners. In: 2022 International Conference on Robotics and Automation (ICRA), pp. 2861–2867. IEEE (2022)
20. Pérez-D'Arpino, C., Liu, C., Goebel, P., Martín-Martín, R., Savarese, S.: Robot navigation in constrained pedestrian environments using reinforcement learning. In: 2021 IEEE International Conference on Robotics and Automation (ICRA), pp. 1140–1146. IEEE (2021)
21. Scharf, L.L., Demeure, C.: Statistical Signal Processing: Detection, Estimation, and Time Series Analysis. Prentice Hall, Upper Saddle River (1991)
22. Zhao, J.S., Liu, X., Feng, Z.J., Dai, J.S.: Design of an Ackermann-type steering mechanism. Proc. Inst. Mech. Engineers, Part C: J. Mech. Eng. Sci. **227**(11), 2549–2562 (2013)
23. Michel, O.: Cyberbotics ltd. webots®: professional mobile robot simulation. Int. J. Adv. Rob. Syst. **1**(1), 5 (2004)
24. Schulman, J., Moritz, P., Levine, S., Jordan, M., Abbeel, P.: High-dimensional continuous control using generalized advantage estimation. arXiv preprint arXiv:1506.02438 (2015)

SPOF-NDN: Forwarding NDN on SDN Switches

Wei Guo[1(✉)], Yu Zhang[1,2], Zhongda Xia[1], Weizhe Zhang[1,2], and Binxing Fang[1]

[1] Harbin Institute of Technology, Harbin, China
guowei@stu.hit.edu.cn, {yuzhang,xiazhongda,wzzhang}@hit.edu.cn, fangbx@cae.cn

[2] Peng Cheng Laboratory, Shenzhen, China

Abstract. Named data networking (NDN) is an instance of information-centric networking (ICN) architecture. Deploying NDN on software-defined network (SDN) switches offers advantages for forwarding throughput. However, it faces fundamental challenges: the flow table pipeline is not suitable for NDN's variable-length TLV packet format and hierarchical names, cannot efficiently implement stateful forwarding (PIT, CS), and controller communication delays compromise low-latency routing mechanisms. This paper introduces SPOF-NDN, a POF-based NDN forwarding scheme that addresses these challenges through three key innovations. First, we design a flow-table-compatible packet format with a fixed-length header containing hashed NDN forwarding information, enabling efficient processing of NDN's variable-length structures. Second, we extend POF switches with a stateful module that implements NDN's stateful functions while leveraging flow tables for stateless functions. Third, we develop a temporary control mechanism that enables instantaneous FIB modifications independent of controller-switch communication latencies. Evaluation in a PINet environment demonstrates correct NDN packet forwarding and support for latency-sensitive routing mechanisms, confirming SPOF-NDN's viability for practical NDN deployment in SDN environments. Per-module analysis reveals optimization potential for enhanced performance.

Keywords: Named Data Networking · Software-Defined Networking · Protocol-Oblivious Forwarding · Network Packet Forwarding

1 Introduction

Named data networking (NDN) [34] is a new Internet architecture. As an instance of information-centric networking (ICN) [3], NDN shows advantages in typical content delivery application scenarios such as content delivery network [8] and video streaming [9,17,18]. In addition, NDN's special communication model can be effectively utilized in applications such as the Internet of Things [16], ad hoc networking [7], and vehicular networking [33].

T. Qiu et al. (Eds.): CCF ChinaNet 2025, CCIS 2810, pp. 130–144, 2026.
https://doi.org/10.1007/978-981-95-8450-5_10

Software-Defined Networking (SDN) [14] provides an attractive platform for NDN deployment through its highly flexible, programmable data plane. SDN-based NDN implementations eliminate the need for specialized hardware while leveraging programmable switch ASICs to achieve superior performance compared to software forwarders like NDN Forwarding Daemon (NFD) [1]. Recent advances demonstrate this potential: Takemasa's Tofino-based implementation [31] achieves 470 Gbps with validated scalability to 10 Tbps, while Long's Pegasus [19] reaches 780 Gbps through enhanced variable-length name parsing and improved PIT design. Additional works, including Signorello's NDN.p4 [29] and Karrakchou's ENDN [13], explore SDN-based NDN functionality extensions.

Despite the programmability offered by SDN technologies such as Protocol-oblivious Forwarding (POF) [30] and Protocol Independent Switch Architecture (PISA) [2], implementing NDN on existing SDN architectures faces fundamental challenges. First, SDN employs flow tables with predetermined field positions and lengths for packet processing, while NDN utilizes TLV format packets [22] with variable-position and variable-length fields and hierarchical names containing variable numbers of components. Second, centralized SDN controllers exclusively manage flow table modifications, introducing communication delays that conflict with NDN's requirements for frequent stateful forwarding information updates and low-latency routing mechanisms such as KITE [35].

This paper extends our previous work [10] presented at ICENAT 2022, introducing SPOF-NDN, a POF-based NDN forwarding scheme designed for compatibility with NFD [1] and deployment in SDN environments (such as PINet [11]). SPOF-NDN addresses these challenges through three key innovations: (1) a specialized packet format containing a fixed-length header consisting of hashed NDN forwarding information to enable efficient flow table processing, (2) a stateful module extending POF capabilities to support NDN's stateful forwarding, and (3) a temporary control mechanism enabling immediate FIB updates through local temporary controllers during the process of flow table modification.

While high-performance forwarding motivates programmable data plane implementations of NDN, our work focuses on a fundamental question: how to implement NDN within POF environments properly. With programmable data plane hardwae achieving 10-Tbps-level performance [2], stateless forwarding operations are unlikely to limit system performance. Since our stateful module implements a subset of NFD functionality, we anticipate that optimized implementations can exceed NFD performance. Additionally, existing performance improvements of software forwarders may also apply to the stateful module to achieve better performance.

The main contributions of this paper are:

- We design an NDN forwarding scheme deployable on SDN switches by dividing NDN functionality into stateful and stateless parts, implementing stateful functions by extending a stateful module for the data plane.
- We introduce a flow-table-compatible NDN packet format containing a fixed-length header consisting of hashed NDN forwarding information, enabling efficient SDN processing of NDN's variable-length structures.

- We develop a temporary control mechanism allowing instantaneous FIB modifications independent of controller-switch communication latencies, supporting low-latency NDN routing mechanisms.
- We validate the scheme on an SDN environment (PINet [11]), demonstrating correct NDN packet forwarding, application support including live video streaming, and latency-sensitive routing mechanisms support such as KITE [35].

2 Background

Our approach leverages two foundational technologies: networking programmability and Named Data Networking, specifically utilizing POF to implement SPOF-NDN.

2.1 Protocol-Oblivious Forwarding (POF)

Traditional network hardware processes packets with fixed logic, limiting developers' ability to implement custom protocols without specialized hardware. SDN [14] addresses this by decoupling control and data planes, enabling software-defined forwarding behavior through programmable controllers. OpenFlow [20] (an instance of SDN) enables programmable packet processing but remains protocol-dependent, supporting only predefined protocols and limiting its applicability to emerging protocols like NDN. POF [30] extends OpenFlow by providing protocol-independent data plane instructions. It uses (offset, length, value) triplets to define packet field matching rules, enabling support for arbitrary network protocols through programmable match-action processing. However, some POF implementations [12] require controller-initiated flow table modifications, introducing multi-second delays in centralized deployments.

2.2 Named Data Networking (NDN)

NDN [34] operates on a name-based communication model where consumers request data via Interest packets and receive corresponding Data packets. Unlike stateless IP forwarding, NDN requires forwarders to maintain state, recording Interest forwarding information until matching Data packets arrive. NDN forwarding comprises stateful functions (the Pending Interest Table (PIT) tracks Interest forwarding paths for Data packet return routing, while the Content Store (CS) provides in-network caching) and stateless functions like the Forwarding Information Base (FIB) for Interest routing decisions. Additionally, NDN supports routing mechanisms as control functions, with protocols like KITE [35] requiring frequent, low-latency FIB modifications for mobility support. NDN packets use variable-length TLV (Type-Length-Value) format [22], supporting flexible hierarchical naming but complicating flow table pipeline parsing in SDN environments.

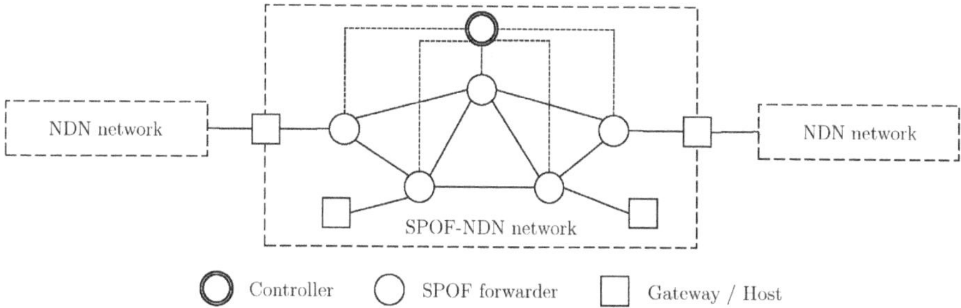

Fig. 1. The overview of a SPOF-NDN network

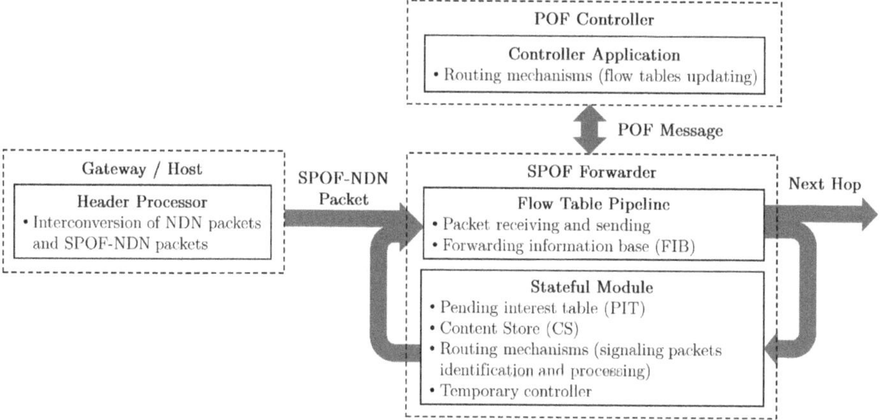

Fig. 2. The overview of the forwarding scheme

3 Design

SPOF-NDN is a POF-based NDN forwarding scheme. As shown in Fig. 1, the SPOF-NDN network consists of SPOF forwarders and one or more centralized controllers, and can connect to other NDN networks via gateways.

As shown in Fig. 2, SPOF-NDN comprises three main components: SPOF forwarders implement NDN's core functions (PIT, FIB, CS) by dividing them between POF switches (stateless FIB via flow tables) and stateful modules (PIT, CS on commodity hardware). NDN routing mechanisms are implemented by the stateful module and POF controllers. The stateful module includes a temporary controller for low-latency FIB updates, while POF controllers manage flow table modifications. Header processors enable seamless interoperability with existing NDN networks through packet format conversion between NDN packets and SPOF-NDN packets.

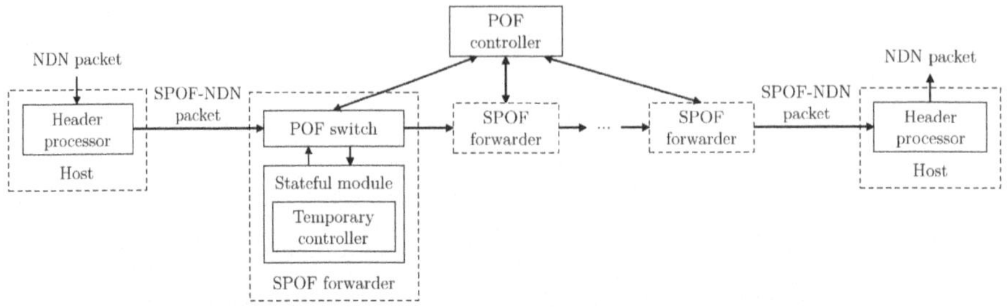

Fig. 3. The process of forwarding an NDN packet

Figure 3 illustrates the packet forwarding process. NDN packets are converted to SPOF-NDN packets at SPOF-NDN network ingress, forwarded through SPOF forwarders where each packet traverses the POF switch pipeline twice (first for input processing and forwarding to the stateful module, then for output processing after stateful operations), and converted back to NDN packets at SPOF-NDN network egress. POF controllers communicate with switches during startup and forwarding processes to manage flow table initialization and updates.

3.1 Packet Parsing

A primary challenge in implementing NDN on flow-table-based SDN switches lies in the inherent incompatibility between NDN's variable-length TLV packet format and the fixed-field matching requirements of flow table pipelines. As flow tables operate on predetermined (offset, length, value) tuples, they cannot directly parse the hierarchical, variable-length names and other fields within a standard NDN packet, as shown in Fig. 4.

To overcome this limitation, SPOF-NDN introduces a specialized packet format, the SPOF-NDN packet, which prepends a fixed-length SPOF header to the standard NDN packet, as shown in Fig. 5. This header translates essential, variable-length NDN forwarding information into a structure that POF flow tables can efficiently process. The conversion between standard NDN packets and SPOF-NDN packets is handled by a header processor at the network edge, which hashes the NDN name components and populates the header fields.

The SPOF header not only facilitates stateless processing in the POF switch but also serves as a communication channel between the flow table pipeline and the stateful module, eliminating the need for separate session state. Its key fields are:

- **type**: A 2-bit field that indicates the packet's payload and processing stage, guiding the packet through the forwarding logic. Its value range includes:
  - UNPROCESSED: Payload is an NDN packet and waiting for the stateful module to check the NDN type.

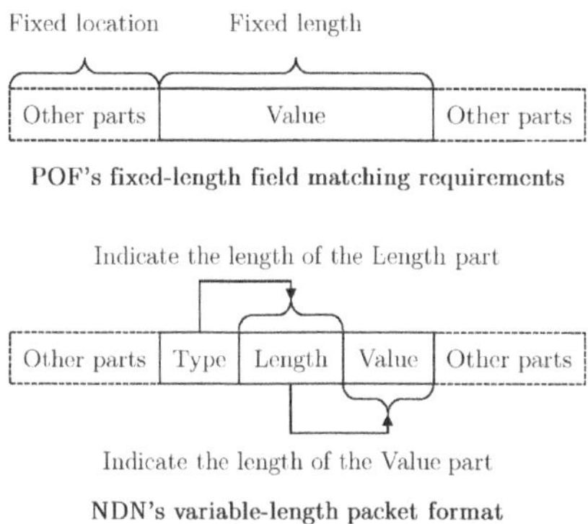

Fig. 4. The incompatibility between the POF flow table's fixed-field matching and the NDN packet's TLV format.

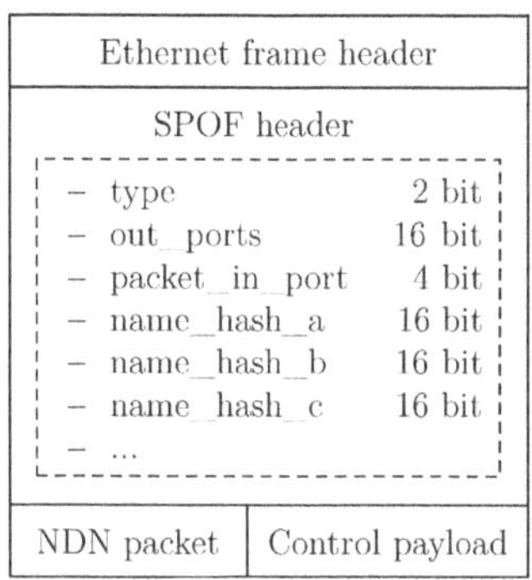

Fig. 5. The SPOF-NDN packet structure with its fixed-length header.

  - INTEREST: Payload is an NDN Interest packet.
  - DATA: Payload is an NDN Data packet.
  - CONTROL: Payload is a control payload, which should be sent to the POF controller instead of the next hop.
- **out_ports**: A 16-bit mask set by the stateful module to communicate its forwarding decision for packets to the flow table pipeline.
- **packet_in_port**: A 4-bit field that records the packet's ingress port, which is essential for the stateful module's PIT logic.
- **name_hash_x**: A set of 16-bit fields storing the hash values of the initial NDN name components. These fields enables the flow table to perform longest prefix matching for the FIB. The number and length of hash fields is a configurable network parameter.

3.2 Stateful Forwarding

NDN forwarding functions are categorized into stateful (PIT, CS) and stateless (FIB) parts, as shown in Fig. 6. Stateless forwarding resembles IP routing, where forwarding decisions depend on static routing rules. Stateful forwarding requires maintaining dynamic state information that both influences and is modified by packet processing.

Standard POF switches rely on flow tables for forwarding decisions, which can only be modified by POF controllers. Since controller communication typically incurs multi-second delays, flow tables cannot effectively implement the frequent state updates required by NDN's stateful forwarding. SPOF-NDN addresses this limitation by extending POF switches with a stateful module running on commodity hardware. This module handles NDN packet parsing, PIT, and CS functionalities using the ndn-cxx library, and communicates with the flow table pipeline via network interfaces.

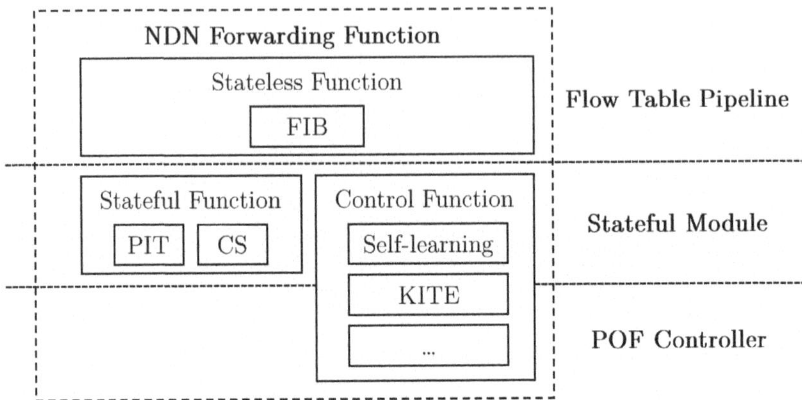

Fig. 6. Categories of NDN forwarding functions

Fields (name components)			Priority	Forward target
Component 1	Component 2	Component 3		
A	B	C	3	#1
A	B	any	2	#2
any	any	any	0	drop

Fig. 7. A flow table implementing longest prefix matching

To fully utilize the performance of programmable data plane hardware, SPOF-NDN implements the FIB within the POF switch's flow table pipeline using priority-based longest prefix matching. Since POF requires predetermined field positions and lengths, the system converts variable-length NDN names into fixed-length hash values stored in the SPOF header's name_hash fields. Flow table entries are assigned priorities corresponding to their prefix length, enabling standard longest prefix matching behavior, as shown in Fig. 7.

SPOF-NDN packet forwarding operates in three stages (Fig. 8):

1. **Input Processing**: The POF switch receives packets and forwards them to the stateful module, recording the ingress port for PIT operations.
2. **Stateful Processing**: The stateful module parses NDN packets and performs PIT/CS operations. For Interest packets, it checks the CS for cached data, manages PIT entries, and consults the temporary FIB. For Data packets, it stores content in the CS, retrieves corresponding PIT entries, and sets forwarding ports.
3. **Output Processing**: The flow table pipeline forwards packets based on their type. Interest packets use either temporary FIB results or flow-table-based FIB lookup, while Data packets follow PIT-determined paths.

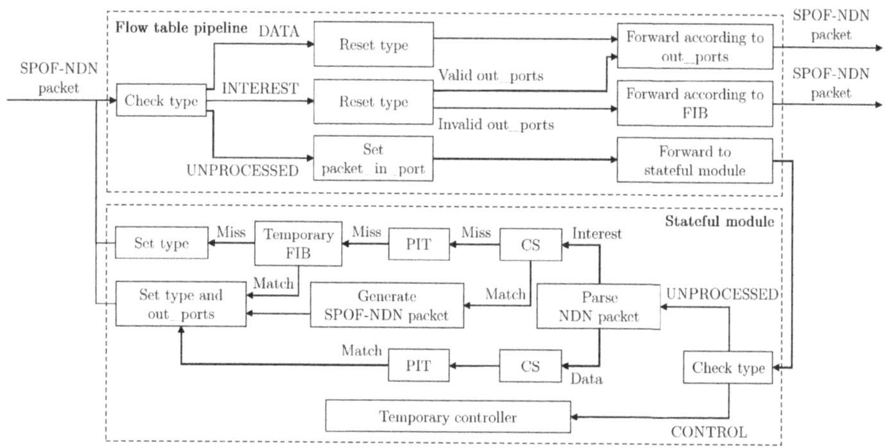

Fig. 8. The forwarding process of the forwarder

Packets traverse the flow table pipeline twice per hop, distinguished by the type field: UNPROCESSED for initial entry and INTEREST/DATA for output processing. This design combines hardware-accelerated stateless operations and software-based stateful processing, maintaining NDN forwarding rules while leveraging SDN performance capabilities.

3.3 Controllers

Control functions in SPOF-NDN encompass flow table initialization, management, and NDN routing mechanism implementations. NDN routing protocols such as KITE [35] require rapid FIB modifications to maintain low-latency mobility support. However, centralized POF deployments [12] restrict flow table mod-

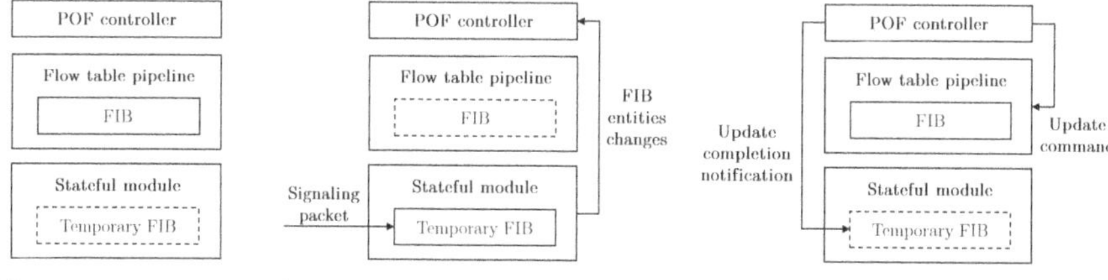

(a) Before the signaling packet arrives, the FIB is enabled and the temporary FIB is disabled.

(b) When signaling packets arrive, the temporary FIB is modified and enabled while the stateful module sends the changes to the POF controller.

(c) The POF Controller updates the FIB table in the flow table pipeline and notifies the stateful module of the update's completion.

Fig. 9. The process of the temporary control mechanism

ifications to POF controllers, introducing multi-second communication delays that compromise routing performance (Figs. 9, 10 and 11).

SPOF-NDN addresses this limitation through a dual-controller architecture combining the centralized POF controller with embedded temporary controllers. The centralized POF controller can update the flow-table-based FIB of switches across the network via POF messages. The temporary controller, integrated within each stateful module, provides immediate local FIB updates without controller communication delays.

The temporary control mechanism operates through coordinated FIB management, as shown in Fig. 9. Upon receiving routing update signaling packets (e.g., KITE's Trace Data packets), the temporary controller immediately applies changes to a local temporary FIB, ensuring zero-delay forwarding information changes. Concurrently, it transmits CONTROL packets containing FIB modification details to the centralized controller via the flow table pipeline. The centralized controller processes these updates, changes flow tables, and signals completion back to the temporary controller. Once FIB synchronization completes, temporary FIB entries are removed, transferring routing responsibility to the updated flow-table-based FIB. This approach ensures consistent routing behavior while eliminating controller communication latency between POF switches and the POF controller.

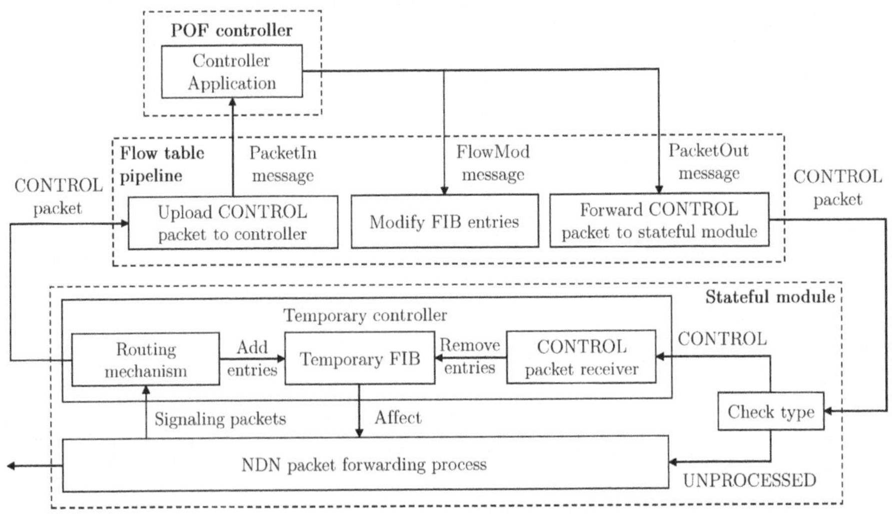

Fig. 10. The process of the dual-controller architecture

The routing mechanism processing workflow comprises eight steps (Fig. 10):

1. **Packet Identification**: The stateful module identifies signaling packets during standard forwarding operations and redirects them to the temporary controller for routing-mechanism-specific processing.

2. **Route Computation**: The temporary controller analyzes signaling packets and determines required FIB modifications according to the routing mechanism logic.
3. **Local FIB Update**: Changes are immediately applied to the temporary FIB, enabling forwarding information changes without communication delays.
4. **Control Message Generation**: Simultaneously, a CONTROL packet containing FIB modification details is generated and transmitted to the POF switch.
5. **Controller Notification**: The POF switch identifies the CONTROL packet and sends a PacketIn message to the POF controller, suspending the packet's forwarding.
6. **FIB Update**: The centralized controller processes the PacketIn message, returns a FlowMod command to update flow tables, and a PacketOut message to resume packet processing.
7. **Synchronization Completion**: The switch applies flow table modifications and forwards the CONTROL packet back to the stateful module, confirming synchronization completion.
8. **Cleanup**: The stateful module receives the returned CONTROL packet and removes the corresponding temporary FIB entries, completing the update cycle.

4 Evaluation

We implemented a SPOF-NDN prototype in a PINet [11] environment, a comprehensive SDN experimental environment that consists of specialized controllers and switches (PINERack [15]) supporting both POF and P4 [5]. The stateful module runs on PINERack hardware, communicating with the POF switch via shared memory. Our POF controller is implemented as an ONOS [4] application on PINet's centralized controller. Header processors are deployed as lightweight software on each host. All SPOF forwarders in the experimental testbed are PINERacks, and hosts are servers (Lenovo SR650 servers equipped with an Intel Xeon 3106 8-core CPU, 32GB memory, and 1Gbps Ethernet cards).

4.1 Application Support Validation

We first validate SPOF-NDN's application compatibility using NDNts-video [23], a live streaming system based on NDNts [24] and Shaka Player [26]. Figure 11 shows the experimental topology where a video source pushes a video stream to a video server using the RTMP protocol [25], and a video player pulls the live video stream through four SPOF forwarders from the video server. The adaptive bitrate mechanism achieved stable playback at 1200×720 resolution with 5859Kbps bitrate and 6938Kbps predicted bandwidth.

This demonstrates SPOF-NDN's correct packet forwarding behavior and practical deployment viability in real SDN environments, supporting applications like live video streaming.

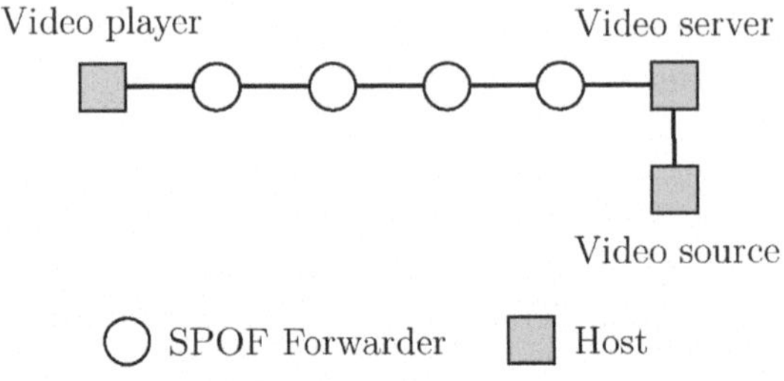

Fig. 11. Application support validation topology

4.2 Performance Evaluation

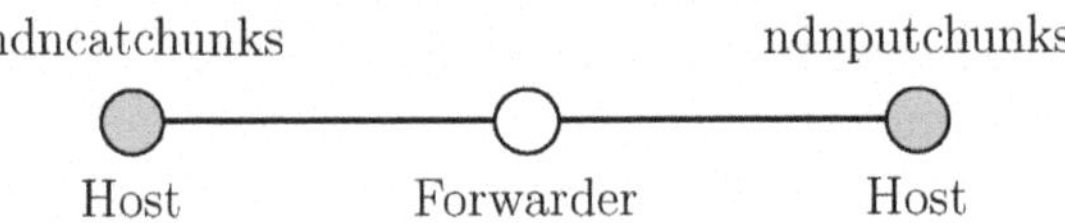

Fig. 12. Performance evaluation topology

We evaluate SPOF-NDN's forwarding performance using ndnputchunks/ ndncatchunks of ndn-tools [21] for random file transfer between two hosts connected through a single forwarder (Fig. 12). Table 1 compares SPOF-NDN and NFD performance.

Table 1. Performances of SPOF-NDN and NFD in file transfer

Forwarder	Goodput (Mbps)	Goodput (pps)	Retransmitted segments (%)	RTT average (ms)
SPOF-NDN	18.34	4585.35	0.42	23.412
NFD	389.13	11055.62	0.92	16.808

The experimental results show that the performance of this prototype has a significant gap compared to NFD, achieving approximately 41% of NFD's packet processing rate (pps). The absence of packet fragmentation protocols like NDNLP [28] also affects the performance, constraining packet sizes to MTU limits.

To identify performance bottlenecks and assess scheme potential, we conducted a per-module evaluation using tcpreplay [32] to replay input packets with varying packet rates and sizes to determine maximum lossless goodput. Table 2 presents individual module performance.

Results indicate that the stateful module constitutes the primary bottleneck, followed by the header processor. Since the stateful module implements

Table 2. Performances of each module

Module	Goodput (Mbps)	Goodput (pps)	Latency (μs)
Header processor	126.34	72000	8
POF switch (first process)	362.88	189000	30
Stateful module	103.62	9152	6744
POF switch (second process)	566.4	295000	20

a subset of NFD functionality and header processing occurs only at network edges, optimized implementations could approach NFD performance levels. Our software-based POF switch cannot fully exploit hardware performance; deploying on 10-Tbps-capable programmable hardware [2] would likely exceed NFD performance. Further optimizations inspired by NDN-DPDK's data structures [27] and MW-NFD's multi-threading [6] could enhance performance significantly.

4.3 Temporary Control Mechanism Validation

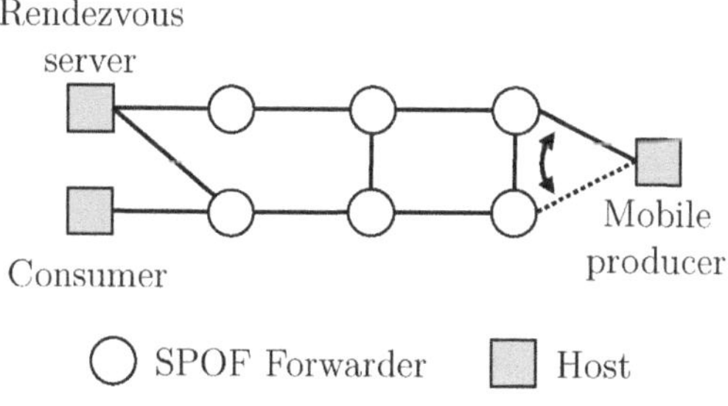

Fig. 13. Temporary control mechanism validation topology

We validate the temporary control mechanism's effectiveness using KITE [35], a mobility-supporting routing mechanism that requires rapid FIB updates when producers change their topological locations in the network. The experimental setup (Fig. 13) includes a KITE rendezvous server, a mobile producer, and a consumer, with continuous video streaming during producer mobility.

The experimental results show a 31.11 ms switch time from producer disconnection to Interest reception after producer reconnection at the new location, maintaining smooth video playback throughout mobility events. This demonstrates that the temporary control mechanism successfully enables low-latency routing in centralized controller environments without stable communication latency between the controller and switches, making routing mechanisms free from inherent controller communication delays in real deployments.

5 Conclusion

This paper presents SPOF-NDN, a POF-based NDN forwarding scheme designed for compatibility with NFD and deployment in SDN environments. By dividing NDN functionality into stateful and stateless parts, SPOF-NDN implements stateful functions (PIT, CS) via an extended data plane module while leveraging flow tables for stateless functions (FIB). The flow-table-compatible SPOF-NDN packet format, featuring a fixed-length header with hashed NDN forwarding information, addresses the fundamental incompatibility between NDN's variable-length TLV structure and SDN's fixed-field matching requirements. The temporary control mechanism enables instantaneous FIB modifications independent of controller-switch communication latencies, supporting low-latency routing mechanisms such as KITE. Evaluation in a PINet environment demonstrates correct NDN packet forwarding and support for latency-sensitive routing mechanisms. The results confirm SPOF-NDN's viability for practical NDN deployment in SDN environments and great potential for further performance improvement.

Acknowledgement. This work is supported by the National Science and Technology Major Project (2022ZD0115303). The authors would like to thank Yi Wang, Chengyu Li, Zuang Hu, and the PINet team for their help with the experiments.

Disclosure of Interests. The authors have no competing interests to declare that are relevant to the content of this article.

References

1. Afanasyev, A., Shi, J., Zhang, B., Zhang, L., Moiseenko, I., Yu, Y., et al.: Nfd developer's guide. Dept. Comput. Sci., Univ. California, Los Angeles, Los Angeles, CA, USA, Technical Report. NDN-0021 (2014)
2. Agrawal, A., Kim, C.: Intel tofino2–a 12.9 tbps p4-programmable ethernet switch. In: 2020 IEEE Hot Chips 32 Symposium (HCS), pp. 1–32. IEEE Computer Society (2020)
3. Ahlgren, B., Dannewitz, C., Imbrenda, C., Kutscher, D., Ohlman, B.: A survey of information-centric networking. IEEE Commun. Mag. **50**(7), 26–36 (2012). https://doi.org/10.1109/MCOM.2012.6231276
4. Berde, P., et al.: Onos: towards an open, distributed sdn os. In: Proceedings of the Third Workshop on Hot Topics in Software Defined Networking, pp. 1–6 (2014)
5. Bosshart, P., Daly, D., Gibb, G., Izzard, M., McKeown, N., Rexford, J., et al.: P4: programming protocol-independent packet processors. SIGCOMM Comput. Commun. Rev. **44**(3), 87–95 (2014). https://doi.org/10.1145/2656877.2656890
6. Byun, S.H., Lee, J., Sul, D.M., Ko, N.: Multi-worker nfd: an nfd-compatible high-speed ndn forwarder. In: Proceedings of the 7th ACM Conference on Information-Centric Networking, ICN '20, pp. 166–168. Association for Computing Machinery, New York (2020). https://doi.org/10.1145/3405656.3420233
7. Fayyaz, S., Atif Ur Rehman, M., Khalid, W., Kim, B.S.: Shm-ndn: a seamless hybrid mobility management scheme for named data mobile ad hoc networks. Internet Things **24**, 100943 (2023). https://doi.org/10.1016/j.iot.2023.100943. https://www.sciencedirect.com/science/article/pii/S2542660523002664

8. Ghasemi, C., Yousefi, H., Zhang, B.: Far cry: Will cdns hear ndn's call?. In: ICN '20, pp. 89–98. Association for Computing Machinery, New York (2020). https://doi.org/10.1145/3405656.3418708
9. Ghasemi, C., Yousefi, H., Zhang, B.: Internet-scale video streaming over ndn. IEEE Netw. **35**(5), 174–180 (2021). https://doi.org/10.1109/MNET.121.1900574
10. Guo, W., Zhang, Y., Fang, B.: SPOF-NDN: a pof-based ndn forwarding scheme. In: Quan, W. (ed.) Emerging Networking Architecture and Technologies, pp. 630–644. Springer, Singapore (2023)
11. Hu, Y., Li, D., Sun, P., Yi, P., Wu, J.: Polymorphic smart network: an open, flexible and universal architecture for future heterogeneous networks. IEEE Trans. Netw. Sci. Eng. **7**(4), 2515–2525 (2020). https://doi.org/10.1109/TNSE.2020.3006249
12. Jing, L., Chen, X., Wang, J.: Design and implementation of programmable data plane supporting multiple data types. Electronics **10**(21) (2021). https://doi.org/10.3390/electronics10212639. https://www.mdpi.com/2079-9292/10/21/2639
13. Karrakchou, O., Samaan, N., Karmouch, A.: Endn: An enhanced ndn architecture with a p4-programmabie data plane. In: Proceedings of the 7th ACM Conference on Information-Centric Networking, ICN '20, pp. 1–11. Association for Computing Machinery, New York (2020). https://doi.org/10.1145/3405656.3418720
14. Kreutz, D., Ramos, F.M.V., Veríssimo, P.E., Rothenberg, C.E., Azodolmolky, S., Uhlig, S.: Software-defined networking: a comprehensive survey. Proc. IEEE **103**(1), 14–76 (2015). https://doi.org/10.1109/JPROC.2014.2371999
15. Li, Z., Hu, Y., Tian, L., Pei, J.: Virtualization of the programmable data plane for supporting coexistence of multiple network functions. J. Electron. Inf. Technol. **45**(10), 3667–3675 (2023)
16. Liang, H., Qian, C., Lu, C., Burgess, L., Mulo, J., Yu, W.: Named data networking (ndn) for data collection of digital twins-based iot systems. In: 2023 IEEE/ACIS 21st International Conference on Software Engineering Research, Management and Applications (SERA), pp. 122–127 (2023). https://doi.org/10.1109/SERA57763.2023.10197693
17. Liang, T., Huang, W., Ma, X., Zhang, W., Zhang, Y., Zhang, B.: Pclive: bringing named data networking to internet livestreaming. In: Proceedings of the 10th ACM Conference on Information-Centric Networking, ACM ICN '23, pp. 36–45. Association for Computing Machinery, New York (2023). https://doi.org/10.1145/3623565.3623711
18. Liang, T., Zhang, Y., Zhang, B., Zhang, W., Zhang, Y.: Low latency internet livestreaming in named data networking. In: Proceedings of the 9th ACM Conference on Information-Centric Networking, ICN '22, pp. 177–179. Association for Computing Machinery, New York (2022). https://doi.org/10.1145/3517212.3559488
19. Long, X., Huang, K., Yang, R., Dai, Q., Li, Z.: Pegasus: a high-speed ndn router with programmable switches and server clusters. In: Proceedings of the 10th ACM Conference on Information-Centric Networking, ACM ICN '23, pp. 12–18. Association for Computing Machinery, New York (2023). https://doi.org/10.1145/3623565.3623713
20. McKeown, N., Anderson, T., Balakrishnan, H., Parulkar, G., Peterson, L., Rexford, J., et al.: Openflow: enabling innovation in campus networks. SIGCOMM Comput. Commun. Rev. **38**(2), 69–74 (2008). https://doi.org/10.1145/1355734.1355746
21. NDN Essential Tools. https://github.com/named-data/ndn-tools. Accessed 30 July 2025
22. NDN Packet Format Specification version 0.3. https://named-data.net/doc/NDN-packet-spec/current/. Accessed 30 July 2025

23. NDNts Adaptive Video. https://github.com/yoursunny/NDNts-video. Accessed 30 July 2025
24. NDNts: Named Data Networking libraries for the Modern Web. https://yoursunny.com/p/NDNts/. Accessed 30 July 2025
25. Parmar, H., Thornburgh, M.: Adobe's real time messaging protocol. Copyright Adobe Systems Incorporated, pp. 1–52 (2012)
26. Shaka Player. https://github.com/shaka-project/shaka-player. Accessed 30 July 2025
27. Shi, J., Pesavento, D., Benmohamed, L.: Ndn-dpdk: Ndn forwarding at 100 gbps on commodity hardware. In: Proceedings of the 7th ACM Conference on Information-Centric Networking, ICN '20, pp. 30–40. Association for Computing Machinery, New York (2020). https://doi.org/10.1145/3405656.3418715
28. Shi, J., Zhang, B.: Ndnlp: A link protocol for ndn. NDN, NDN Technical Report NDN-0006 (2012)
29. Signorello, S., State, R., François, J., Festor, O.: Ndn.p4: programming information-centric data-planes. In: 2016 IEEE NetSoft Conference and Workshops (NetSoft), pp. 384–389 (2016). https://doi.org/10.1109/NETSOFT.2016.7502472
30. Song, H.: Protocol-oblivious forwarding: unleash the power of sdn through a future-proof forwarding plane. In: Proceedings of the Second ACM SIGCOMM Workshop on Hot Topics in Software Defined Networking, HotSDN '13, pp. 127–132. Association for Computing Machinery, New York (2013). https://doi.org/10.1145/2491185.2491190
31. Takemasa, J., Koizumi, Y., Hasegawa, T.: Vision: toward 10 tbps ndn forwarding with billion prefixes by programmable switches. In: Proceedings of the 8th ACM Conference on Information-Centric Networking, ICN '21, pp. 13–19. Association for Computing Machinery, New York (2021). https://doi.org/10.1145/3460417.3482973
32. Tcpreplay. https://github.com/appneta/tcpreplay. Accessed 30 July 2025
33. Threet, Z., Papadopoulos, C., Shannigrahi, S.: An argument for ndn bridges in hierarchical in-vehicle networks. In: 2023 IEEE Vehicular Networking Conference (VNC), pp. 49–52 (2023). https://doi.org/10.1109/VNC57357.2023.10136279
34. Zhang, L., Afanasyev, A., Burke, J., Jacobson, V., claffy, k., Crowley, P., et al.: Named data networking. SIGCOMM Comput. Commun. Rev. **44**(3), 66–73 (2014). https://doi.org/10.1145/2656877.2656887
35. Zhang, Y., Xia, Z., Mastorakis, S., Zhang, L.: Kite: producer mobility support in named data networking. In: Proceedings of the 5th ACM Conference on Information-Centric Networking, ICN '18, pp. 125–136. Association for Computing Machinery, New York (2018). https://doi.org/10.1145/3267955.3267959

Traffic-Based Faulty AP Detection in Enterprise WLAN via Variational Auto-Encoder

Junjun Chen[1], Zhongnan Fu[1(✉)], Wending Liu[1], Jingzhou Sun[2], Naiwen Wei[2], and Hao Ma[1]

[1] Computer Center, Peking University, Beijing, China
fuzhongnan@pku.edu.cn
[2] Huawei Technologies Co., Ltd., Beijing, China

Abstract. Large-scale enterprise Wireless Local Area Networks (WLANs) often consist of tens of thousands of access points (APs), rendering manual detection of faulty devices a challenging task. While severe failures are easily identifiable, subtle issues frequently remain undetected until reported by end users. A key challenge in this context is the scarcity of labeled performance data and the highly imbalanced distribution of fault occurrences. To tackle this, we propose a traffic-based anomaly detection framework grounded in unsupervised learning. Leveraging the Variational Auto-Encoder (VAE), our approach learns normal traffic behavior patterns and identifies anomalies without depending on labeled data. Specifically, we integrate dilated convolution into the VAE to capture temporal dependencies across different time scales. For evaluating the proposed method, real-world enterprise WLAN traffic data were collected from a university network. Extensive experiments demonstrate robust detection performance, with a best F1-score of 0.88, outperforming other unsupervised methods.

Keywords: WLAN · Anomaly Detection · VAE · Traffic Monitoring

1 Introduction

In recent years, WLAN has witnessed rapid development, revolutionizing the way people communicate. Enterprise WLAN, in particular, has become indispensable in large organizations such as campuses and corporate facilities. Managing such a vast network is challenging, especially with the booming growth of user demands and network devices. While severe faults (e.g., offline APs) are easy to detect, subtle issues (e.g., slow speed or intermittent disruptions) often go unnoticed until users complain, severely impairing user experience. However, manual monitoring is inefficient for large-scale networks, and traditional tools may miss these transient problems. This necessitates automated and scalable solutions to detect abnormal AP behavior. In this work, we explore a data-driven approach to address this challenge using unsupervised anomaly detection.

T. Qiu et al. (Eds.): CCF ChinaNet 2025, CCIS 2810, pp. 145–157, 2026.
https://doi.org/10.1007/978-981-95-8450-5_11

A rich body of literature has explored device identification in WLAN. However, most of these studies focus on identifying Internet of Things (IoT) devices by analyzing traffic patterns, while the detection of faulty APs has received relatively little attention.

In this work, we propose a framework for detecting faulty APs in enterprise WLAN. Given the scarcity of labeled data, we adopt an unsupervised approach based on VAE to identify abnormal AP traffic patterns. To capture traffic correlations across different time scales, we incorporate parallel dilated convolution into the encoder and decoder of VAE. The contributions of this paper are summarized as follows:

- Given the scarcity of labeled traffic data in real-world enterprise WLAN, we propose a faulty AP detection framework based on VAE. As a reconstruction-based approach, VAE compresses the traffic patterns into a latent space of low dimension. Such compression works like a low-pass filter. During reconstruction, abnormal traffic segments will result in large reconstruction errors and thus be detected.
- To capture temporal dependencies across different time scales, we use dilated convolution as a building block for VAE. Dilated convolution enhances time series modeling by expanding the receptive fields of CNN. Compared with recursive architectures such as LSTM, dilated convolution is easier to train and better suited to our problem.
- To evaluate the performance of the proposed method, we collect real-world traffic data from a university network. Through extensive experiments, our algorithm achieves a best F1-score of 0.88, outperforming other reconstruction-based anomaly detection algorithms.

2 Related Works

2.1 Device Identification Base on Network Traffic

A significant body of research has focused on device identification based on network traffic. This research area can be roughly divided into two categories. The first category mainly aims to identify specific types of IoT devices [1,2,5,6,15]. For instance, in [1], a genetic algorithm is employed to extract relevant features from different protocol headers. Subsequently, various machine learning algorithms are utilized to classify the types of IoT devices. This approach leverages the unique characteristics embedded within network traffic to distinguish among different device types.

The second category of research focuses on detecting malicious devices [7,10,17]. In [17], recurrent neural networks (RNNs) are harnessed to identify attackers. These studies analyze network traffic patterns to recognize abnormal behaviors that may indicate the presence of malicious entities. By leveraging the sequential nature of network traffic data, RNN-based methods can effectively capture temporal dependencies and anomalies, enabling the detection of malicious devices in network environments.

2.2 Time Series Anomaly Detection

Time series anomaly detection is a highly active area of research. It can be broadly categorized into three main types: traditional statistical learning, supervised learning, and unsupervised learning.

Traditional statistical learning algorithms for time series anomaly detection usually make simple assumptions about the features of time series [4,9,14]. These assumptions, often based on prior knowledge, may not fully capture the complexity of real-world time series data. Moreover, selecting an appropriate algorithm for anomaly detection heavily relies on human expertise.

Supervised learning methods [3,11,13,18] primarily focus on learning the features of anomalies. They utilize classifiers trained on labeled data to identify abnormal patterns. For instance, Opprentice [13] employs a random forest algorithm to effectively integrate the outputs of multiple detectors. Although these methods can achieve high accuracy when complete and reliable labels are available, such ideal scenarios are uncommon.

Unsupervised learning approaches aim to learn the normal patterns of time series and detect anomaly points that significantly deviate from these learned patterns [19–22,24]. Generative models have gained popularity in this field due to their powerful data generation capabilities. By comparing the input data with the generated samples, anomalies can be identified.

3 Framework

In this section, we elaborate on the faulty AP detection framework. We first briefly introduce the fundamentals of VAE. Subsequently, we present the architecture of the entire network and discuss the training and detection procedures.

3.1 Background of VAE

As a generative learning approach, the goal of VAE [8] is to develop a model that can accurately represent the distribution of observed data $\mathbf{x}$, denoted as $p_\theta(\mathbf{x})$. In the context of faulty AP detection, once such a model is obtained, the identification process simply involves evaluating the value of $p_\theta(\mathbf{x})$, where $\mathbf{x}$ represents the KPI of an AP. If the observation probability of $\mathbf{x}$ is low, it is likely to be an anomaly. This intuitive approach forms the basis of our anomaly detection strategy.

However, directly modeling the distribution $p_\theta(\mathbf{x})$ is often a challenging task due to its potentially complex form. As a class of deep Bayesian networks, VAE offers a solution by introducing a low dimension latent space. The marginal distribution $p_\theta(\mathbf{x})$ of the observed data can be expressed as an integral over the latent variable $\mathbf{z}$:

$$p_\theta(\mathbf{x}) = \int p_\theta(\mathbf{x}|\mathbf{z})p_\theta(\mathbf{z})d\mathbf{z}, \tag{1}$$

where $p_\theta(\mathbf{x}|\mathbf{z})$ is the conditional probability of generating $\mathbf{x}$ given $\mathbf{z}$, and $p_\theta(\mathbf{z})$ is the prior distribution of the latent variable $\mathbf{z}$. For $\mathbf{z}$, a simple prior distribution is chosen, usually a diagonal normal distribution $\mathcal{N}(\mathbf{0}, \mathbf{I})$.

To learn the stochastic mapping between the observed data $\mathbf{x}$ and the latent variable $\mathbf{z}$, we first map $\mathbf{x}$ to the latent space according to $p_\theta(\mathbf{z}|\mathbf{x})$, and then regenerate it according to $p_\theta(\mathbf{x}|\mathbf{z})$. Training is performed by enforcing the regenerated result to be close to the original input $\mathbf{x}$. However, the interdependence between the posterior distribution $p_\theta(\mathbf{z}|\mathbf{x})$ and the conditional distribution $p_\theta(\mathbf{x}|\mathbf{z})$ presents a significant challenge during the training process.

Since $p_\theta(\mathbf{z}|\mathbf{x})$ is intractable, VAE takes variational inference techniques to approximate this posterior distribution by another network, parameterized by ϕ, as shown in Fig. 1. The posterior is assumed to be a normal distribution, with mean $\mu_\mathbf{z}(\mathbf{x})$ and deviation $\sigma_\mathbf{z}(\mathbf{x})$.

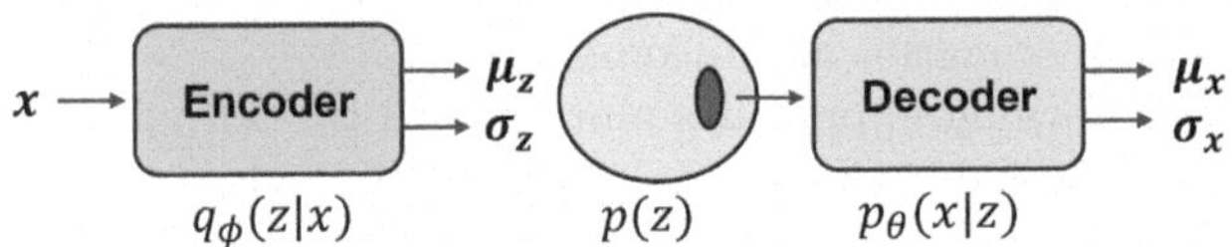

Fig. 1. Variational autoencoder architecture

The optimization objective of VAE is the *evidence lower bound*, abbreviated as ELBO. ELBO is derived as follows,

$$\begin{aligned}\log p_\theta(\mathbf{x}) =& \mathbb{E}_{q_\phi(\mathbf{z}|\mathbf{x})}\left[\log p_\theta(\mathbf{x})\right]\\ =& \mathbb{E}_{q_\phi(\mathbf{z}|\mathbf{x})}\left[\log\left[\frac{p_\theta(\mathbf{x},\mathbf{z})}{p_\theta(\mathbf{z}|\mathbf{x})}\right]\right]\\ =& \mathbb{E}_{q_\phi(\mathbf{z}|\mathbf{x})}\left[\log\left[\frac{p_\theta(\mathbf{x},\mathbf{z})}{q_\phi(\mathbf{z}|\mathbf{x})}\frac{q_\phi(\mathbf{z}|\mathbf{x})}{p_\theta(\mathbf{z}|\mathbf{x})}\right]\right]\\ =& D_{KL}(q_\phi(\mathbf{z}|\mathbf{x})||p_\theta(\mathbf{z}|\mathbf{x})) + \underbrace{\mathbb{E}_{q_\phi(\mathbf{z}|\mathbf{x})}\left[\log\left[\frac{p_\theta(\mathbf{x},\mathbf{z})}{q_\phi(\mathbf{z}|\mathbf{x})}\right]\right]}_{=\mathcal{L}_{\theta,\phi}(\mathbf{x})\ (\text{ELBO})}.\end{aligned} \tag{2}$$

Since $D_{KL}(q_\phi(\mathbf{z}|\mathbf{x})||p_\theta(\mathbf{z}|\mathbf{x})) \geq 0$, ELBO serves as a lower bound of the log-likelihood. During training, the approximate posterior $q_\phi(\mathbf{z}|\mathbf{x})$ and the generative model $p_\theta(\mathbf{x}|\mathbf{z})$ are jointly trained to maximize ELBO. Because ELBO is a lower bound of the log-likelihood, maximizing ELBO will simultaneously optimize two key objectives. First, the log-likelihood $\log p_\theta(\mathbf{x})$ gets larger, indicating a more effective generative model. Second, the KL divergence between $q_\phi(\mathbf{z}|\mathbf{x})$ and $p_\theta(\mathbf{z}|\mathbf{x})$ is minimized, which enhances the approximation quality.

3.2 Network Architecture

In this subsection, we present the network architecture of the VAE. The input dimension of the VAE is denoted by W. During both the training and detection phases, a sliding window of size W is applied to the traffic records. For a specific traffic record at time t, the sequence of data points $x_{t-W+1}, \ldots, x_t$ is selected as the input $\mathbf{x}_t$ for the VAE.

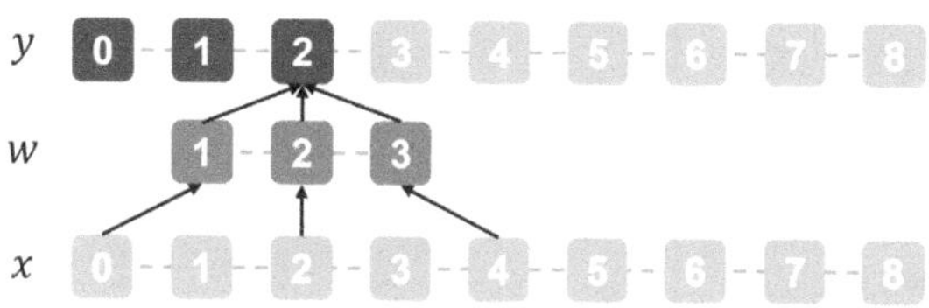

Fig. 2. Illustration of dilated convolution with $d = 1$.

To capture temporal dependencies and patterns in traffic data, dilated convolution [23] is employed as a building block for the encoder and decoder of VAE. Dilated convolution expands the receptive field by inserting gaps into the original input. Figure 2 shows a dilated convolution with $d = 1$, where the input x_i is sampled with a step size of d. In the one-dimension case, Eq. (3) shows the operation of a d-dilated convolution,

$$y[i] = \sum_{k=0}^{K-1} w[k] \cdot x \left[i + k \cdot (d+1) - \left\lfloor \frac{(K-1)(d+1)}{2} \right\rfloor \right]. \tag{3}$$

The overall network architecture is illustrated in Fig. 3. For brevity, batch normalization and activation function layers are omitted from this figure. To capture temporal dependencies across different time scales, parallel dilated convolutions are incorporated into both the encoder and decoder. For instance, in layer 2 of the encoder, three distinct dilated convolution modules are employed, with dilation rates $d = 1, 3, 5$ respectively. Following the dilated convolution operation, the outputs are concatenated along the channel dimension. Detailed specifications of the network are provided in Table 1.

The VAE features a latent space of dimension K. This latent space functions as a compressed representation of the input traffic data, allowing the model to learn the underlying structure and inherent characteristics of normal traffic patterns.

Following standard VAE, the prior $p(\mathbf{z})$ is chosen to be a centered normal distribution $\mathcal{N}(\mathbf{0}, \mathbf{I})$. The conditional distribution $p_\theta(\mathbf{x}|\mathbf{z})$ and the approximate posterior distribution $q_\phi(\mathbf{z}|\mathbf{x})$ are chosen to be diagonal normal distribution. That is $p_\theta(\mathbf{x}|\mathbf{z}) = \mathcal{N}(\boldsymbol{\mu}_\mathbf{x}, \boldsymbol{\sigma}_\mathbf{x}^2\mathbf{I})$ and $q_\phi(\mathbf{z}|\mathbf{x}) = \mathcal{N}(\boldsymbol{\mu}_\mathbf{z}, \boldsymbol{\sigma}_\mathbf{z}^2\mathbf{I})$, where the mean and deviation are output of encoder(decoder).

3.3 Training and Detection

In the training phase, we maximize the ELBO using Stochastic Gradient Variational Bayes (SGVB) algorithm [8], which employs reparameterization trick to

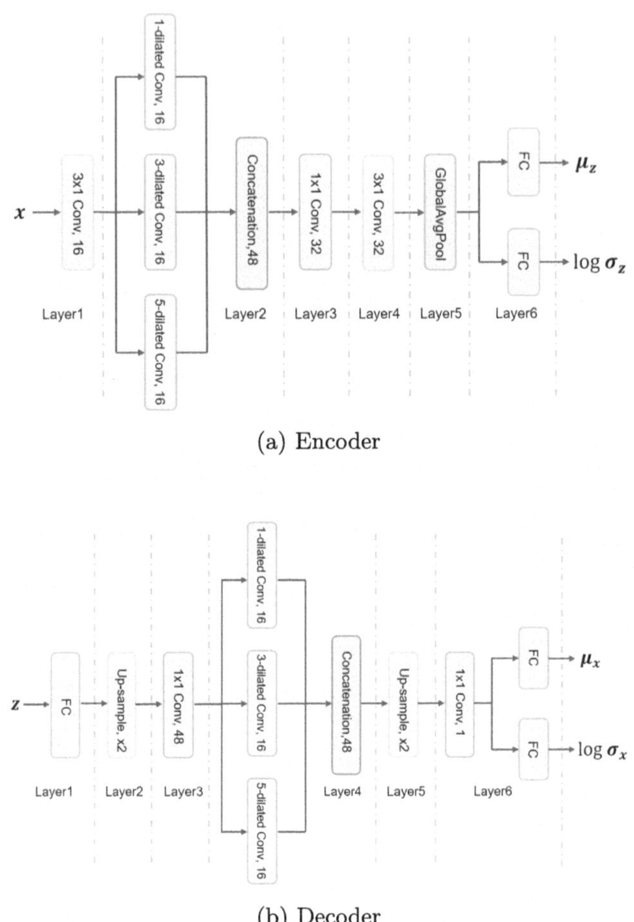

Fig. 3. The architecture of VAE with parallel dilated convolutions.

allow backpropagation through the sampling process in $q_\phi(\mathbf{z}|\mathbf{x})$, which corresponds to the expectation operator in ELBO.

During the training process, ELBO is estimate by sampling from $q_\phi(\mathbf{z}|\mathbf{x})$. As reported in [8], we approximate ELBO by taking one single sample from the latent space per data point. Let the batch size be B, ELBO is estimated as Eq. (4). Then, ELBO is maximized by using stochastic gradient ascent based on the gradient of ELBO.

$$\mathcal{L}_{\theta,\phi} \approx \frac{1}{B}\sum_{i=1}^{B}\left(\log p_\theta(\mathbf{x}_i|\mathbf{z}_i) + \log p_\theta(\mathbf{z}_i) - \log q_\phi(\mathbf{z}_i|\mathbf{x}_i)\right). \tag{4}$$

After the training phase, an effective model for compressing the original traffic data is obtained. Similar to all lossy compression methods, noise in the origi-

Table 1. Network Parameter

Module	Layer	Input	Output
Encoder	Layer 1	[W, 1]	[W/2, 16]
	Layer 2	[W/2, 16]	[W/2, 48]
	Layer 3	[W/2, 48]	[W/2, 32]
	Layer 4	[W/2, 32]	[W/4, 32]
	Layer 5	[W/4, 32]	[32, 1]
	Layer 6	[32, 1]	[K, 2]
Decoder	Layer 1	[K, 1]	[W/4, 32]
	Layer 2	[W/4, 32]	[W/2, 32]
	Layer 3	[W/2, 32]	[W/2, 48]
	Layer 4	[W/2, 48]	[W/2, 48]
	Layer 5	[W/2, 48]	[W, 16]
	Layer 6	[W, 16]	[W, 2]

nal data is filtered out after compression. When the compressed latent variables are used to reconstruct the traffic data, extreme values or abnormal patterns are likely to be assigned a relatively low probability. That is, if $\mathbf{x}$ contains an abnormal traffic pattern, $p_\theta(\mathbf{x}|\mathbf{z})$ is expected to be small.

Taking L samples from $q_\phi(\mathbf{z}|\mathbf{x})$, Eq. (5) can be used as the reconstruction probability based on this intuition. In some reference [12,16], reconstruction error is used as metric. In these works, the decoder would directly output the value of $\mathbf{x}$ instead of the probability. In fact, these two approaches share the same root. If the reconstruct error is large, the output value is likely to deviate largely from the mean, and thus has a low reconstruction probability.

$$\mathbb{E}_{q_\phi(\mathbf{z}|\mathbf{x})}\left[\log p_\theta(\mathbf{x}|\mathbf{z})\right] \approx \frac{1}{L}\sum_{l=1}^{L} \log p_\theta(\mathbf{x}|\mathbf{z}^{(l)}). \tag{5}$$

During detection, for each input $\mathbf{x}$, we calculate the reconstruction probability for each point within $\mathbf{x}$ using Eq. (5). The procedure is detailed in Algorithm 1. First, we iterate over all sliding windows containing the target point x_t. For each sliding window, if the reconstruction probability of x_t is smaller than a threshold P_{thres}, we increase the abnormal count by 1. To mitigate noise interference, a point is labeled as abnormal only when over 30% of the sliding windows containing it identify it as abnormal. To evaluate the performance of our detection method, we computed the precision and recall corresponding to each threshold. In the experiment, we exhaustively tested all possible thresholds and calculated the F1-score for each. The highest F1-score was selected as our evaluation metric, as it reflects the optimal performance of our model.

Algorithm 1: Detection Procedure

Data: All sliding windows containing target point x_t: $\mathbf{x_1}, \mathbf{x_2}, \ldots, \mathbf{x_W}$
Initialization $i = 0$, count=0;
while $i < W$ **do**
  $\boldsymbol{\mu_z}, \boldsymbol{\sigma_z}$ = Encoder($\mathbf{x}_i$) ;
  Take L samples from $q_\phi(\mathbf{z}|\mathbf{x}_i)$;
  Calculate Eq. 5 ;
  if $\frac{1}{L}\sum_{l=1}^{L} \log p_\theta(x_t|\mathbf{z}^{(l)}) \leq P_{thres}$ **then**
    count = count + 1;
  end
  $i = i + 1$;
end
if *count is larger than threshold* **then**
  x_t is tagged as anomaly point.
end

4 Evaluation

4.1 Dataset Preparation

We conducted data collection in a university network with approximately 20,000 APs. To collect fine-grained traffic data, we deployed a monitoring system on the switch gateway, as depicted in Fig. 4. In this setup, network traffic is mirrored to the monitor for data collection. The traffic logs obtained from the monitor are session-based. Once a network session ends, detailed information about this session is recorded. This session-based logging approach captures data regarding network interactions, including source and destination IP addresses, session start/end timestamps, and traffic volume etc.

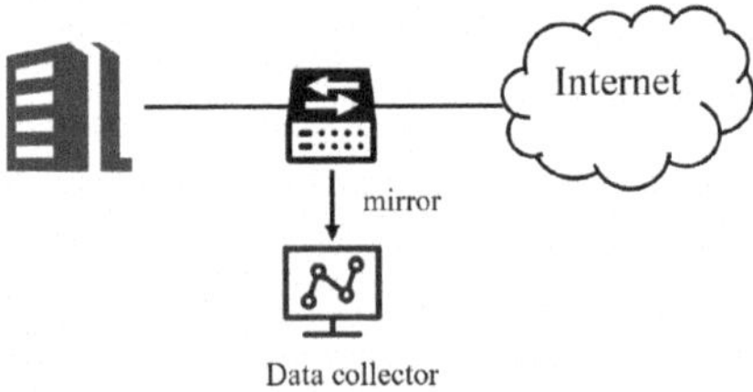

Fig. 4. Data Collection System

Based on this monitoring system, we collected traffic data over a 3-day period. As a result, each AP generates a traffic data sequence of length 4,320, where each data point represents the total uplink and downlink traffic through the AP within one minute. To ensure data quality, we filtered out inactive APs and selected 1,000 APs for the experiments.

During dataset collection, we still rely on user reports to identify faulty APs. However, daily reports of faulty APs are typically rare, making it difficult to build the dataset. To test the performance of the VAE, we first study real anomalous traffic patterns based on user reports, and then generate artificial noise based on them. In the experiment, we randomly select APs to inject with artificial noise. The total number of anomaly points is 3,638, distributed across 215 anomalous intervals, each lasting approximately 15 min.

During both training and detection phases, we exclude windows where zero-traffic data accounts for more than 80% of the entire window. Periods with such characteristics contribute little to the training process.

4.2 Experiment Setup

In the experiment, the window size W is set to 120, corresponding to a time span of 2 h. A window size that is too small would cause the VAE to focus primarily on local noise rather than capturing meaningful traffic trends. Conversely, an excessively large window size would necessitate expanding the network architecture and increasing the volume of training data, thereby elevating the risk of overfitting. With $W = 120$, the total number of windows for detection is 2,539,224. Among these, the number of windows containing anomaly points is 29,455, accounting for approximately 1.1% of the total.

The latent dimension K is set to 16. The impact of different values of K on the model's performance will be investigated later. During the training process, an L2 regularization penalty is applied to the hidden layers to prevent overfitting. To address potential numerical instabilities, the gradient norms were clipped, with a maximum limit set at 20.0. Before training and detection, the traffic data are normalized.

4.3 Performance Analysis

To evaluate the performance of the proposed method, we compare our approach with three baseline methods. These baselines also adopt a generative approach to detect anomaly points.

- DONUT [21]: DONUT uses fully-connect layers as building blocks of VAE. It also incorporates other tricks like missing value imputation and modified ELBO.
- CNN-VAE: This is the same as ours, except that dilated convolution is replaced by normal convolution.
- LSTM-VAE [12]: VAE is used to capture local features over short windows, and LSTM is built on top of VAE to capture long term trends.

Table 2 compares the results of these approaches. For DONUT and LSTM-VAE, we follow the architecture used in the reference and test different latent space dimensions to find the best performance. As for CNN-VAE, the only difference between CNN-VAE and our method is that we use dilated convolution instead of normal convolution.

Table 2. Precision, Recall and F1-score comparison of anomaly detection methods.

Method	Precision	Recall	F1
DONUT [21]	0.72	0.76	0.74
CNN-VAE	0.80	0.84	0.82
LSTM-VAE [12]	0.84	0.78	0.81
Ours	**0.86**	**0.90**	**0.88**

As in Table 2, our method achieves the best performance in all three key evaluation metrics. It achieves a F1 score of 0.88, markedly exceeding CNN-VAE (0.82), LSTM-VAE (0.81), and DONUT (0.74). This highlights the balance our model strikes between precision and recall. In terms of individual metrics, our method achieves the highest precision of 0.86, indicating the lowest false positive rate among all tested models. More notably, it yields a high recall of 0.90. This recall is particularly significant as it shows our model's robust capability to identify the vast majority of true anomalies, thereby minimizing false negatives—a critical requirement in many real-world anomaly detection systems.

An interesting observation is the suboptimal performance of LSTM-VAE in this specific application. We attribute this to the nature of the traffic patterns in our dataset. Although LSTMs are adept at modeling seasonal or long-term temporal dependencies, anomaly detection in our scenario is more dependent on local contextual information and abrupt deviations from neighboring points.

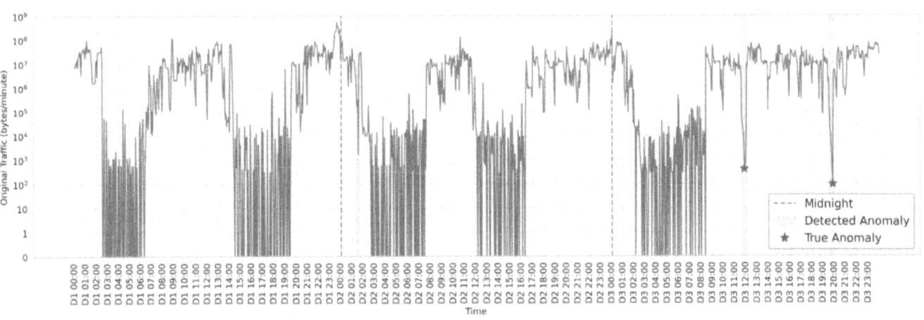

Fig. 5. Traffic log in a dormitory. Three anomalies are reported, with two of them are true anomalies.

To examine the data and detection results in greater detail, we present two case studies. Figure 5 illustrates the traffic log of an AP in a dormitory room, where the traffic exhibits two distinct patterns. During late nights, the traffic volume is low and discontinuous. In these periods—when there is no human activity—traffic spikes are attributed to background traffic. Two sudden traffic dip anomalies were detected on the last day; however, our method also falsely identified an anomaly on the first day. This might be because the minimum traffic volume during that period was close to the level of background traffic. For LSTM-VAE, such short-term temporal correlations are lost after compression in the LSTM cells, which impairs its performance.

Figure 6 shows the traffic log of a classroom AP, where an anomaly occurred on the first day. This anomaly arose when the AP failed to provide data services and only handled background traffic (e.g., management frames), and our approach successfully detected it.

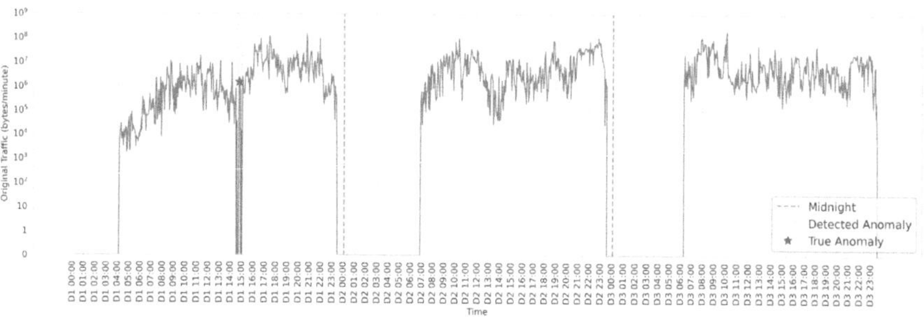

Fig. 6. Traffic log in a classroom. Traffic pattern suddenly changes for a while.

The impact of the latent dimension K on the model's performance is depicted in Fig. 7. Empirically, when the latent dimension is too small, the model tends to underfit, as it lacks the capacity to capture the complex patterns in the data. As shown in the figure, there is an increasing trend in the F1-score as K increases, indicating that a larger latent dimension allows the model to better represent the underlying traffic patterns. However, when K becomes excessively large, the model is prone to overfitting. In this case, the model may learn the noise of the training data too well, leading to poor generalization on unseen data.

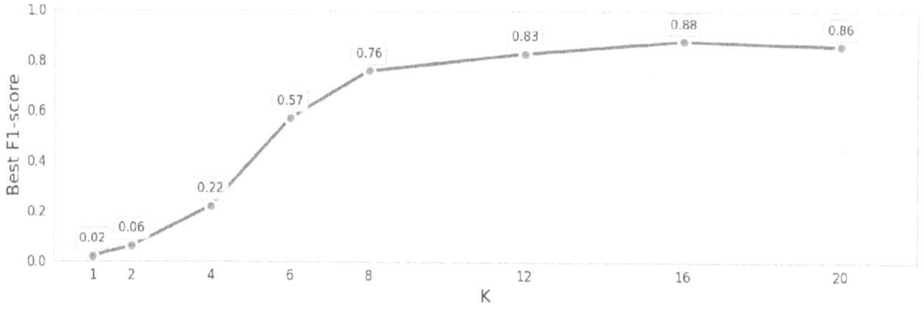

Fig. 7. The influence of latent space dimension.

5 Conclusion

In this work, we addressed the challenge of detecting faulty APs in enterprise WLANs. We formulated this problem as an unsupervised learning task. Specifically, we developed tools to collect traffic records for each AP and trained a VAE model for fault detection. To enhance the model's performance, we incorporated parallel dilated convolutions into the architecture to capture temporal dependencies across different time scales. Our experiments yielded a best F1-score of 0.88, outperforming other generative-based methods.

Looking ahead, future work will involve exploring multi-modal data. For instance, we can leverage the location information of APs and wireless KPIs such as RSSI. Co-located APs are likely to exhibit similar patterns, and wireless KPIs can offer valuable information about the wireless environment and connection quality. Such information can further improve the accuracy and reliability of our faulty AP detection system.

References

1. Aksoy, A., Gunes, M.H.: Automated IoT device identification using network traffic. In: ICC 2019-2019 IEEE International Conference on Communications (ICC), pp. 1–7. IEEE (2019)
2. Al-Garadi, M.A., Mohamed, A., Al-Ali, A.K., Du, X., Ali, I., Guizani, M.: A survey of machine and deep learning methods for internet of things (IoT) security. IEEE Commun. Surv. Tutorials **22**(3), 1646–1685 (2020)
3. Carmona, C.U., Aubet, F.X., Flunkert, V., Gasthaus, J.: Neural contextual anomaly detection for time series. arXiv preprint arXiv:2107.07702 (2021)
4. Chen, Y., Mahajan, R., Sridharan, B., Zhang, Z.L.: A provider-side view of web search response time. ACM SIGCOMM Comput. Commun. Rev. **43**(4), 243–254 (2013)
5. Chowdhury, R.R., Idris, A.C., Abas, P.E.: Identifying sh-iot devices from network traffic characteristics using random forest classifier. Wirel. Netw. **30**(1), 405–419 (2024)
6. Hamad, S.A., Zhang, W.E., Sheng, Q.Z., Nepal, S.: Iot device identification via network-flow based fingerprinting and learning. In: 2019 18th IEEE International Conference on Trust, Security and Privacy in Computing and Communications/13th IEEE International Conference on Big Data Science and Engineering (TrustCom/BigDataSE), pp. 103–111. IEEE (2019)
7. Iglesias, F., Zseby, T.: Analysis of network traffic features for anomaly detection. Mach. Learn. **101**, 59–84 (2015)
8. Kingma, D.P., Welling, M., et al.: Auto-encoding variational bayes (2013)
9. Knorn, F., Leith, D.J.: Adaptive Kalman filtering for anomaly detection in software appliances. In: IEEE INFOCOM Workshops 2008, pp. 1–6. IEEE (2008)
10. Kumari, R., Singh, M., Jha, R., Singh, N., et al.: Anomaly detection in network traffic using k-mean clustering. In: 2016 3rd International Conference on Recent Advances in Information Technology (RAIT), pp. 387–393. IEEE (2016)
11. Laptev, N., Amizadeh, S., Flint, I.: Generic and scalable framework for automated time-series anomaly detection. In: Proceedings of the 21th ACM SIGKDD International Conference on Knowledge Discovery and Data Mining, pp. 1939–1947 (2015)

12. Lin, S., Clark, R., Birke, R., Schönborn, S., Trigoni, N., Roberts, S.: Anomaly detection for time series using vae-lstm hybrid model. In: ICASSP 2020-2020 IEEE International Conference on Acoustics, Speech and Signal Processing (ICASSP), pp. 4322–4326. IEEE (2020)
13. Liu, D., et al.: Opprentice: towards practical and automatic anomaly detection through machine learning. In: Proceedings of the 2015 Internet Measurement Conference, pp. 211–224 (2015)
14. Lu, W., Ghorbani, A.A.: Network anomaly detection based on wavelet analysis. EURASIP J. Adv. Sig. Process. **2009**, 1–16 (2008)
15. Meidan, Y., et al.: Profiliot: a machine learning approach for IoT device identification based on network traffic analysis. In: Proceedings of the Symposium on Applied Computing, pp. 506–509 (2017)
16. Niu, Z., Yu, K., Wu, X.: LSTM-based vae-gan for time-series anomaly detection. Sensors **20**(13), 3738 (2020)
17. Radford, B.J., Apolonio, L.M., Trias, A.J., Simpson, J.A.: Network traffic anomaly detection using recurrent neural networks. arXiv preprint arXiv:1803.10769 (2018)
18. Ren, H., et al.: Time-series anomaly detection service at Microsoft. In: Proceedings of the 25th ACM SIGKDD International Conference on Knowledge Discovery & Data Mining, pp. 3009–3017 (2019)
19. Su, Y., Zhao, Y., Niu, C., Liu, R., Sun, W., Pei, D.: Robust anomaly detection for multivariate time series through stochastic recurrent neural network. In: Proceedings of the 25th ACM SIGKDD International Conference on Knowledge Discovery & Data Mining, pp. 2828–2837 (2019)
20. Wang, Z., et al.: Revisiting vae for unsupervised time series anomaly detection: a frequency perspective. In: Proceedings of the ACM Web Conference 2024, pp. 3096–3105 (2024)
21. Xu, H., et al.: Unsupervised anomaly detection via variational auto-encoder for seasonal kpis in web applications. In: Proceedings of the 2018 World Wide Web Conference, pp. 187–196 (2018)
22. Xu, J., Wu, H., Wang, J., Long, M.: Anomaly transformer: time series anomaly detection with association discrepancy. arXiv preprint arXiv:2110.02642 (2021)
23. Yu, F., Koltun, V.: Multi-scale context aggregation by dilated convolutions. arXiv preprint arXiv:1511.07122 (2015)
24. Zhou, H., et al.: Informer: beyond efficient transformer for long sequence time-series forecasting. In: Proceedings of the AAAI Conference on Artificial Intelligence, vol. 35, pp. 11106–11115 (2021)

FeRN: Hybrid Node-to-Node Loss Recovery in Overlay Network

Yixin Shen[1], Bo Wang[1(✉)], Wufan Wang[2], Yixuan Gao[1], and Mingwei Xu[1]

[1] Tsinghua University, Beijing 100084, China
syx@ieee.org, {wangbo2019,xumw}@tsinghua.edu.cn,
gaoyx22@mails.tsinghua.edu.cn

[2] Beijing University of Posts and Telecommunications, Beijing 100876, China
wufanwang@bupt.edu.cn

Abstract. Utilizing Internet links in an overlay network to save costs is becoming a widespread solution for enterprise cloud service architectures. However, existing methods struggle to effectively transfer data through cross-region Internet links with high loss rates and latency, which makes it challenging to reduce the 95th percentile bandwidth cost. We propose FeRN, a hybrid node-to-node loss recovery design that focuses on the optimization of Internet links between each pair of nodes, decreasing the end-to-end loss rate of various applications, including bulk data transfer, latency-sensitive and short-lived ones. FeRN employs real-time forward error correction (FEC) coding with dynamic redundancy to address varying loss patterns on Internet links. Experiments with real-world traces demonstrate that compared to TCP Cubic, FeRN can effectively reduce end-to-end loss rate, thus increasing throughput by 200%, reducing 99th percentile tail latency by 32%, and reducing short flow completion time by 17%.

Keywords: Overlay Network · Loss Recovery · Cloud Service

1 Introduction

Cloud services play a crucial role in modern society, encompassing a wide range of applications, including video conferencing [14,28,30], cloud PC [1,7,20], as well as file backup [17,18]. With enterprises operating across countries and regions, cross-regional node interconnection becomes essential for collaborative tasks like international video conferencing. Consequently, cloud service providers must ensure high-quality cross-regional interconnection to maintain a high Quality of Experience (QoE) for cloud services.

Typically, cross-regional interconnection relies on either public Internet links or premium links. Premium links deliver superior performance but are costly, whereas Internet links are more affordable but lack performance guarantees [31]. To balance between quality and cost, current cloud service providers often

T. Qiu et al. (Eds.): CCF ChinaNet 2025, CCIS 2810, pp. 158–169, 2026.
https://doi.org/10.1007/978-981-95-8450-5_12

employ both Internet links and premium links. For instance, XRON [29] utilizes premium links as backups, swiftly switching to them when the Internet link underperforms due to packet loss or other issues.

However, existing solutions have not effectively reduced the dependency on premium links, resulting in persistent high costs. The root cause of this challenge lies in the high packet loss rates observed on Internet links. Our measurements (Sect. 2.2) reveal that cross-regional Internet links frequently suffer from prolonged packet loss, especially during peak hours. The average packet loss rate during peak periods reaches 5%, with spikes up to 30%. Even some good quality links experience some peak periods where the average packet loss rate exceeds 5%.

When packet loss rates are high (e.g., exceed 5%), application performance deteriorates significantly. For flows with loss-based congestion control algorithms (CCA), frequent window reductions caused by high packet loss result in a substantial throughput drop. For latency-sensitive flows, increased retransmissions exacerbate tail latency and impair QoE. Similarly, for short flows, frequent tail retransmissions due to high packet loss can greatly increase flow completion time, negatively impacting their performance.

Given the poor performance of Internet links, they often struggle to carry traffic effectively during peak periods due to packet loss, resulting in premium links bearing the majority of the traffic load. As premium link pricing is calculated based on the 95th percentile of traffic volume (i.e., peak traffic) [25], the inability to reduce peak-period traffic on premium links perpetuates the high-cost problem.

To fully harness the potential of Internet links, this work aims to improve their transmission performance, enabling them to share a larger portion of the traffic load. This approach eases the burden on premium links and helps lower overall costs.

This paper proposes FeRN, a transport-layer solution for node-to-node loss recovery over Internet links, avoiding bandwidth waste of the entire path from end-to-end recovery. The main challenge FeRN faces is the bursty nature of losses on Internet links and the temporal variability of loss patterns. To overcome it, FeRN employs a three-state loss model to capture bursty packet loss behaviors and uses Dynamic Real-time forward error correction (FEC) Coding for redundancy-based recovery between nodes.

We collected extensive real-world data to analyze the characteristics of Internet links and validated FeRN in Mininet emulation environment using real-world traces. The results demonstrate that for various applications, including bulk data transfer, latency-sensitive and short-lived flows, FeRN improves average node-to-node throughput by 200%, reduces 99th-percentile latency at the frame level by 17%, and significantly decreases flow completion time for short flows by 32%, compared to TCP Cubic.

2 Background and Motivations

2.1 Hybrid Overlay Network

The rising demand for large-scale cloud services has significantly increased cross-region traffic in overlay networks, making cost-efficient deployment a priority for enterprises. Hybrid overlay networks [16,29] offer a solution by strategically combining Internet and premium links to optimize traffic costs.

Lossy Internet Links. Cross-region Internet links, unlike premium ones, offer inconsistent performance, with higher packet loss rates and latency that vary by time of day [29]. To understand their transmission characteristics, we analyzed packet loss rates and latency over 24 h between a pair of transcontinental nodes.

As shown in Fig. 1, Internet links consistently exhibit high packet loss and latency. During peak hours, packet loss averages 5%, peaking at 15%, while the average Round-Trip Time (RTT) rises from 250 to 300 ms. A 5% loss rate severely degrades throughput for bulk transfers, and an RTT of 300 ms adds significant latency to end-to-end retransmissions, greatly affecting latency-sensitive applications and short flows.

Saving 95th Bandwidth Cost. Hybrid overlay networks use Internet links as cost-saving complements to premium links, reducing over-all bandwidth costs. A strawman approach involves utilizing Internet links during off-peak periods and switching to premium links during peak periods to achieve temporal complementarity. While this avoids Internet link performance issues during peak hours, it offers limited cost savings. Premium link pricing by ISPs is typically based on the 95th percentile bandwidth [25], calculated over billing cycles of one day to one month. This means that lowering the 95th percentile bandwidth is the only way to achieve substantial cost reductions. However, on a daily scale, the 95th percentile often coincides with traffic peaks, which align with degraded Internet link performance.

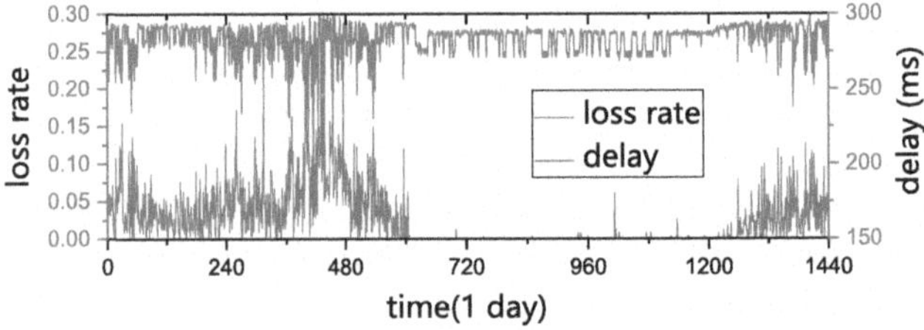

Fig. 1. Loss rate and delay of Internet link.

Figure 2 illustrates the 24-hour traffic between intercontinental nodes and the loss rate of their Internet link. The two trends are highly similar, with peak packet loss coinciding with traffic surges, and the 95th percentile bandwidth falling exactly within the highest loss period. Thus, the strawman approach

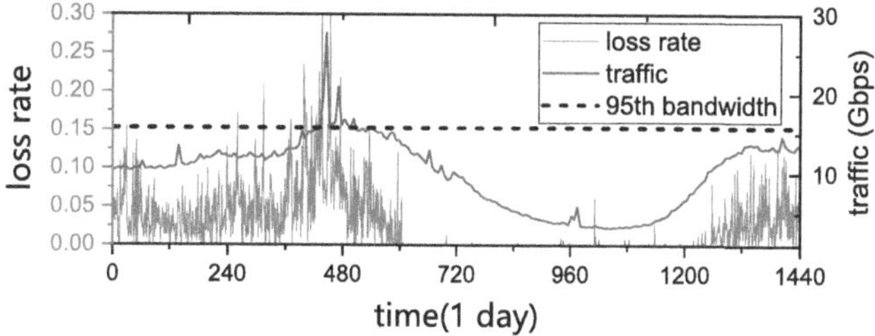

Fig. 2. Loss rate correspond to node traffic.

struggles to utilize Internet links during peaks, making the temporal complementarity strategy ineffective.

Therefore, relying solely on temporal complementarity to reduce costs is insufficient. To lower the 95th percentile bandwidth cost, Internet links must be utilized even during high-loss periods to balance traffic across all links during peaks.

2.2 Loss Recovery on Internet Links

Using Internet links with high packet loss and latency requires effective loss recovery to protect application QoE. Overlay networks host various cloud applications, including latency-sensitive video conferencing, bulk data transfers, and short HTTP flows, which suffer varying performance impacts from degraded Internet links. As shown in Table 1, packet loss nearly doubles the 99th percentile delay of latency-sensitive applications, cuts bulk transfer throughput by half or more, and increases short flow completion time by 59%. This highlights the need to design loss recovery mechanisms that address diverse application requirements, optimizing both throughput and latency with a focus on reducing end-to-end loss rates.

Adaptive forward error correction (FEC) is a common end-to-end loss recovery strategy but adds overhead along the entire path, increasing congestion risks at bottlenecks. End-to-end retransmission, meanwhile, causes significant delays in high-latency Internet links. For short flows, tail packet loss often triggers retransmission timeouts (RTO), severely impacting flow completion time.

We argue that node-to-node loss recovery is ideal for Internet links, as it can be optimized specifically for Internet links and deployed at the node level without altering user-end applications. Additionally, operating on shorter network paths enables faster retransmissions and quicker link state updates, enhancing real-time responsiveness. This approach not only addresses Internet link challenges but also improves end-host performance.

To optimize loss recovery design for Internet links, we collected traces of Internet links between two intercontinental nodes and analyzed the packet loss pattern.

We analyzed packet loss events on the Internet link between two nodes over 24 h, classifying them by burst length. Figure 3 shows that burst losses constitute

Table 1. Performance degradation of different types of flows in lossy network.

loss rate	latency-sensitive 99th delay(s)	bulk transfer thpt(Mbps)	short flow FCT(s)
0%	0.223	9.5	1.12
2%	0.596	5.2	1.48
5%	0.618	3.9	1.79

40% of all events. The distribution of n-burst losses follows an approximately geometric pattern, with 2- or 3-packet bursts being relatively common. This aligns with previous findings [8,24]. A likely explanation is that the heavily utilized Internet link experiences short congestion bursts at gateways, causing burst losses [13]. Additionally, ISPs can employ queue management policies to alleviate transient congestion, resulting in variable loss rates and burst loss patterns observed by applications [4,9,23].

Our findings indicate that Internet links generally have sufficient potential bandwidth. Node experiments show that loss-tolerant designs like BBR achieve desirable throughput even during peak periods. To mitigate transient and persistent packet loss, we applied dynamic interleaved coding to reduce end-to-end loss rates. However, interleaving FEC introduces additional decoding latency, making it essential to improve its real-time performance and minimize end-to-end delays.

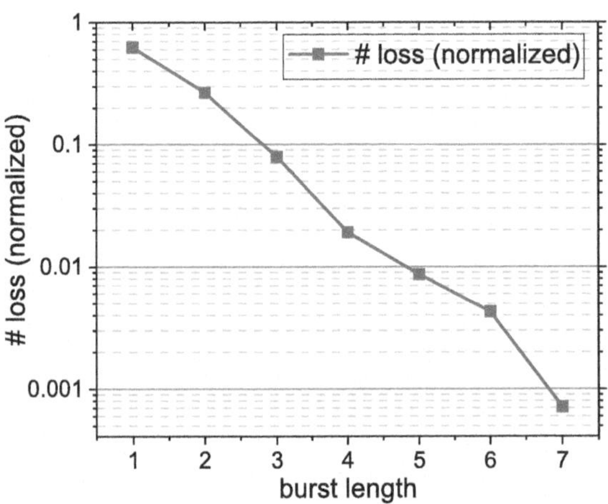

Fig. 3. Distribution of packet loss with different burst length.

2.3 Related Works

Overlay Network. Overlay networks have been extensively studied and applied in both academia and industry [3,6,15,26]. Skyplane [13] focuses on throughput optimization of bulk transfer on cross-region links. XRON [29] uses network layer approach to balance between Internet links and premium links. In comparison, FeRN mainly focuses on transport-layer Internet link optimization.

Redundancy Coding. There are many previous studies about redundancy codings [5,11,12,24,33]. Interleaving FEC are also investigated [19,32] and applied in scenarios such as wireless network [22] and RDMA [34]. There are also works that try to make joint optimization of redundancy and retransmission [2,10,27]. To the best of our knowledge, FeRN is the first to (1) modeled interleaving coding with 3-state loss model in Internet links (2) tail loss detection and mitigation with retransmission.

3 Design

FeRN is a transmission optimization system deployed at gateway nodes, combining coding-based and retransmission-based loss recovery to optimize node-to-node performance.

FeRN employs dynamic real-time FEC encoding to adapt to changing network conditions and traffic patterns. To address the dynamic changes in latency and loss rates, each node monitors packet loss patterns, determining optimal FEC parameters, which are periodically synchronized with the sender. Additionally, FeRN tracks real-time throughput, dynamically adjusting the size of the FEC coding blocks to minimize the potential decoding delay at the receiver, ensuring efficient data recovery while maintaining low latency.

Packet Loss Model. The granularity of loss characterization heavily influences coding parameter selection. As shown in §2.1, peak hours see higher packet loss rates with predominantly burst losses, while off-peak periods have lower loss rates but still exhibit notable burst loss events. FeRN must dynamically track evolving loss patterns and adjust coding parameters to enhance recovery rates while minimizing redundancy.

FeRN computes coding parameters by monitoring real-time network loss conditions. Since naive loss models fail to capture burst loss patterns, FeRN uses a state-transition Markov model to characterize packet loss behavior for better coding decisions. Figure 4 presents a three-state Markov model with states for no loss, random loss, and burst loss. State transition probabilities represent the likelihood of link degradation or recovery. Compared to the naive model, the three-state model effectively captures burst loss patterns while remaining statistically simple.

Packet Coding Pattern. To minimize computational overhead and since the Internet links predominantly experience packet erasures (packet loss), rather bit-errors, FeRN uses XOR-based encoding for packet-level redundancy. For n

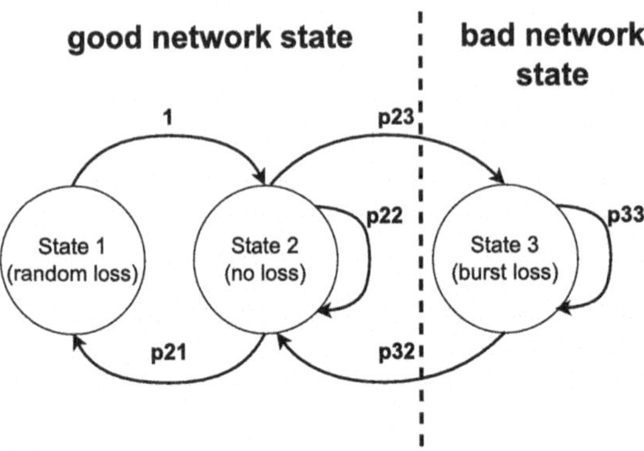

Fig. 4. Three-state markov model of packet loss.

original packets, the encoder generates one FEC redundant packet via XOR operations. The value of n, controlled by the redundancy rate, is dynamically updated by the encoding controller. To mitigate burst losses, FeRN employs interleaving coding, rearranging data so consecutive symbols are distributed across the coding group. Each group forms an $n * d$ matrix, with vertical columns as FEC blocks. The interleaving depth d determines tolerance for up to d-burst losses. Since interleaving adds decoding latency, d must be carefully calibrated to maintain acceptable end-to-end latency.

Dynamic Real-time Coding Model. FeRN's coding model must consider dynamic loss patterns and real-time requirements. Its optimization objective is to use the transition probabilities of the three-state loss model to dynamically determine the coding block length n and interleaving depth d, ensuring the end-to-end packet loss rate stays below $loss_{th}$ while maintaining recovery delay under $delay_{th}$.

Loss Rate Constraint. Given the coding parameter set (n, gap) and the state transition probabilities of the loss model, our goal is to quantify how much the end-to-end packet loss rate can be mitigated. This establishes the loss rate constraint condition. With interleaving coding, burst losses shorter than d are treated as random losses within a single coding block. Thus, coding fails in only two scenarios:

1. Burst length exceeds d
2. Multiple random losses (≥ 2) occur within a single coding block of size $n + 1$

For random packet loss, the loss occurrence rate is defined as $lhr = p_{21} + p_{23}$, representing the probability of a single packet loss event regardless of the burst length. In every coding block of $n+1$ packets, one redundancy packet is encoded. If more than one packet is lost within this block, recovery becomes impossible. Consequently, the expected end-to-end packet loss rate can be expressed as follows:

$$lr_{random} = E(x|x > 1, x \sim B(n + 1, lhr)) \tag{1}$$

For burst losses, we define burst length as $burst$. Recovery becomes impossible if $burst$ exceeds the interleaving depth d. Consequently, the expected end-to-end packet loss rate is calculated as follows:

$$lr_{burst} = E(x = \lceil \frac{burst}{d} \rceil | burst > d, burst \sim G(p33)) \tag{2}$$

Thus, the end-to-end loss rate after coding, lr_{code}, is derived as the weighted sum of the above two values. It should be limited by $loss_{th}$, thereby satisfying the packet loss constraint:

$$lr_{code} = (lr_{random} + p_{23} * lr_{burst}) < loss_{th} \tag{3}$$

Latency Constraint. Given coding parameters (n, d), the objective is to ensure that the maximum recovery latency $delay_{code}$ remains within a threshold $delay_{th}$, limiting the worst-case end-to-end latency increase to $delay_{th}$. FeRN estimates this delay by monitoring real-time throughput $thpt$ at the receiver node.

$$delay_{code} = \frac{n * d}{thpt} < delay_{th} \tag{4}$$

4 Evaluation

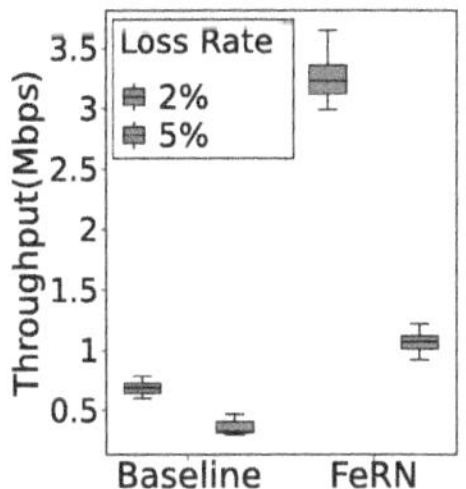

Fig. 5. Bulk transfer

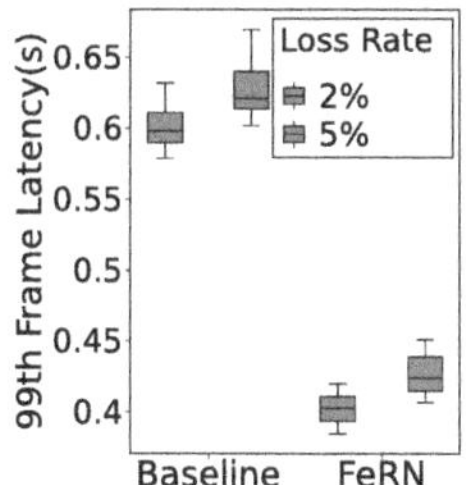

Fig. 6. Latency-sensitive

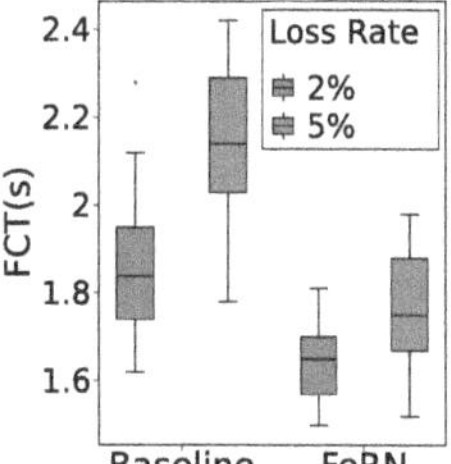

Fig. 7. Short-lived

We evaluate FeRN in the Mininet emulation environment. FeRN is integrated into the encapsulation layer of nodes within the VxLAN protocol, incorporating custom packet headers to enable loss recovery functionality.

In the Mininet emulation environment, we created a typical node forwarding topology, where n endpoints communicate through a single pair of node links, with n set based on experimental needs. We also collected application traces from production nodes across three countries over a month and selected representative datasets to evaluate FeRN's performance.

4.1 FeRN Performance

We compare the performance of bulk transfer flows, latency-sensitive flows, and short-lived flows on Mininet. To emulate real-world scenarios, we set the number of endpoints to $n = 10$ and initiated random traffic flows of various types from different endpoints. Figure 5, 6, 7 show the performance of these traffic types on network links with 2% and 5% average packet loss.

The baseline group does not incorporate any loss recovery strategies, while the FeRN group employs dynamic real-time node-to-node FEC. Results show varying improvements across traffic types. Bulk transfer flows saw the greatest enhancement in throughput, attributed to TCP's spurious retransmission as local recovery replaces end-to-end retransmission. For latency-sensitive and short flows, FeRN significantly reduced latency by mitigating packet loss.

4.2 FeRN Overhead

We define transmission *overhead* as the proportion of redundant packets and retransmitted packets. We analyze FeRN's overhead under different $loss_{th}$ with BBR flows and the associated changes in end-to-end packet loss rate. Figure 8 shows the relationship between FeRN's overhead and performance (end-to-end loss rate) under a 2% link loss rate, alongside the theoretical overhead curve.

The results show that FeRN's overhead approaches the optimal level, with higher overhead achieving performance closer to the theoretical maximum. This is because increasing the coding block length n reduces accuracy loss from rounding effects.

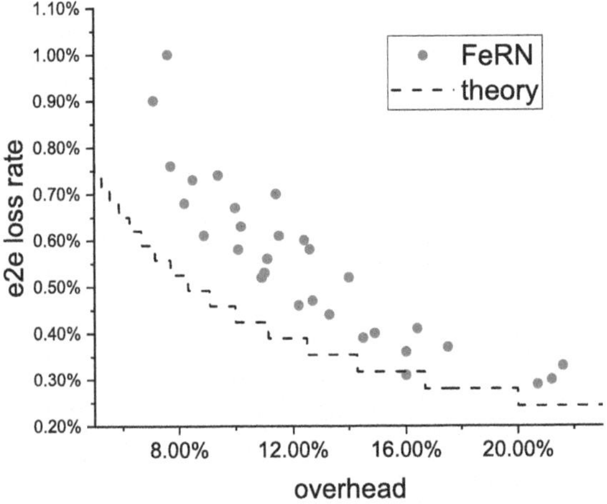

Fig. 8. FeRN overhead vs performance.

5 Conclusion and Future Works

This paper focuses on optimizing data transmission on Internet links with high packet loss and latency in overlay networks. We analyze the necessity of optimizing Internet links to save costs and collect real-world data on traffic patterns and packet loss patterns. To improve end-to-end performance, we propose FeRN, a node-to-node solution employing real-time dynamic FEC. Validated with real-world traces, FeRN effectively reduces packet loss and enhances performance. However, there is still room for improvement and future work will explore the following directions.

Coding Redundancy. Using FEC encoding to mitigate packet loss introduces significant bandwidth overhead. FeRN currently adjusts FEC aggressiveness via $loss_{th}$ but lacks a mechanism to better coordinate FEC and retransmission. Inspired by Hairpin [21], we believe greater focus is needed on balancing FEC and retransmission. For FeRN, developing a dynamic mechanism to balance coding redundancy and retransmission delay is a key area for future work.

Real-World Experiment. Currently, FeRN lacks sufficient real-world experimentation. Further testing is required to evaluate its performance and robustness in production environments and to quantify the extent of cost optimizations it can achieve.

References

1. Abimbola, B.: Cloud computing concept and roots. arXiv preprint arXiv:2102.00981 (2021)
2. Ahmed, A., Al-Dweik, A., Iraqi, Y., Mukhtar, H., Naeem, M., Hossain, E.: Hybrid automatic repeat request (harq) in wireless communications systems and standards: a contemporary survey. IEEE Commun. Surv. Tutorials **23**(4), 2711–2752 (2021)
3. Andersen, D., Balakrishnan, H., Kaashoek, F., Morris, R.: Resilient overlay networks. In: Proceedings of the Eighteenth ACM Symposium on Operating Systems Principles, pp. 131–145 (2001)
4. Baltrunas, D., Elmokashfi, A., Kvalbein, A., Alay, Ö.: Investigating packet loss in mobile broadband networks under mobility. In: 2016 IFIP Networking Conference (IFIP Networking) and Workshops, pp. 225–233. IEEE (2016)
5. Bolot, J.C., Fosse-Parisis, S., Towsley, D.: Adaptive fec-based error control for internet telephony. In: IEEE INFOCOM'99. Conference on Computer Communications. Proceedings. Eighteenth Annual Joint Conference of the IEEE Computer and Communications Societies. The Future is Now (Cat. No. 99CH36320), vol. 3, pp. 1453–1460. IEEE (1999)
6. Cai, C.X., Le, F., Sun, X., Xie, G.G., Jamjoom, H., Campbell, R.H.: Cronets: cloud-routed overlay networks. In: 2016 IEEE 36th International Conference on Distributed Computing Systems (ICDCS), pp. 67–77. IEEE (2016)
7. Chhabra, S., Singh, A.K.: A comprehensive vision on cloud computing environment: Emerging challenges and future research directions. arXiv preprint arXiv:2207.07955 (2022)

8. Commission, F.C.: Measuring broadband America (2021). https://www.fcc.gov/reports-research/reports/measuring-broadband-america/measuring-fixed-broadband-eleventh-report
9. Dischinger, M., Haeberlen, A., Gummadi, K.P., Saroiu, S.: Characterizing residential broadband networks. In: Proceedings of the 7th ACM SIGCOMM conference on Internet measurement, pp. 43–56 (2007)
10. Flach, T., et al.: Reducing web latency: the virtue of gentle aggression. In: Proceedings of the ACM SIGCOMM 2013 conference on SIGCOMM, pp. 159–170 (2013)
11. Fong, S.L., Khisti, A., Li, B., Tan, W.T., Zhu, X., Apostolopoulos, J.: Optimal streaming codes for channels with burst and arbitrary erasures. IEEE Trans. Inf. Theory **65**(7), 4274–4292 (2019)
12. Garrido, P., Sanchez, I., Ferlin, S., Aguero, R., Alay, O.: rquic: Integrating fec with quic for robust wireless communications. In: 2019 IEEE Global Communications Conference (GLOBECOM), pp. 1–7 (2019). https://doi.org/10.1109/GLOBECOM38437.2019.9013401
13. Jain, P., Kumar, S., Wooders, S., Patil, S.G., Gonzalez, J.E., Stoica, I.: Skyplane: optimizing transfer cost and throughput using {Cloud-Aware} overlays. In: 20th USENIX Symposium on Networked Systems Design and Implementation (NSDI 23), pp. 1375–1389 (2023)
14. Jiang, J., et al.: Via: improving internet telephony call quality using predictive relay selection. In: Proceedings of the 2016 ACM SIGCOMM Conference, pp. 286–299 (2016)
15. Jiang, J., et al.: Via: Improving internet telephony call quality using predictive relay selection. In: Proceedings of the 2016 ACM SIGCOMM Conference, pp. 286–299 (2016)
16. Kataria, B., et al.: Saving private wan: using internet paths to offload wan traffic in conferencing services. Proc. ACM Netw. **2**(CoNEXT4), 1–22 (2024)
17. Kaur, R., Chana, I., Bhattacharya, J.: Data deduplication techniques for efficient cloud storage management: a systematic review. J. Supercomput. **74**, 2035–2085 (2018)
18. Leesakul, W., Townend, P., Xu, J.: Dynamic data deduplication in cloud storage. In: 2014 IEEE 8th International Symposium on Service Oriented System Engineering, pp. 320–325. IEEE (2014)
19. Liu, J., Zhang, X., Blow, K., Fowler, S.: Performance analysis of packet layer fec codes and interleaving in fso channels. IET Commun. **11**(13), 2042–2048 (2017)
20. Luo, X., Zhang, W., Li, H., Bose, R., Chung, Q.B.: Cloud computing capability: its technological root and business impact. J. Organ. Comput. Electron. Commer. **28**(3), 193–213 (2018)
21. Meng, Z., et al.: Hairpin: rethinking packet loss recovery in edge-based interactive video streaming. In: 21st USENIX Symposium on Networked Systems Design and Implementation (NSDI 24), pp. 907–926 (2024)
22. Pathak, P., Bhatia, R.: Investigation of ldpc codes with interleaving for 5g wireless networks. Ann. Telecommun. pp. 1–11 (2024)
23. Raghavendra, R., Belding, E.M.: Characterizing high-bandwidth real-time video traffic in residential broadband networks. In: 8th International Symposium on Modeling and Optimization in Mobile, Ad Hoc, and Wireless Networks, pp. 597–602. IEEE (2010)

24. Rudow, M., Yan, F.Y., Kumar, A., Ananthanarayanan, G., Ellis, M., Rashmi, K.: Tambur: efficient loss recovery for videoconferencing via streaming codes. In: 20th USENIX Symposium on Networked Systems Design and Implementation (NSDI 23), pp. 953–971 (2023)
25. Tian, Y., Li, Z., Liu, M.Y., Mao, J., Tyson, G., Xie, G.: Cost-saving streaming: Unlocking the potential of alternative edge node resources. In: Proceedings of the 2024 ACM on Internet Measurement Conference, pp. 580–587 (2024)
26. Tootaghaj, D.Z., Ahmed, F., Sharma, P., Yannakakis, M.: Homa: An efficient topology and route management approach in sd-wan overlays. In: IEEE INFOCOM 2020-IEEE Conference on Computer Communications, pp. 2351–2360. IEEE (2020)
27. Uberti, J.: Webrtc forward error correction requirements. Internet Eng. Task Force (IETF) Doc. RFC **8854**, 10 (2021)
28. Ukani, A., Mirian, A., Snoeren, A.C.: Locked-in during lock-down: undergraduate life on the internet in a pandemic. In: Proceedings of the 21st ACM Internet Measurement Conference, pp. 480–486 (2021)
29. Wu, B., et al.: Xron: A hybrid elastic cloud overlay network for video conferencing at planetary scale. In: Proceedings of the ACM SIGCOMM 2023 Conference, pp. 696–709 (2023)
30. Wu, Y., Wu, C., Li, B., Lau, F.C.: vskyconf: cloud-assisted multi-party mobile video conferencing. In: Proceedings of the second ACM SIGCOMM workshop on Mobile cloud computing, pp. 33–38 (2013)
31. Yeganeh, B., Durairajan, R., Rejaie, R., Willinger, W.: A case for performance-and cost-aware multi-cloud overlays. In: 2023 IEEE 16th International Conference on Cloud Computing (CLOUD), pp. 560–566. IEEE (2023)
32. Yin, H.H., Ng, K.H., Zhong, A.Z., Yeung, R.W., Yang, S., Chan, I.Y.: Intrablock interleaving for batched network coding with blockwise adaptive recoding. IEEE J. Selected Areas Inf. Theory **2**(4), 1135–1149 (2021)
33. Zuo, T., et al.: Lowar: Enhancing rdma over lossy wans with transparent error correction. In: 2024 IEEE/ACM 32nd International Symposium on Quality of Service (IWQoS), pp. 1–10 (2024). https://doi.org/10.1109/IWQoS61813.2024.10682853
34. Zuo, T., et al.: Lowar: Enhancing rdma over lossy wans with transparent error correction. In: 2024 IEEE/ACM 32nd International Symposium on Quality of Service (IWQoS), pp. 1–10 (2024). https://doi.org/10.1109/IWQoS61813.2024.10682853

Interpretable Fault Prediction via Fusion of Static and Temporal Knowledge Graphs

Hanlin Liu[1], Yu Yang[1], Mingyue Li[1], Aliya Bao[1], and Hua Li[1,2,3(✉)]

[1] Inner Mongolia University, Hohhot 010021, China
cslihua@imu.edu.cn
[2] Inner Mongolia Engineering Research Center of Ecological Big Data Ministry of Educdation, Hohhot 010021, China
[3] Inner Mongolia Engineering Laboratory for Cloud Computing and Service, Hohhot 010021, China

Abstract. Fault prediction in network operations and maintenance (O&M) has become increasingly challenging due to the complexity and scale of modern AI workloads. Traditional topology-based AI for IT Operations methods fail to capture the temporal dynamics of fault propagation, which constrains accurate fault localization. Although knowledge graphs (KGs) have been introduced to alleviate this problem, they still fail to effectively capture static fault factual knowledge and neglect the temporal dynamics of network systems. To fill these gaps, this paper designs FFE-TKG, which fuses static fault factual knowledge with temporal information to build temporal KGs (TKGs). Based on the TKGs, a fault prediction architecture, FRP-TKG, is proposed, which leverages entity frequencies and contextual relationships in TKGs and employs reinforcement learning to enhance interpretability. Experiments on real datasets demonstrate that FRP-TKG outperforms existing baselines, enabling more effective and reliable O&M decision-making.

Keywords: Temporal Knowledge Graph · Network Operations and Maintenance · Fault Pediction

1 Introduction

The rapid growth of large-scale Artificial Intelligence (AI) models, such as Generative AI and Large Language Models (LLMs), has introduced increasingly severe operations and maintenance (O&M) challenges to modern data centers and network infrastructures, including resource conflicts, software defects, hardware malfunctions, etc. As these issues threaten system stability and may lead to service disruptions and economic losses, AI for IT Operations (AIOps) has emerged as an effective solution [1].

AIOps leverages machine learning (ML) techniques to improve the efficiency and intelligence of fault detection and diagnosis [2]. Although traditional AIOps

T. Qiu et al. (Eds.): CCF ChinaNet 2025, CCIS 2810, pp. 170–184, 2026.
https://doi.org/10.1007/978-981-95-8450-5_13

approaches based on physical or logical topology graphs can effectively monitor faults [3], they primarily focus on real-time fault detection but often overlook the systematic modeling of underlying fault propagation processes, thus struggling to construct a comprehensive O&M knowledge base. This makes it difficult for O&M personnel to quickly locate and handle faults.

Motivated by these challenges, recent research has turned to constructing O&M knowledge graphs (KGs) for more effective fault root cause analysis. These studies have modeled various entities and their relationships across different operational scenarios. In microservices environments, KGs are constructed by capturing performance metrics and their relationships [4], network service dependencies [5], and hardware-software interactions [6]. Similarly, in cloud-native settings, KGs primarily represent physical and logical system components, anomaly alerts, and application events along with their interconnections [7]. For Function-as-a-Service scenarios, the focus shifts to modeling clusters and their operational relationships [8].

However, existing approaches lack comprehensive modeling of static fault factual knowledge from fault cases. For instance, the fact that persistent high CPU usage on a gateway node often leads to downstream service timeouts is rarely captured explicitly. The absence of such factual knowledge limits a system's ability to recognize recurring fault patterns, which may result in less accurate fault localization and delayed resolution. Moreover, they largely overlook the temporal dependencies inherent in O&M data, which are critical for capturing the dynamic behavior of network systems.

Therefore, it is essential to construct Temporal Knowledge Graphs (TKGs) [17] that integrate fault factual knowledge with dynamic network behaviors. For example, DFSFED [9] leverages temporal and spatial associations to fuse service-oriented trouble reports with real-time alarm messages. Subsequently, TKGs are introduced to more accurately model dependencies and prior knowledge among network components [10]. To further overcome the limitations of relying solely on localized information, an STKGN model [11] is proposed to capture spatio-temporal correlations. Despite these advancements, existing fault prediction methods still suffer from limited accuracy and poor interpretability, hindering their adoption in real-world O&M scenarios.

To address the limitations of insufficient O&M data mining and inadequate predictive capability with poor interpretability of fault prediction approaches, this paper proposes a novel KG fusion method. It lays the foundation for a dual-module collaborative architecture, FRP-TKG, which enhances fault prediction by identifying fault triggers and tracing potential propagation paths. The main contributions of this paper are summarized as follows:

1. We design a KG fusion method, FFF-TKG, which integrates static fault factual knowledge with temporal fault information to construct network O&M TKGs tailored for fault prediction.
2. Building on these TKGs, we propose a fault prediction architecture, named FRP-TKG, which enables accurate fault prediction while enhancing interpretability through reinforcement learning (RL).

3. We evaluate the performance of the proposed FRP-TKG model against multiple baselines for the fault prediction task using real-world datasets.

2 Related Work

Current fault prediction methods generally fall into two categories: ML-based and KG-based methods. ML-based methods, such as Support Vector Machine (SVM) [13] and LSTM [14], have shown strong potential in network O&M fault prediction. SVMs perform well on small datasets but are sensitive to kernel and penalty settings. LSTM-based models, known for their ability to capture temporal dependencies, achieve improved accuracy when enhanced with attention mechanisms. For example, Cinar et al. [15] proposed an attention-enhanced recurrent neural network to handle periodic time-series data with missing values, while Liang et al. [16] introduced a multi-level encoder-decoder architecture to capture dynamic spatiotemporal patterns. However, ML-based approaches rely heavily on numerical features and lack the semantic abstraction necessary to represent and reason about the factual nature of fault events.

Recently, KG-based methods have gained attention by integrating multi-source data and modeling complex entity relationships. Liu et al. [9] developed the DFSPED system that combines service topology with fault reports for proactive fault management, but it requires extensive historical data and complex data engineering. Zhang et al. [10] proposed a TKG-based framework for Remaining Useful Life (RUL) prediction, which improved temporal reasoning but overlooked model interpretability. Similarly, Huai et al. [11] emphasized the benefits of capturing spatiotemporal correlations through KGs, yet their approach did not fully consider the structured modeling of fault factual knowledge.

Despite their Progress, Existing Approaches Exhibit Two Major Limitations. First, they often overlook fault factual knowledge, which is critical for understanding and generalizing fault propagation and solutions. Such knowledge abstracts and generalizes historical fault events, capturing high-level causal patterns beyond raw monitoring data. Second, most current methods function as black boxes, providing little interpretability for their predictions. This hinders the trustworthiness and usability of these models in O&M decision-making scenarios.

3 Methodology

To effectively leverage high-level fault factual knowledge and improve the transparency of fault prediction, we design a two-phase framework, as illustrated in Fig. 1. The core idea is to construct Network O&M TKGs that encode both static fault semantics and dynamic system evolution. Based on these, an interpretable prediction method is developed, which integrates entity-level statistics, contextual relationships, and RL-based reasoning to reveal the decision path.

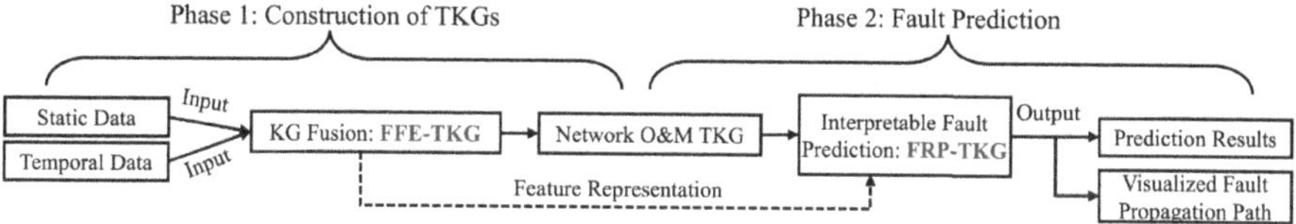

Fig. 1. Overview of the proposed fault prediction framework.

In the first phase, static and temporal data are used to construct static KGs and TKGs, which are then fused through the proposed FFE-TKG method into unified Network O&M TKGs. In the second phase, the FRP-TKG model operates on the fused TKGs to perform interpretable fault prediction by visualizing fault propagation paths and generating final predictions to support O&M decision-making.

3.1 KG Fusion Method: FFE-TKG

To capture both high-level semantic knowledge and fine-grained temporal dynamics, we construct two types of KGs. However, these two graph types differ significantly in entity representations, structural patterns, and temporal characteristics, leading to a semantic gap that hinders unified reasoning. To address this, we propose FFE-TKG, as shown in Fig. 2, a fusion framework that aligns and integrates static KGs and TKGs into a unified O&M TKG, enabling consistent and expressive knowledge representation for downstream interpretable fault prediction.

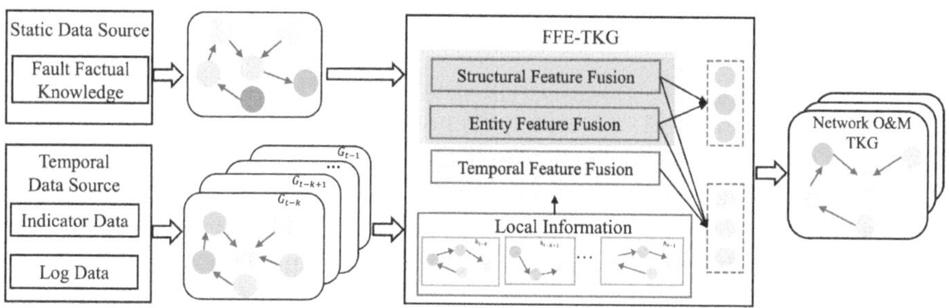

Fig. 2. Overall architecture of FFE-TKG.

Specifically, FFE-TKG comprises three fusion components: (1) the **Entity Feature Fusion Component**, which aggregates similar entities in both KGs and TKGs; (2) the **Structural Feature Fusion Component**, which integrates neighborhood structural information; and (3) the **Temporal Feature Fusion Component**, which captures the temporal dynamics of entities and relations in TKGs. We detail each component below.

Structural Feature Fusion: The FFE-TKG fuses neighborhood information of the target entity e_s, and iteratively updates the entity's feature representation. The l-th layer representation of the target entity e_s, denoted as $h_{e_s}^{(l)}$, is defined in Eq. 1.

$$h_{e_s}^{(l)} = \sigma\left(\sum_{r\in R}\sum_{e_o\in\mathcal{N}_r(e_s)}\frac{1}{c_{ij}^r}W_r^{(l-1)}h_{e_o}^{(l-1)} + W_{e_o}^{(l-1)}h_{e_s}^{(l-1)}\right), \tag{1}$$

where, $N_r(e_s)$ denotes the set of neighboring entities connected to the target entity e_s via relation r, $W_r^{(l)}$ represents the weight matrix associated with relation r at the l-th layer, c_{ij}^r is a normalization constant specific to relation r, and non-linear activation function σ is set to ReLU.

Entity Feature Fusion: This module represents the target entity e_s using a generated d-dimensional vector $v_i \in \mathbb{R}^d$ and performs entity feature fusion by computing the similarity between vectors. The similarity is calculated based on the principle of cosine similarity:

$$\text{similarity}(v_i, v_j) = \frac{v_i \cdot v_j}{\|v_i\|\,\|v_j\|} = \frac{\sum_{k=1}^{d} v_{ik}v_{jk}}{\sqrt{\sum_{k=1}^{d} v_{ik}^2}\sqrt{\sum_{k=1}^{d} v_{jk}^2}} \tag{2}$$

where, $(\cdot)$ denotes the dot product between vectors, and $\|v_i\|$, $\|v_j\|$ represent their Euclidean norms, respectively.

Temporal Feature Fusion: To avoid the problem of vanishing gradients, the module uses LSTM to capture the temporal properties of entities in the TKGs:

$$D_{e_s}^{(t)} = \text{LSTM}\left(h_{e_s}^{(t-1)} \oplus v_{e_s} \oplus v_{e_o} \oplus D_{e_s}^{(t-1)}\right), \tag{3}$$

where $h_{e_s}^{(t-1)}$ denotes the structural representation of the target entity e_s aggregated from time step $t-1$. v_{e_s} and v_{e_o} represent the embedding vectors of the subject and object entities, respectively. $D_{e_s}^{(t-1)}$ denotes the encoded information related to e_s up to time step $t-1$.

Overall, these components enable FFE-TKG to generate informative TKGs that serve as a reliable foundation for downstream fault prediction. Finally, Algorithm 1 describes the KG fusion process based on FFE-TKG.

3.2 Fault Prediction Method: FRP-TKG

Based on the TKGs constructed by the FFE-TKG method, the FRP-TKG is proposed to address the limited interpretability of existing fault prediction models. FRP-TKG consists of two collaborative modules: the Historical Information-Based Prediction (HIP) module and the Temporal Correlation Information-Based Prediction (TCIP) module. As illustrated in Fig. 3, the model performs fault prediction by jointly leveraging historical patterns and temporal correlations.

Algorithm 1. Knowledge Graph Fusion via FFE-TKG

Input: Static KG $\mathcal{G}_{static}$; Temporal KGs $\mathcal{G}_{dynamic} = \{\mathcal{G}_1, \mathcal{G}_2, \dots, \mathcal{G}_t\}$
Output: Fused Knowledge Graph $\hat{\mathcal{G}}$

$H_{static} \leftarrow$ AggregateGraphInformation($\mathcal{G}_{static}$) //Extract structural features from static KG
$H_{dynamic} \leftarrow [\,]$ //Initialize list to store features of temporal graphs
for $i \leftarrow 1$ to t **do**
  $H_{dynamic}.append$(AggregateGraphInformation($\mathcal{G}_i$))
end for
$H_{dynamic} \leftarrow$ LSTM_Process($H_{dynamic}$)
for $i \leftarrow 1$ to t **do**
  $\mathcal{G}_i \leftarrow$ UpdateGraph($\mathcal{G}_i$, MultiHeadAttention($H_{static}, H_{dynamic}[i]$))
end for
for $i \leftarrow 1$ to t **do**
  $\mathcal{G}_i \leftarrow$ EntityMatching($\mathcal{G}_{static}, \mathcal{G}_i$) //Align static and dynamic graph entities
  if IsSimilarity($\mathcal{G}_{static}, \mathcal{G}_i$) **then**
    $\hat{\mathcal{G}} \leftarrow$ FuseGraphs($\mathcal{G}_{static}, \mathcal{G}_i$) //Fuse when KGs are similar
  else
    $\hat{\mathcal{G}} \leftarrow$ AppendGraphs($\mathcal{G}_{static}, \mathcal{G}_{dynamic}$)
  end if
end for
return $\hat{\mathcal{G}}$

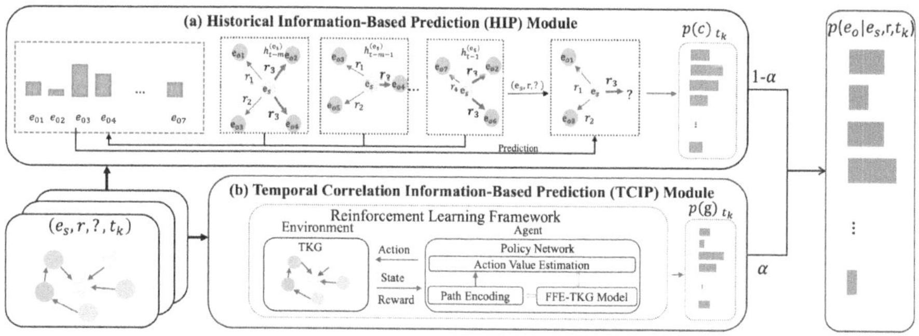

Fig. 3. Overall architecture of FRP-TKG model.

3.2.1 HIP Module

As shown in module (a) of Fig. 3, we illustrate the prediction task with a typical TKG fact in the form of a quadruple $(e_s, r, ?, t_k)$ [12], where the tail entity is missing. In consecutive temporal subgraphs $\{\mathcal{G}_1, \mathcal{G}_2, ..., \mathcal{G}_{k-1}\}$ [10], the neighboring entities of the given entity e_s are denoted as $\{e_{o1}, e_{o2}, ..., e_{on}\}$, and the relations between e_s and its neighbors are denoted as $\{r_1, r_2, \dots, r_m\}$. At timestamp t_k, by analyzing the frequency of tail entities $\{e_{o1}, e_{o2}, \dots, e_{on}\}$ that co-occur with e_s under a given relation r, we can estimate the probability over potential tail entities, and build the vector H_t by Eq. 4.

$$H_{tk}^{(e_s,r)} = h_{t1}^{(e_s,r)} + h_{t2}^{(e_s,r)} + \cdots + h_{tk-1}^{(e_s,r)}. \quad (4)$$

Subsequently, the HIP module encodes the input, which consists of the representation vectors of the entity e_s and the relation r, using a multilayer perceptron. Subsequently, a non-linear transformation is applied via an activation function to generate an index vector $z_s = \tanh\left([e_s \oplus e_r]\right)$, where z_s is an N-dimensional vector, and N denotes the total number of entities.

To incorporate the query condition into historical statistical information, the index vector z_s is added to the historical frequency vector $H_{t_k}^{(e_s,r)}$, as shown in Eq. 5. In the resulting vector c_z, entities that do not satisfy the query condition $(e_s, r, ?, t_k)$ are assigned significantly lower values. Then the vector c_z is processed to produce a probability distribution over candidate tail entities, enabling the prediction at time t as formulated in Eq. 6.

$$\mathrm{c_z} = \mathrm{z}_s + H_{t_k}^{(e_s,r)} \quad (5) \qquad p(c)_{t_k} = \mathrm{softmax}(c_z). \quad (6)$$

Finally, the HIP module yields a probability distribution over candidate entities for future time steps and facilitates fault prediction by utilizing historical information.

3.2.2 TCIP Module

To enhance model interpretability and improve prediction performance for infrequent entities, the TCIP module incorporates RL and entity representations learned from the FFE-TKG model. The overall framework is illustrated in Fig. 3 (b). We model the agent's interaction with the TKGs as a Markov Decision Process (MDP), defined by the tuple (S, A, δ, ρ). The MDP components are specified as follows.

Environment: The environment is represented as TKGs. We introduce cross-temporal edges to link the same entity across different time points, facilitating cross-graph search.

State: In the state space S, each state s_l is represented as $s_l = (e_l, t_l, e_s, t, r)$, where e_l denotes the nodes currently visited by the agent at time t_l, and e_s, t, r corresponds to the elements of the query quadruple $(e_s, r, ?, t)$.

Action: At a given state s_l, the action space A_l, as a subset of A, represents the set of possible actions the agent can take at timestep l. The transition function δ defines the probability of moving from one state to another, based on the selected action.

Reward: The agent receives a final reward of $+1$ only when it successfully reaches the correct target entity. Otherwise, the Dirichlet distribution is used to determine the reward value [18].

Agent: The agent's behavior is determined by the policy network, which takes the current state as input and outputs an action probability distribution. First, the model needs to decide in each state based on the target entity e_s as well as the previous entity e_i and relation r_i as shown in Eq. 7.

$$h_l = \left(\left(e_s, t\right), r_1, \left(e_1, t_1\right), \ldots, r_l, \left(e_l, t_l\right)\right). \tag{7}$$

LSTM is then employed as a sequence encoder to encode the history path:

$$h_l = \text{LSTM}\left(h_{l-1}, \left[r_{l-1}; e_{l-1}^{t_{l-1}}\right]\right). \tag{8}$$

Subsequently, a common approach to selecting the best path for a policy network is to evaluate the optional actions and calculate the state transfer probabilities as shown in Eq. 9.

$$\phi\left(a_n, s_l\right) = \beta_n \left\langle \tilde{e}, e_n^{t_n} \right\rangle + \left(1 - \beta_n\right) \left\langle \tilde{r}, r_n \right\rangle, \tag{9}$$

where $e_n^{t_n}$ denotes the candidate entity at step l, and r_n represents the corresponding candidate relation. The vectors $\tilde{e}$ and $\tilde{r}$ are the expected representations of the target entity and relation, obtained by encoding the state information through a multilayer perceptron, as shown in Eqs. 10. W_1, W_e, and W_r are learnable parameters.

$$\tilde{e} = W_e \,\text{ReLU}\left(W_1 \left[h_l; e_q^{t_q}; r_q\right]\right), \tilde{r} = W_r \,\text{ReLU}\left(W_1 \left[h_l; e_q^{t_q}; r_q\right]\right). \tag{10}$$

After calculating the similarity between the expected nodes and the candidate entities, the score is weighted using β_n, which is represented as shown in Eq. 11, where W_β is a parameter for model learning, and variables subscripted with q are associated with the query.

$$\beta_n = \text{sigmoid}\left(\mathrm{W}_\beta \left[h_l; e_q^{t_q}; r_q; e_n^{t_n}; r_n\right]\right). \tag{11}$$

In summary, the parameters of the policy network $\pi_\theta(a_l|s_l)$ are influenced by FFE-TKG model representations, path encoding, and the action scoring function. At each step, the agent selects actions based on this policy to navigate toward the target entity.

Objective Function: To maximize the long-term reward, the objective function, representing the expected reward obtained under the strategy π_θ, is formulated as follows:

$$J(\theta) = \mathbb{E}_{(e_s, r, e_o, t) \sim F_{\text{train}}} \left[\mathbb{E}_{a_1, \ldots, a_L \sim \pi\theta} \left[\tilde{R}(s_L \mid e_s, r, t)\right]\right], \tag{12}$$

where, $\mathbb{E}$ is the expected value, which represents the average of the rewards for all possible sequences. $a_1, \ldots, a_L$ is a sequence of actions taken by the agent. $\tilde{R}(s_L \mid e_s, r, t)$ is a adjusted reward function. The optimization strategy is tuned using a policy gradient method as in Eq. 13.

$$\nabla_\theta J(\theta) \approx \nabla_\theta \sum_{l=1}^{L} \tilde{R}(s_L \mid e_s, r, t) \log \pi_\theta(a_l \mid s_l), \tag{13}$$

where, $\nabla_\theta J(\theta)$ is the gradient of the objective function concerning the model parameters θ, guiding the policy update. $\tilde{R}(s_L \mid e_s, r, t) \log \pi_\theta(a_l \mid s_l)$ is an approximation of the gradient of the objective function, where $\log \pi_\theta(a_l \mid s_l)$ denotes the log-probability of taking action a_l under state s_l according to the policy.

Finally, by weightedly combining the probability distributions of the above two modules, the model can generate a composite probability distribution, as shown in Eq. 14.

$$p\left(e_o \mid e_s, r, t_k\right) = \alpha \cdot p(c)_{t_k} + (1-\alpha) \cdot p(g)_{t_k}, \tag{14}$$

where $p\left(e_o \mid e_s, r, t_k\right)$ represents the model's predicted probability of the entity, which combines the probabilistic predictions of the two modules and weights the probabilities of the candidate entities to obtain the final prediction output.

4 Evaluation

To evaluate the effectiveness of the proposed FRP-TKG model in fault prediction tasks, we conduct extensive experiments against a variety of baselines. To assess the impact of the FFE-TKG fusion method, we compare the performance of fault prediction using TKGs before and after fusion. In addition, we conduct an interpretability analysis of FRP-TKG.

4.1 Datasets and Experimental Settings

To construct the fused network O&M TKGs as the datasets, the fault factual knowledge is derived from a large number of fault reports and historical operational experiences accumulated during the operation of the Kubernetes (K8s) [19] platform. The TKGs are built from 20 days of continuous real-time monitoring data collected from the Train-ticket system deployed on an Alibaba Cloud K8s cluster [20], combined with temporal fault simulation data generated using the Kube-monkey and ChaosBlade tools. In addition, the datasets are divided into training, validation, and test sets in the ratio of 8:1:1.

All experiments are conducted on Windows 11 with the following hardware: -GPU: NVIDIA GeForce GTX 3080Ti; -CPU: Intel(R) Core(TM) i7-9700E @2.60 GHz; -RAM: 16 GB. Besides, we set the learning rate to 0.001, the batch size to 1024, the embedding dimension to 200, the hidden layer size to 768, and the dropout rate to 0.5.

4.2 Baselines and Evaluation Metrics

The experiments thoroughly validate the effectiveness of our proposed FFE-TKG model by conducting comprehensive comparisons against a range of state-of-the-art methods for fault prediction tasks, including TTransE [21], HyTE [22], RE-NET [23], RE-GCN [24], CyGNet [25], xERTE [26], TITer [27].

Table 1. Performance on Tail Entity Prediction

Model	MRR	Hits@1	Hits@3	Hits@10
TTransE	31.32	29.14	39.86	45.19
HyTE	26.28	24.53	29.94	35.45
RE-NET	77.23	72.96	80.33	85.03
RE-GCN	79.42	75.81	82.61	87.44
CyGNet	69.23	65.45	71.33	80.03
xERTE	81.19	78.34	85.33	**89.73**
TITer	81.47	77.90	**85.90**	89.10
FRP-TKG	**83.54**	**80.19**	85.12	88.62

Table 2. Performance on Head Entity Prediction

Model	MRR	Hits@1	Hits@3	Hits@10
TTransE	27.42	23.66	33.26	38.62
HyTE	23.41	19.74	25.80	32.83
RE-NET	70.67	68.59	71.93	82.39
RE-GCN	69.62	63.19	73.70	78.93
CyGNet	60.88	57.32	66.07	75.03
xERTE	75.54	73.84	77.83	86.78
TITer	75.21	73.77	77.56	86.99
FRP-TKG	**76.34**	**73.95**	**79.96**	**87.12**

In the fault prediction task, two kinds of standard measures are used to evaluate the experiment's performance, including Mean Reciprocal Ranking (MRR) and Hits@K, which is the average proportion of triples that rank less than K. For each metric, a higher score indicates a better effect. The MRR and Hits@K (K=1,3,10) can be calculated as follows:

$$\text{MRR} = \frac{1}{|N_t|}\sum_{i=1}^{|N_t|}\frac{1}{\text{rank}_i}, \quad (15) \qquad \text{Hits@}K = \frac{1}{|N_t|}\sum_{i=1}^{|N_t|}\mathbb{1}(\text{rank}_i \leq K), \quad (16)$$

where $|N_t|$ is the length of the triple set N_t, rank_i refers to the prediction ranking of the i-th triple, and $\mathbb{1}(\cdot)$ is an indicator function equal to 1 if the condition is true, otherwise it is 0.

4.3 Prediction Results

The overall results are shown in Table 1 and Table 2. It can be observed that FRP-TKG achieves outstanding performance in both tail entity and head entity prediction tasks.

Compared to our proposed method, FRP-TKG, dynamic reasoning models such as TTransE and HyTE perform less effectively. Although these models incorporate temporal embeddings, they often overfit to specific timestamps and fail to capture broader historical patterns, resulting in lower overall accuracy. In contrast, models like RE-NET, RE-GCN, CyGNet, xERTE, and TITer show improved performance by modeling temporal dynamics more effectively. However, these methods still struggle to adapt to evolving graph structures under highly dynamic conditions. Notably, while some baselines achieve competitive Hits@10 scores in certain cases, their lower MRR and Hits@1 values indicate weaker overall ranking performance and reduced precision in top-ranked predictions. Overall, although FRP-TKG performs slightly below certain baselines in specific metrics for the tail entity prediction task, it consistently achieves strong overall performance across both tail and head predictions, particularly in MRR and Hits@1, demonstrating its advantage in accurate and interpretable fault prediction.

Furthermore, to evaluate the effectiveness of the FFE-TKG, we conduct comparative experiments using both the fused TKGs and the original TKGs without integrating fault knowledge. Taking the task of tail entity prediction as an example, the experimental results are presented in Table 3.

Table 3. Comparison experiment results before and after KG fusion

KG	MRR	Hits@1	Hits@3	Hits@10
Original TKGs	73.11	69.87	75.91	80.46
Fused TKGs	83.54	80.19	85.12	88.62

As shown in Table 3, the experimental results validate the effectiveness of the proposed FFE-TKG fusion method. By integrating fault factual knowledge into the TKGs, FFE-TKG significantly enhances the quality of O&M data, leading to notable improvements in fault prediction performance.

4.4 Hyperparameter Settings and Analysis

In this section, we conduct parameter analysis on hyperparameter α, which is designed to balance the HIP and TCIP modules in FRP-TKG. It means that only use the HIP module for fault prediction when α is set to 1, and only use the TCIP module when it is set to 0.

As shown in Fig. 4, our model can obtain the optimal performance when α is 0.4, which shows that it is necessary to use both modules to work together to improve prediction accuracy.

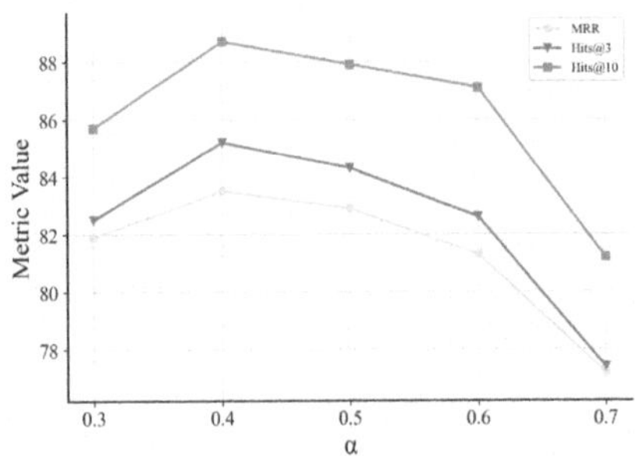

Fig. 4. Hyperparameter α analysis.

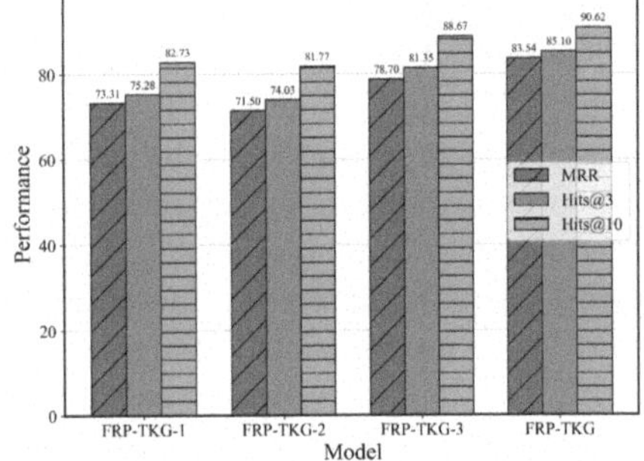

Fig. 5. Overall results of ablation experiments.

4.5 Ablation Studies

To evaluate the effectiveness of different components in the FRP-TKG model, additional ablation experiments were conducted on three model variants for tail entity prediction, with similar results observed for head entity prediction.

Specifically, the FRP-TKG-1 variant removes the HIP module to evaluate its contribution to model performance. The FRP-TKG-2 variant excludes the TCIP module to assess its effectiveness. The FRP-TKG-3 variant focuses on removing the RL component from the TCIP module to examine the impact of policy optimization on prediction performance. The overall ablation results are illustrated in Fig. 5.

The experimental results demonstrate that the FRP-TKG-1 variant exhibits a performance decline across all evaluation metrics, most notably in the critical Hits@1 score. This indicates that the HIP module plays a vital role in enhancing prediction accuracy by enabling the model to better interpret and leverage historical information. Similarly, the FRP-TKG-2 variant also shows a noticeable drop in performance, underscoring the importance of capturing temporal dependencies. In contrast, while the FRP-TKG-3 variant exhibits a slight decrease in performance, it still maintains relatively high accuracy compared to the other ablation variants. It suggests that while RL contributes to improved reasoning, the core performance gains of FRP-TKG stem from the integration of historical information and temporal correlations, captured by the HIP and TCIP modules, respectively.

4.6 Interpretability Analysis

The interpretability of the FRP-TKG model is primarily reflected in its ability to visualize reasoning paths based on TKGs. Taking the "Key Server" in Fig. 6 as an example, the model predicts tail entities by analyzing contextual entities and relationship patterns across temporal subgraphs. The graph shows that the "Key Server" is frequently connected to entities such as "Overload" and "CPU usage exceeds threshold" through relations like CAUSES and TRIGGERS, forming a clear fault evolution pathway.

The model determines that the most probable tail entity in the current subgraph is "Overload" with a probability of 85%, followed by "Service Latency" (65%) and "Throughput Decrease" (55%). This reasoning approach, grounded in the evolutionary patterns of historical temporal graphs and causal chain inference, enhances the interpretability of the prediction results, enabling O&M personnel to identify potential issues and locate fault sources more efficiently.

4.7 Complexity Analysis

Based on the above results, we further analyze the computational complexity of the proposed framework. The complexity of the framework mainly comes from FFE-TKG and FRP-TKG. In FFE-TKG, structural aggregation (Eq. (1)) costs $\mathcal{O}(L|E|d)$ for L layers, entity similarity (Eq. (3)) is $\mathcal{O}(|V|^2d)$ in the worst case,

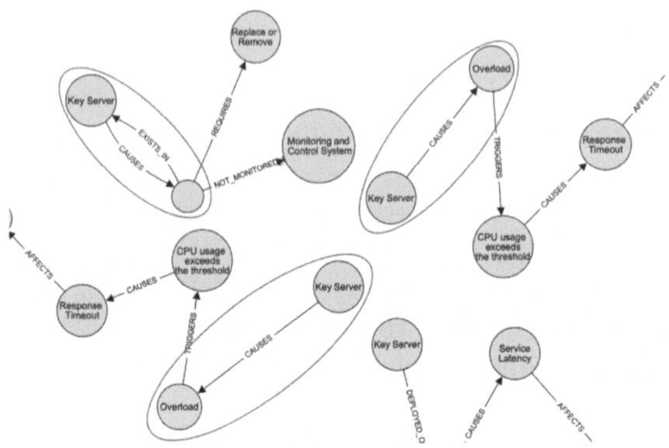

Fig. 6. Visualization of the fault occurrence path.

and temporal fusion (Eq. (2)) requires $\mathcal{O}(|V|Td^2)$ for T time steps. In FRP-TKG, the HIP module (Eqs. (4)–(6)) is lightweight with $\mathcal{O}(dN + T)$, while the TCIP module (Eqs. (7)–(9)) is more expensive due to reinforcement learning, with path exploration complexity about $\mathcal{O}(mBRL_p\bar{a}d + L_pd^2)$, where m is the batch size, B the beam width, R the number of rollouts, L_p the maximum path length, $\bar{a}$ the average branching factor of the graph, and d the embedding dimension.

In practice, training overhead mainly arises from graph fusion and RL optimization, whereas inference is efficient, especially when HIP contributes more. The framework can be scaled to larger graphs through neighbor sampling, temporal windowing, and beam-pruned RL, ensuring applicability in large-scale O&M scenarios.

5 Conclusion

We propose a two-phase framework for fault prediction to address the lack of fault factual knowledge and limited interpretability in existing approaches. In the first phase, we develop FFE-TKG, a fusion method that incorporates fault factual knowledge into TKGs from entity, structural, and temporal dimensions. In the second phase, we introduce FRP-TKG, which captures historical and temporal relational patterns and leverages RL to enhance prediction interpretability. Extensive experiments on real datasets demonstrate that our framework outperforms competitive baselines. The framework's ability to identify critical fault triggers and visualize potential propagation pathways offers significant advantages for real-world troubleshooting and decision-making processes.

References

1. Diaz-de-Arcaya, J., Torre-Bastida, A.I., Zárate, G., Miñón, R., Almeida, A.: A joint study of the challenges, opportunities, and roadmap of MLOps and AIOps: a systematic survey. ACM Comput. Surv. **56**(4), 1–30 (2023). https://doi.org/10.1145/3625289

2. Notaro, P., Cardoso, J., Gerndt, M.: A survey of aiops methods for failure management. ACM Trans. Intell. Syst. Technol. (TIST) **12**(6), 1–45 (2021). https://doi.org/10.1145/3483424
3. Remil, Y., Bendimerad, A., Mathonat, R., Kaytoue, M.: AIOps Solutions for Incident Management: Technical Guidelines and A Comprehensive Literature Review (Version 1) (2024). arXiv https://doi.org/10.48550/ARXIV.2404.01363
4. Meng, Y., et al.: Localizing failure root causes in a microservice through causality inference. In: 2020 IEEE/ACM 28th International Symposium on Quality of Service (IWQoS). Hang Zhou, China, pp. 1–10 (2020). https://doi.org/10.1109/IWQoS49365.2020.9213058
5. Brandón, Á., Solé, M., Huélamo, A., Solans, D., Pérez, M.S., Muntés-Mulero, V., Graph-based root cause analysis for service-oriented and microservice architectures. J. Syst. Softw. **159**, 110432 (2020). ISSN **0164–1212**. https://doi.org/10.1016/j.jss.2019.110432
6. Qiu, J., Qingfeng, D., Yin, K., Zhang, S.-L., Qian, C.: A causality mining and knowledge graph based method of root cause diagnosis for performance anomaly in cloud applications. Appl. Sci. **10**, 2166 (2020). https://doi.org/10.3390/app10062166
7. Wang, H., et al.: GRANO: interactive graph-based root cause analysis for cloud-native distributed data platform. Proc. VLDB Endow. **12**(12), 1942–1945 (2019). https://doi.org/10.14778/3352063.3352105
8. Fatouros, G., et al.: Knowledge graphs and interoperability techniques for hybrid-cloud deployment of FaaS applications. In: 2022 IEEE International Conference on Cloud Computing Technology and Science (CloudCom), Bangkok, Thailand, pp. 91–96 (2022). https://doi.org/10.1109/CloudCom55334.2022.00023
9. Liu, K., Li, Z., Wang, Z., Zhang, J., Tang, Y.: Towards more intelligent network management: service-oriented proactive fault management using KDD techniques. In: Proceedings of the 3rd World Congress on Intelligent Control and Automation (Cat. No.00EX393), Hefei, vol. 1, pp. 715–718 (2000). https://doi.org/10.1109/WCICA.2000.860069
10. Zhang, Y., Zhou, W., Huang, J., Jin, X., Xiao, G.: Temporal knowledge graph informer network for remaining useful life prediction. IEEE Trans. Instrument. Meas. **72**, 1–10, Art no. 3528610 (2023). https://doi.org/10.1109/TIM.2023.3309395
11. Huai, Z., Zhang, D., Yang, G., Tao, J.: Spatial-temporal knowledge graph network for event prediction. Neurocomputing **553**, 126557 (2023). ISSN **0925–2312**. https://doi.org/10.1016/j.neucom.2023.126557
12. Ji, S., Pan, S., Cambria, E., Marttinen, P., Yu, P.S.: A survey on knowledge graphs: representation, acquisition, and applications. IEEE Trans. Neural Netw. Learn. Syst. **33**(2), 494–514 (2022). https://doi.org/10.1109/TNNLS.2021.3070843
13. Drucker, H., Burges, C.J.C., Kaufman, L., Smola, A., Vapnik, V.: Support vector regression machines. In: Proceedings of the 10th International Conference on Neural Information Processing Systems (NIPS'96), pp. 155–161. MIT Press, Cambridge (1996)
14. Hochreiter, S., Schmidhuber, J.: Long short-term memory. Neural Comput. **9**(8), 1735–1780 (1997). https://doi.org/10.1162/neco.1997.9.8.1735
15. Cinar, Y.G., Mirisaee, H., Goswami, P., Gaussier, E., Ait-Bachir, A., Strijov, V.: Time Series forecasting using RNNs: an extended attention mechanism to model periods and handle missing values (2017). https://doi.org/10.48550/arXiv.1703.10089

16. Liang, Y., Ke, S., Zhang, J., Yi, X., Zheng, Y.: GeoMAN: multi-level attention networks for geo-sensory time series prediction. In: Proceedings of the 27th International Joint Conference on Artificial Intelligence (IJCAI'18), pp. 3428–3434. AAAI Press (2018)
17. García-Durán, A., Dumančić, S., Niepert, M.: Learning sequence encoders for temporal knowledge graph completion. In: Proceedings of the 2018 Conference on Empirical Methods in Natural Language Processing, pp. 4816–4821. Association for Computational Linguistics, Brussels (2018)
18. Yang, H., Park, H., Lee, K.: A selective portfolio management algorithm with off-policy reinforcement learning using Dirichlet distribution. Axioms **11**, 664 (2022)
19. Bernstein, D.: Containers and cloud: from LXC to docker to kubernetes. IEEE Cloud Comput. **1**(3), 81–84 (2014). https://doi.org/10.1109/MCC.2014.51
20. In: Proceedings of the 40th International Conference on Software Engineering: Companion Proceeedings. Association for Computing Machinery, New York (2018)
21. Leblay, J., Chekol, M.W.: Deriving validity time in knowledge graph. In: Companion Proceedings of the The Web Conference 2018 (WWW '18). International World Wide Web Conferences Steering Committee, Republic and Canton of Geneva, CHE, pp. 1771–1776 (2018). https://doi.org/10.1145/3184558.3191639
22. Dasgupta, S.S., Ray, S.N., Talukdar, P.: HyTE: hyperplane-based temporally aware knowledge graph embedding. In: Proceedings of the 2018 Conference on Empirical Methods in Natural Language Processing, pp. 2001–2011. Association for Computational Linguistics, Brussels (2018)
23. Visin, F., Kastner, K., Cho, K., Matteucci, M., Courville, A., Bengio, Y.: ReNet: a recurrent neural network based alternative to convolutional networks. arXiv Prepr. arXiv. 1505 (2015)
24. Li, Z., et al.: Temporal knowledge graph reasoning based on evolutional representation learning. In Proceedings of the 44th International ACM SIGIR Conference on Research and Development in Information Retrieval (SIGIR '21), pp. 408–417. Association for Computing Machinery, New York (2021). https://doi.org/10.1145/3404835.3462963
25. Zhu, C., Chen, M., Fan, C., Cheng, G., Zhang, Y.: Learning from history: modeling temporal knowledge graphs with sequential copy-generation networks. In: Proceedings of the AAAI Conference on Artificial Intelligence, vol. 35, no. 5, pp. 4732–4740 (2021). https://doi.org/10.1609/aaai.v35i5.16604
26. Han, Z., Chen, P., Ma, Y., Tresp, V.: xERTE: explainable reasoning on temporal knowledge graphs for forecasting future links (2020). https://doi.org/10.48550/arXiv.2012.15537
27. Sun, H., Zhong, J., Ma, Y., Han, Z., He, K.: TimeTraveler: reinforcement learning for temporal knowledge graph forecasting. In: Proceedings of the 2021 Conference on Empirical Methods in Natural Language Processing, Online and Punta Cana, Dominican Republic, pp. 8306–8319. Association for Computational Linguistics (2021)

Author Index

T. Qiu et al. (Eds.): CCF ChinaNet 2025, CCIS 2810, pp. 185–186, 2026.
https://doi.org/10.1007/978-981-95-8450-5

The manufacturer's authorised representative in the EU is Springer Nature Customer Service Centre GmbH, Europaplatz 3, 69115 Heidelberg, Germany. If you have any concerns regarding our products, please contact ProductSafety@springernature.com

Printed and bound by CPI Group (UK) Ltd, Croydon, CR0 4YY

07/07/2026

02160913-0002